WHY
MINSKY
MATTERS

WHY
MINSKY
MATTERS

*An Introduction to the Work
of a Maverick Economist*

L. Randall Wray

PRINCETON UNIVERSITY PRESS

Princeton and Oxford

Copyright © 2016 by Princeton University Press
Published by Princeton University Press, 41 William Street,
Princeton, New Jersey 08540
In the United Kingdom: Princeton University Press, 6 Oxford Street,
Woodstock, Oxfordshire OX20 1TW

press.princeton.edu

Jacket photograph © Beringer-Dratch.
Courtesy of the Levy Economics Institute of Bard College.

ISBN 978-0-691-15912-6

Library of Congress Control Number 2015945043

British Library Cataloging-in-Publication Data is available

This book has been composed in Garamond Pro and Filosofia

Printed on acid-free paper. ∞

Printed in the United States of America

1 3 5 7 9 10 8 6 4 2

CONTENTS

PREFACE

Minsky matters, and this book will explain why he should matter to you.

This is not a biography of Hyman P. Minsky. Nor is it really an exercise in "the history of Minsky's thought." Rather, I am trying to make Minsky's ideas accessible to a wider audience. Minsky's writing style is notoriously opaque. Even those who want to understand him, including trained economists, find his work difficult.

This book will explain Minsky's most important contributions in jargon-free plain English. I explain "why Minsky matters" for those who might have heard the name Minsky in recent years and want to delve into the man's contributions—much as one might try to figure out why Charles Darwin matters, or Sigmund Freud, or Milton Friedman.

You probably already know of Friedman, and you might even have read some of his books. He wrote for a general audience in a simple but lively style. Minsky's style is much more turgid, and he rarely targeted anything he wrote for a general audience. Even when he did, he usually missed. He needs to be translated.

But a straight translation is not sufficient if one is trying to hit a general audience. The writing must also draw the reader in; it must make the topic (Minsky) interesting. The angle that makes Minsky interesting right now, is that he saw the Global Financial Crisis coming. But this crisis will not be the last one, and he also saw the next one coming—and the one after that.

Yet, this is not really a book about the crisis, although you will have a much better understanding of financial crises—and what to do about them—after reading this book. Minsky's work enables one to understand our most recent crash but also to recognize the forces that will bring on the next one.

I organized the book around three main themes one finds in Minsky's publications: the financial instability writings that led up to his now famous book *Stabilizing an Unstable Economy*; his early work on employment, inequality, and poverty; and his last work from the mid-1980s to his death—that led to the Money Manager Capitalism analysis. Although all of these are linked, it was useful to treat them as phases of his career.

A theme running throughout his work is that the "vision" of most economists is wrong. Market processes are not stabilizing. Adding bells and whistles to accepted economic doctrine does not make up for the wrong vision. Minsky matters because his vision was different.

Minsky—the man—was larger than life. He always wanted to be the center of attention, and he usually was. He was the smartest guy in the room, in every room. He was tall and gregarious, with a head full of wild hair. Even in old age he was impish; in pictures as a young man, he looked rakish with his cigarette.

I vividly remember the first time I laid eyes on him. Actually, I heard him first, as he was shuffling into the classroom while mumbling to himself: "Too many students; every year there are more of them. I'd really like the last one who enters the classroom to close the door because we don't want anyone *out there* to know what's going on *in here*." He then launched into the most incredible lecture that ranged from the "Cross of Gold" speech of William Jennings Bryan, through the *Wizard of Oz*'s indictment of New York bankers, and on to the previous day's St. Louis Cardinals baseball game, with all loose ends neatly tied by the end of class.

When I was his teaching assistant, he called me into his office to lecture me that "you can be radical in your thoughts, but not in your dress"—telling me I must always keep dress pants, a dress shirt, and a tie in my office as he frowned at my preferred dress of tank top, shorts, and flip-flops. As I found out years later, it was the same lecture Professor Lange had given him when he was a graduate student.

As his TA, I spent most of the time trying to convince him that he was far too generous in assigning grades to his undergrads. I suppose he felt guilty for his lecture style, which stumped at least half the class. He rarely came with notes, never followed a syllabus, and mostly avoided discussing assigned readings. Generosity was his restitution.

Minsky began many conversations with, "You have to remember . . ." as he then discussed the minutiae of obscure events that occurred decades before you were born. He had developed his own language that required time and some effort to pierce. One does not "buy an asset" in Minsky-speak, rather one "takes a position in an asset." When one has to sell assets to make payments on debts, this is "selling position to make position." To some extent, this was because he wanted to be precise and had picked up terms from Wall Street, but I suspect that he enjoyed some mystery and notoriety for obscurantism.

He'd give a little wink after offering a pearl of wisdom that he knew was just beyond your grasp.

Minsky always said he stood on the shoulders of giants. He had little interest in mining the scribblings of defunct economists in an attempt to divine "what they really meant." He would probably have little patience with anyone who tries too hard to interpret his own writing. But he did love to be the center of attention, and he was a giant on whose shoulders we can stand.

I thank Seth Ditchik, executive editor at Princeton University Press, for suggesting this project. Eric Tymoigne and some anonymous referees offered useful comments. Thanks to the Levy Economics Institute for funding during a sabbatical year that gave me time to complete this book, and for the efforts of Dimitri Papadimitriou and Jan Kregel to make Minsky's work available at the Minsky Archive.[1] I also thank Esther Minsky, Diana Minsky, and Alan Minsky for their friendship over many years. Most of all, I thank Hyman Minsky for his support and inspiration.

WHY
MINSKY
MATTERS

Introduction

Stability—even of an expansion—is destabilizing in that the more adventuresome financing of investment pays off to the leaders and others follow.

—*Minsky, 1975, p. 125*[1]

There is no final solution to the problems of organizing economic life.

—*Minsky, 1975, p. 168*[2]

Why does the work of Hyman P. Minsky matter? Because he saw "it" (the Global Financial Crisis, or GFC) coming. Indeed, when the crisis first hit, many of those familiar with his work (and even some who knew little about it) proclaimed it a "Minsky crisis." That alone should spark interest in his work.

The queen of England famously asked her economic advisors why none of *them* had seen it coming. Obviously the answer is complex, but it must include reference to the evolution of macroeconomic theory over the postwar period—from the "Age of Keynes," through the rise of Milton Friedman's monetarism and the return of neoclassical economics in the particularly extreme form developed by Robert Lucas, and finally on to the new monetary consensus adopted by Chairman Bernanke on the precipice of the crisis. The story cannot leave out the parallel developments in finance theory—with its "efficient markets hypothesis"—and the "hands-off" approach to regulation and supervision of financial institutions.

What passed for macroeconomics on the verge of the global financial collapse had little to do with reality. The world modeled by mainstream economics bore no relation to our economy. It was based on rational expectations in which everyone bets right, at least within a random error, and maximizes anything and everything while living in a world without financial institutions. There are no bubbles, no speculation, no crashes, and no crises in these models. And everyone always pays all debts due on time.

By contrast, Lake Wobegon appears to be impossibly unruly. No wonder mainstream economists never saw anything coming.

In short, expecting the queen's economists to foresee the crisis would be like putting flat-earthers in charge of navigation for NASA and expecting them to accurately predict points of reentry and landing of the space shuttle. The same can be said of the U.S. president's Council of Economic Advisers (CEA)— who actually had served as little more than cheerleaders for the theory that so ill-served policy makers.

This book provides an introduction to Minsky's alternative approach to economic theory and policy and explains why Minsky matters. Although there were a handful of economists who had warned as early as 2000 about the possibility of a crisis, Minsky's warnings actually began a half century earlier— with publications in 1957 that set out his vision of financial instability. Over the next forty years, he refined and continually updated the theory. It is not simply that he was more prescient than others. His analysis digs much deeper. For that reason, his work can continue to guide us not only through the next crisis, but even those that will follow.

Minsky's view can be captured in his memorable phrase: "Stability is destabilizing." What appears initially to be contradictory or perhaps ironic is actually tremendously insightful: to the degree that the economy achieves what looks to be robust and stable growth, this is setting up the conditions in which a crash becomes ever more likely. It is the *stability* that changes behaviors, policy making, and business opportunities so that the *instability* results.

Back in 1929, the most famous American economist, Irving Fisher, announced that the stock market had achieved a "permanent plateau," having banished the possibility of a market crash. In the late 1960s, Keynesian economists such as Paul Samuelson announced that policy makers had learned how to "fine-tune" the economy so that neither inflation nor recession would ever again rear their ugly heads. In the mid-1990s, Chairman Greenspan argued that the "new economy" reflected in the NASDAQ equities boom had created conditions conducive to high growth without inflation. In 2004, Chairman Bernanke announced that the era of "the Great Moderation" had arrived so that recessions would be mild and financial fluctuations attenuated.

In every case, there was ample evidence to support the belief that the economy and financial markets were more stable, that the "good times" would continue indefinitely, and that economists had finally gotten it right. In every case, the prognostications were completely wrong. In every case, the "stability is destabilizing" view had it right. In every case, Minsky was vindicated.

But Minsky left us with much more than a colorful and useful phrase.

The Wall Street Paradigm

Minsky had his feet firmly planted in two worlds. One was the world of "high theory"—the academic environment in which economists create theories and models and occasionally test them with economic data. Unfortunately, as mainstream macroeconomic theory has so vividly demonstrated in recent years, this can be about as useful as debating "angels on pinheads" when it comes to developing an understanding of the way the world actually works.

However, Minsky had his other foot firmly planted out in the real world of financial markets. Indeed, he always claimed that he began from a "Wall Street paradigm." To be clear, that did not mean that he was one of those "1 percenters" that Occupy Wall Street has been demonstrating against! What Minsky meant was that you've got to understand "high finance" in order to understand our modern economy. And Minsky had a deep understanding of banks and other financial institutions as well as of financial markets.

This understanding helped Minsky to develop an alternative approach. He not only saw it coming, but all along the way he warned that "it" (another Great Depression) could happen again.[3] In retrospect, he had identified in "real time" those financial innovations that would eventually create the conditions that led to the GFC—such as securitization, rising debt ratios, layering debts on debts, and leveraged buyouts.

Furthermore, from the beginning he had formulated policies that if applied would have attenuated the thrust toward instability. As the financial system evolved over that half century during which Minsky developed his theories and policies, he continually updated his recommendations.

Ironically, mainstream economics went in precisely the *opposite* direction: as the financial system became increasingly complex and dominant, orthodox thinking actually simplified its approach to finance and relegated Wall Street's role to insignificance in the models that came out of academic ivory towers.

As if that were not bad enough, the government officials in charge of regulating and supervising these behemoths frequently adopted simplistic and ultimately dangerous mainstream beliefs.

It Happened Again!

Even the U.S. government's own investigation of the causes of the GFC pointed a finger at the failure of our "public stewards" to constrain the runaway financial system. *The Financial Crisis Inquiry Report*[4] makes a strong case that the crisis was foreseeable and avoidable. It did not "just happen," and it had nothing to do with "black swans with fat tails." It was created by the biggest banks under the noses of our regulators.

According to the report, the GFC represents a dramatic failure of corporate governance and risk management, in large part a result of an unwarranted and unwise focus on trading (actually, gambling) and rapid growth (a good indication of fraud, as William Black[5] argues). Indeed, the biggest banks were aided and abetted by government overseers who not only refused to do their jobs but also continually pushed for deregulation and desupervision in favor of self-regulation and self-supervision. For example, President Clinton's Secretary of the Treasury Larry Summers—a nephew of Paul Samuelson and the most prominent Harvard Keynesian of today—famously pushed for deregulation of "derivatives" that played a critical enabling role in creating the financial tsunami that sank the economy.

There is a danger in focusing on bad actors, bad financial practices, and bad events.[6] To be sure, it is a scandal that those most responsible for the crisis—top management at the biggest banks and "shadow banks"—have not faced prosecution. Still, it is important to understand longer term trends. Minsky helps us to put the crisis in the context of the postwar transformation of the financial system, and he would agree that we should not pin all the blame on bad apples.

Lessons from the GFC

As Minsky would say, financial fragility had grown on trend from the 1960s to the latest crash, making "it" (another "Great Crash" like that of the 1930s) likely to "happen again." For that reason, although the GFC was not strictly inevitable, the financial structure made a crisis highly probable. In many important respects, we had produced conditions similar to those that existed on the eve of the Great Depression—and we experienced a similar crisis.

The most important difference, however, was the response. As Minsky would say, the "Big Bank" (the U.S. Federal Reserve Bank, or Fed) and the "Big Government" (Uncle Sam's Treasury) saved us from the worst—we did not fall into a depression. Yes, we had a terrible recession (that we still had not fully escaped even six years later), and we had a monstrous collapse of the financial system that wiped out trillions of dollars of wealth. But though unemployment reached into the double digits— perhaps 25 million workers were without jobs—the social safety net originally put in place during President Roosevelt's New Deal and President Johnson's War on Poverty prevented the extent of suffering we saw in the 1930s.

President Obama's "Big Government" budget deficit grew to a trillion dollars (in part due to a hastily formulated stimulus package), which helped to prop up the economy.

And Fed Chairman Benjamin Bernanke put together a "Big Bank" rescue package of $29 trillion (yes, you read that correctly!) to save the world's banking system.[7] As a result, we saw very few runs on banks and remarkably few bank failures given that this was by far the worst financial crisis since the Great Depression (when President Roosevelt had to declare a bank "holiday" to stop runs, with only half of all the banks allowed to reopen).

As Minsky argued, the only sensible response to a financial crisis is for the Fed to act as "lender of last resort" to prevent what Irving Fisher called a "debt deflation" caused by fire sales of financial assets as panicked households, firms, and banks try to liquidate their wealth.[8] President Hoover's Treasury Secretary at the start of the Great Depression, Andrew Mellon, had infamously recommended liquidation as a solution to the crisis: "liquidate labor, liquidate stocks, liquidate farmers, liquidate real estate . . . it will purge the rottenness out of the system."[9] But by selling everything, prices collapsed, bankrupting farmers, firms, and households—making the depression much worse.

Although Chairman Bernanke's response was clumsy, there is little doubt that the Fed played the critical role in saving the banks and preventing asset prices from a free fall.

Still, the outcome was far from rosy. Whereas we emerged from the Great Depression with a robust financial system, strict regulation, and strong safety nets, as of 2015, we have only managed to prop up the financial institutions that caused the crisis—and have left the economy in a much weaker state than it had been in either 2006 or 1940. Tens of millions of U.S. homeowners remain deeply underwater in their mortgages, and millions have already lost their homes.

Although official unemployment rates came down, much of the improvement is illusory—millions of workers have given up all hope and left the labor force. Even after years of "recovery," both the homeownership rate (percentage of Americans who own their homes) and the employment rate (percentage of the adult population with jobs) are stuck well below where they were before the GFC. Inequality has actually increased, and all of the gains in the recovery have gone to the very top of the income and wealth distribution.

And because the federal government in Washington did not follow Roosevelt's example in undertaking a thorough reform of the financial system, our biggest banks are actually even bigger and more dangerous than they were on the eve of the GFC. They've resumed many of the same practices that created the GFC. Our public stewards are again allowing this to happen. We didn't seem to learn much from the GFC.

The Mainstream Discovers Minsky

As mentioned at the outset of this introduction, when the crisis hit, prominent economists discovered Minsky. The most famous U.S. Keynesian, Paul Krugman, even devoted a number of his *New York Times* columns to Minsky's work. In May 2009, Krugman announced to his readers that he was going to delve into Minsky's 1986 book:

> So I'm actually reading Hyman Minsky's magnum opus[10], here in Seoul . . . And I have to say that the Platonic ideal of Minsky is a lot better than the reality. There's a deep insight in there; both the concept of financial fragility and his insight, way ahead of anyone else, that as the memory of the Depression faded the system was in fact becoming more fragile. But that insight takes up part of Chapter 9. The rest is a long slog through turgid writing, Kaleckian income distribution theory (which I don't think has anything to do with the fundamental point), and more. To be fair, it took me several decades before I learned to appreciate Keynes in the original. Maybe a reread will make me see the depths of Minsky's insight across the board. Or maybe not.[11]

Krugman went on to give three lectures at the London School of Economics (LSE), the third of which he titled "The Night They Reread Minsky." During his talk, he claimed "I was into

Minsky before Minsky was cool," and he gave Minsky credit for recognizing the growing fragility of the economy long before it finally collapsed into the GFC.

Similarly, speaking at the annual "Minsky Conference" in April 2009,[12] Janet Yellen (who would later replace Chairman Bernanke as the head of the Fed) commented:

> It's a great pleasure to speak to this distinguished group at a conference named for Hyman P. Minsky. My last talk here took place 13 years ago when I served on the Fed's Board of Governors. My topic then was "The 'New' Science of Credit Risk Management at Financial Institutions." It described innovations that I expected to improve the measurement and management of risk. My talk today is titled "A Minsky Meltdown: Lessons for Central Bankers." I won't dwell on the irony of that. Suffice it to say that, with the financial world in turmoil, Minsky's work has become required reading. It is getting the recognition it richly deserves. The dramatic events of the past year and a half are a classic case of the kind of systemic breakdown that he—and relatively few others—envisioned.[13]

So if the foremost orthodox Keynesians "reread Minsky" and found much to like, why hasn't this led to a substantial reform of economic thinking and policy making?

Minsky's Rejection of the Presumption of Stability

In his LSE lecture, Krugman explained that Minsky's problem is that he rejected the mainstream's orthodox, neoclassical economics in favor of a heterodox approach. That is why his ideas are not having the impact that they should.

In 2014 Krugman returned to that theme, arguing that in spite of its failure to "see it coming," good old mainstream economics is able to explain the problem with 20–20 hindsight:

> [T]he heterodox need to realize that they have, to an important extent, been working with the wrong story line. Here's the story they tell themselves: the failure of economists to predict the global economic crisis (and the poor policy response thereto), plus the surge in inequality, show the failure of conventional economic analysis. So it's time to dethrone the whole thing—basically, the whole edifice dating back to Samuelson's 1948 textbook—and give other schools of thought equal time.
>
> Unfortunately for the heterodox (and arguably for the world), this gets the story of what actually happened almost completely wrong.
>
> It is true that economists failed to predict the 2008 crisis (and so did almost everyone). But this wasn't because economics lacked the tools to understand such things—we've long had a pretty good understanding of the logic of banking crises. What happened instead was a failure of real-world observation—failure to notice the rising importance of shadow banking. . . . This was a case of myopia—but it wasn't a deep conceptual failure. And as soon as people *did* recognize the importance of shadow banking, the whole thing instantly fell into place: we were looking at a classic financial crisis.[14]

According to Krugman, mainstreamers had simply failed to notice the rise of shadow banking—something Minsky had been talking about at least since the early 1980s. Minsky had even written an insightful piece on securitization in 1987, predicting "That which can be securitized will be securitized."[15]

As this book makes clear, however, Krugman makes two fundamental errors. First, he does not understand banking. By contrast, Minsky had a deep understanding of bank operations, gained in part from his Wall Street connections and as well from his experience sitting on the board of a St. Louis bank. That is a topic for chapter 4.

More importantly, Krugman and other mainstream economists do not understand Minsky's "beef" with orthodoxy. For Minsky, the main problem is not that orthodoxy failed to "notice" the rise of shadow banks; he would argue that their theory cannot be made good by adding this detail to their analysis.

Minsky's critique was much more fundamental than that: mainstream economics begins with the presumption that the economy is naturally stable. Market forces are supposed to move the economy back to "equilibrium"—where demand equals supply. This is precisely what Minsky rejected.

The Economist's *Mea Culpa*

With the benefit of hindsight, orthodox economists now recognize a number of factors that they claim to have led to the crisis. These are the things that Krugman and others wish they had noticed because then they would have seen the crisis coming.

1. Black Swans with Fat Tails. In the euphoric boom of the early 2000s, financial markets had priced the risks based on relatively short time horizons—typically the previous five years. They had also presumed that "tail risks" (the probability of something bad happening) were small. Note, however, that this was during the period proclaimed by Chairman Bernanke to be the "Era of the Great Moderation"—an unusually quiescent period in which asset prices marched

ever-upward. That was particularly true of U.S. residential real estate—which was the main driver of the boom. With home prices rising steadily, defaults on mortgages and foreclosures were rare. Using this period to calculate risk of default as well as to gauge tail risk would necessarily lead markets to massively underprice risk. They should have set aside bigger loss reserves in case a "black swan event" came along so that they could cover the "fat tail" losses. We know better now.

2. The Fed Kept Interest Rates Too Low for Too Long. Coming out of the "Bush Recession" at the beginning of the twenty-first century, the Fed kept rates low because the recovery was not creating enough jobs. With no inflation on the horizon, the Fed saw no reason to tighten monetary policy. But those low interest rates induced speculators to borrow to fuel asset price booms in real estate, commodities, and stocks. The Fed ignored "asset price inflation" as it focused only on prices of the "real stuff" consumers buy— which were rising slowly. If the Fed had been paying attention to the speculative bubble, it could have nipped it in the bud by raising rates. We know better now.

3. No One Noticed the Rise of Shadow Banking (Krugman's personal favorite). Paul McCulley of PIMCO (which runs the biggest bond mutual fund in the world) is credited with coining the term "shadow bank" to refer to financial institutions that are not regulated and supervised as banks— things like pension funds, money market mutual funds, mortgage companies, and various kinds of securitization vehicles. Over the two decades leading up to the GFC, these grew to be much larger than the commercial banks in terms of assets. They do many of the things banks do— including offering deposits and making loans—but without much government oversight. Most importantly, they

operate with much higher leverage ratios (the ratio of assets to capital or net worth). With very little of their "own money" at risk, they mostly use "other people's money" to buy assets. Even a very small decline in the value of the assets they hold can wipe out all the capital, at which point the "other people" start losing. Our regulators should have forced them to hold more capital, putting more of their "own money" at risk. We know better now.

So, there was nothing wrong with the orthodox economics. We just need to put fat tail risk, asset price bubbles, and shadow banks into the conventional models. Then we'll see the next crisis coming. Or so the orthodox economists assure us!

The policy response since the GFC has largely been based on that view. The main recommendation is to adopt "macro-prudential regulation" to reduce "systemic risk." This is a huge topic, and there is plenty of disagreement over what it really means. However, the most important proposals have been to increase capital requirements, to force financial institutions to have "skin in the game" (more of their own money at risk), and to return some segmentation to the financial system. The idea is that we want to have a segment of the system that is relatively safe, where most people obtain their financial services, and keep that mostly separate from a segment that takes greater risks for those willing and able to bear them.

Minsky's Alternative Vision

Even if we took the three factors listed above as contributing causes to the GFC (which we should not do, as all three arguments are confused),[16] Minsky would argue that adding these to mainstream economics would do little good. It is the mainstream *vision* that is wrong—the belief that market forces are fundamentally stabilizing.

Most people have heard of Adam Smith's metaphor of the invisible hand.[17] The idea is that a market economy in which every individual seeks to satisfy her own desires will naturally reach the best possible outcome. More technically, those individuals are supposed to react to "price signals," which will bring about equality between demand and supply at a market-clearing equilibrium price.

For example, if the demand for engineers exceeds supply, their salaries rise and induce more college students to choose that profession. An equilibrium salary is reached, where demand equals supply. Similarly, if the supply of widgets exceeds the demand, producers cut back on production and lower prices until demand equals supply at the equilibrium price.

That seems like common sense; the "trick" was to show that the market economy can reach an equilibrium where *every market is simultaneously in equilibrium*—a "general equilibrium"—with supplies equal to demands throughout the entire economy. Not only that, but it had to be shown that the general equilibrium is "stable," meaning that the *invisible hand of market forces* would invariably nudge the economy toward equilibrium if it ever got out of equilibrium.

The neoclassical "vision" is that Smith's metaphor applies to our real world. To be sure, no neoclassical economist argues that the real-world economy is always in equilibrium (although a lot of their models do start from that presumption). They believe that our economy is subject to "shocks"—one of those black swan fat tail events—that move it away from equilibrium. However, the *market forces* operate to move the economy back to equilibrium after such shocks.

There is a debate within the mainstream over just how fast the market forces operate in the real world. Krugman has made a famous distinction between "saltwater" (U.S. east coast economists at Harvard, Yale, and Princeton) and "freshwater" (University of Chicago) economists. The former believe that there are stubborn "frictions" that forestall the return to equilibrium, whereas the latter believe that the equilibrating forces are strong. As a result, saltwater economists advocate a greater role for government to remove or counteract such frictions; freshwater economists think that government policy would be impotent or even make matters worse.

By contrast, Minsky argued that the internal dynamics of our modern economy are not equilibrium-seeking. There's no invisible hand operating that way. Furthermore, if we ever did achieve the mainstream's beloved "equilibrium," those internal dynamics would push us away—the system is not stable. And if by some miracle we were to get twice lucky—achieving an *equilibrium* that was *stable*—stability is *destabilizing*.

This is because quiescence changes behavior, policy making, and business opportunities. Chairman Bernanke's "Great Moderation" could not have been a stable equilibrium because market participants took into account the "moderation," discounting the likelihood of black swans and fat tails. They took on more risk. A stable economy also makes it ever more difficult to find profitable opportunities as markets tend to become saturated. Finally, economic stability promotes fiscal tightening (through automatic stabilizers that increase tax revenue and lower some kinds of spending) and monetary policy tightening; it also promotes financial deregulation on the argument that the system is more stable. These policy tendencies promote risk-taking. All of these elements ensured that the system would move from a robust structure to a fragile financial profile.

That is the fundamental insight that Minsky left with us. And it is the insight that is rejected by freshwater and saltwater economists alike. They desperately want to keep their equilibrium methods, building models of the economy that *require* stability. They need that invisible hand. Without it, their whole theoretical edifice crumbles.

Some saltwater Keynesians might object: if Minsky is right, then our modern economic system's dynamics are such that (a) stability is fleeting and (b) anything we do to make the system more stable will eventually be destabilizing. However, it seems that we actually had a very long period in the postwar years with relative stability. Stabilizing policy seemed to work. Minsky must be too pessimistic.

As we'll see, the long period of relative stability, followed by increasing instability and a series of financial crises actually proves Minsky right. According to Minsky, in the New Deal and during the immediate postwar period, we developed sets of institutions that contained the natural instability. However, over time, those institutions became less potent, in part because profit-seeking firms found ways to get around restraints but also because we gradually relaxed regulations and supervision of financial institutions.

The financial structure evolved gradually, from one that promoted stability toward one that generates greater instability. The task, then, is to come up with new sets of institutions to "reconstitute" finance (as Minsky put it), and as well to constrain the inevitable thrust toward boom and bust.

This is not just a matter of bringing back the old constraints that Roosevelt's New Deal had imposed. Times have changed. We need a *new* New Deal.

In the following chapters, we examine Minsky's contributions with a view to outlining the reforms that are necessary to constrain the instability we now face. This requires abandonment of the narrow orthodox view—neither saltwater nor freshwater can save us because both rely on the same flawed vision. We need Minsky's vision of an economy that is not necessarily equilibrium-seeking and that evolves from relative stability toward rising instability.

In chapter 1, we briefly summarize Minsky's main areas of contribution. In chapter 2, we examine the postwar development of economic theory and policy and contrast that with Keynes's revolution in theory and policy. Minsky always argued that in important ways, the Keynesian revolution was aborted because Keynes's vision was dropped as his less controversial ideas were synthesized with the old neoclassical economics. Much of Minsky's work provided a reinterpretation of Keynes and an extension to take account of the increasingly important role played by finance.

In the remaining chapters, we examine in more detail Minsky's work, which in a very important sense follows Keynes's vision while extending his revolution of theory and policy. Chapter 2, in particular, contrasts the mainstream's interpretation of Keynes with Minsky's reinterpretation.

Chapter 3 examines Minsky's early work in developing his most famous contribution, the Financial Instability Hypothesis (FIH). While beginning with Keynes's "investment theory of the cycle," Minsky adds the "financial theory of investment." Over the course of an upswing, the financial position of firms and thus of the economy as a whole becomes more fragile. Minsky began working on this model of financial instability in the late 1950s and essentially completed it in his 1975 book, *John Maynard Keynes*.[18] In spite of the title, this was most certainly *not* a biography of Keynes, nor is it even an exposition of Keynes's thought. Instead, as Minsky often put it, he "stood on the shoulders of giants"—most importantly, the shoulders of Keynes—to produce his own novel contribution to our understanding of the economy.

In chapter 4, we look at Minsky's view of banking and contrast it with the view of orthodox Keynesians like Paul

Krugman. While that orthodox approach is based on a simple "deposit multiplier," Minsky's view was based on a much deeper understanding of real-world banking. Indeed, it is even broader than that because Minsky began with balance sheets and position-taking in assets—something that he argued can be applied to all firms, households, and governments. So, in an important sense, "anyone can create money"—as he frequently argued—but "the problem is to get it accepted."

Chapter 5 explores Minsky's contributions on employment and poverty. While not as well-known as his work on the financial sector, this work—undertaken while he was at Berkeley—offered an alternative to the Kennedy–Johnson, orthodox Keynesian-based War on Poverty. From the beginning, Minsky argued that this "war" would fail because it did not contain a job creation component. For Minsky, the solution to most poverty is to eliminate involuntary unemployment. Hence he recommended a program based on the New Deal's Works Progress Administration, which created 8 million jobs during the Great Depression. It might seem strange for Minsky to have spent much of the 1960s and early 1970s working on this topic—as it seems to be only tangentially related to his preoccupation with financial instability. However, Minsky believed that maintenance of full employment and reduction of poverty and inequality were essential to promoting financial and economic stability. We'll see why in chapter 5.

Chapter 6 examines Minsky's later work, mostly produced after he had retired and moved to the Levy Economics Institute. This represents a major extension to, and revision of, his earlier work on the FIH. Rather than focusing on the evolution of financial positions over the course of a business cycle, Minsky emphasized the longer term transformation of the financial system as a whole. In some respects, this represents a return to his studies with his original dissertation advisor, the great Joseph

Schumpeter, who also was concerned with the evolution over time of the capitalist economy. Minsky developed a stages approach, according to which the capitalist economy has evolved through several different forms. As we'll see, he argued that the U.S. economy emerged from World War II with a very stable form of capitalism, but over the following half century, the financial system had evolved toward fragility. We entered a new phase of capitalism—money manager capitalism—that collapsed into the Global Financial Crisis (GFC) in 2007–2008. This chapter will provide a Minskian analysis of the GFC from that perspective.

From the 1960s on, Minsky worked on proposals to improve bank regulations and oversight. Chapter 7 begins with early work on "prudent banking"—how a "good" bank runs its business. We next examine the essential functions that need to be provided by the financial system of a developed capitalist economy. We then look at a number of Minsky's proposals that are intended to promote prudent banking while fulfilling those functions.

Chapter 8 is the concluding chapter, presenting Minsky's general reforms to promote stability, democracy, security, and equality. His interest was in policies, regulations, and programs that would reduce the natural thrust to instability that is inherent to modern capitalism, while also promoting democracy. Minsky strongly believed that rising insecurity and inequality over recent decades have made the system much more unstable. The question he addressed is how this instability can be attenuated while preserving the freedoms that democracies value.

The book also contains a list of references (Further Reading) and a list of Minsky's writings (The Collected Writings of Hyman P. Minsky). Of course there is some duplication between the two lists, but the reader should use Further Reading to look up the full source for any short citation found in the text.

1
■

Overview of Minsky's Main Contributions

The lessons I learned from [Paul] Douglas are that any formal
analytical tool—such as the Cobb-Douglas production
function—explains but little of what happens in the world,
and that to be useful, analytical tools have to be embedded in
an understanding of the institutions, traditions and legalities
of the market.

— *Minsky, 1988, p. 174*[1]

A capitalist economy can be described by a set of interrelated
balance sheets and income statements. The liabilities of the
balance sheet are commitments to make payments either on
demand, when a contingency occurs or at specified dates.

— *Minsky, 1992*[2]

Although this book is not a biography of Minsky, we begin with
a short introduction to his life.[3]

Hyman Minsky (1919–1996) studied mathematics as an
undergraduate at the University of Chicago, graduating in 1941
with a major in math and a minor in economics. He was offered
a fellowship to remain and study for a graduate degree in economics. However, he left for Harvard after only one semester
to join a research group in postwar planning, working with

Professor Wassily Leontief. He had planned to return to Chicago to resume studies, but Harvard offered a more generous fellowship to stay. That was short-lived, as he was drafted by the U.S. Army after only one semester. He was discharged in Berlin in 1946 but accepted a six-month civilian assignment in the Manpower Division of the Office of Military Government. He later said that his appreciation for the importance of specific institutions and historical circumstances grew out of that assignment.

Minsky received graduate fellowship offers from both Chicago and Harvard, but he chose Harvard because several of the professors he preferred to work with at Chicago would be absent. In 1949, he took his first permanent academic position at Brown University; like many Ph.D. candidates, he had to finish his dissertation while teaching. He was writing it under the direction of Harvard Professor Joseph Schumpeter, who, Minsky joked, "committed the cardinal sin of a dissertation advisor—he died" before Minsky could finish. Professor Leontief volunteered to fill in, even though the topic was outside his area of interest. Minsky finished in 1954. While at Brown, he married Esther De Pardo in 1955 and they had two children—one is a professor of art history, and the other is a producer for progressive radio programs.

He temporarily left Brown for a visiting position at the University of California at Berkeley, which led to a permanent position in 1957. He had a leave to work at the National Bureau of Economic Research in 1960 but remained at Berkeley until 1965. While there, he published articles in many of the top economics journals; his research included multiplier-accelerator models, central banking and money markets, employment and growth, and financial crises.

By the mid-1960s, the student movement was gearing up. While Minsky was a leftist who supported the goals, he did not always approve of the methods. He used to say that one of the reasons he left Berkeley for Washington University in St. Louis was to get some peace and quiet. In truth, there were two other reasons: a generous salary and the opportunity to be associated with Mark Twain Bank in St. Louis. That association helped to develop his understanding of financial institutions, instruments, and practices.

In 1969–1970, Minsky spent a sabbatical year at Cambridge University, UK, where he was able to engage influential economists like Joan Robinson and Frank Hahn and begin a close friendship with Jan Kregel (who wrote his dissertation with Robinson). Some years later, Kregel helped to create the Trieste Summer School of Advanced Economic Studies, held annually in the late summer on the coast of northern Italy; Minsky gave lectures there and debated fellow post-Keynesian economists, such as Paul Davidson and Pierangelo Garegnani. He would often sit in the middle of the audience and read a newspaper while others lectured—appearing to ignore them—but then launch penetrating questions in the discussion that followed.

When he retired from teaching in 1990, he moved to the Levy Economics Institute at Bard College as a distinguished scholar, where he remained until his death in 1996. At the Levy Institute, he established two of the institute's ongoing research programs: Monetary Policy and Financial Structure, and the State of the U.S. and World Economies; he was also a driving force behind the institute's efforts to influence policy formation. For example, he formulated a proposal to develop a national system of community development banks—and some of the ideas were incorporated into a bill signed by President Clinton to fund a (smaller) program.

He was a recipient in 1996 of the Veblen–Commons Award, given by the Association for Evolutionary Economics in recognition of exemplary standards of scholarship, teaching, public service, and research in the field of evolutionary institutional economics. Though he is commonly identified as a post-Keynesian, he preferred "financial Keynesian" as a description of his work and felt close to the American institutionalists.

Minsky's politics were idiosyncratically leftist. On one hand, he was active in leftist—even self-described radical—political activities as a student. His parents were Mensheviks, Russian refugees who met in America at a party to celebrate the 100th birthday of Karl Marx, sponsored by the Socialist Party of the United States. During the years in Berkeley, he participated in political groups that were on the left wing of the Democratic Party. His politics played a role in his decisions to leave both Brown and Berkeley as he had angered top administrators at both universities sufficiently that further promotion was endangered.

On the other hand, as a student in Chicago he became a close friend of Paul Douglas (of Cobb–Douglas production function fame and future U.S. Senator), who saw him as a safe opponent of Leninism. He befriended many bankers and Wall Street traders, including Leon Levy and Henry Kaufman. Many of his closest friends in academic economics were mainstream and not particularly liberal (in the American sense). He had no desire to partition the discipline into "us" versus "them." In the last months of his life, he asked his colleagues at the Levy Institute to reach out to the mainstream, telling all of us that the time was right "to move the discipline"—at least a little.

He loved to shock his more left-wing students by railing against the welfare state—sometimes sounding like President Reagan. (I found out later what he had against welfare—it is discussed in chapter 5.)

He rarely taught or even talked about Marx and infrequently mentioned him in his writing. He could be fairly scathing in his criticism of work done by many economists on the left. As discussed below, his two most important influences during his studies at the University of Chicago were Henry Simons and Oscar Lange. This adds to the confusion about his politics, as most economists today would include Simons in Chicago's "free-market" branch of economics and Lange in the socialist camp—or worse, a *communist*.

However, in Minsky's views, each of them was offering a (different) way to make markets "work." Minsky would later report that it broke his heart when Lange left Chicago to work for the new Communist government in Poland. While Minsky credited Lange as a major influence, Minsky avoided him later in the 1940s when Lange came to New York—presumably because of his association with the communist government. It is safe to say that few of his fellow economists would have labeled his politics as radical—even if he, himself, occasionally did!

His biggest influences were the Chicago school's institutionalist tradition (especially Henry Simons and Paul Douglas, but he also worked with those outside the camp, including Lange, Jacob Viner, and Frank Knight) and Harvard's Joseph Schumpeter. The way he saw it, "the socialism of Lange had more in common with the capitalism of Simons than with the socialism of Stalin, and the capitalism of Simons had more in common with the socialism of Lange than with the capitalism of Hitler."[4] He also noted that among the senior faculty at Chicago, only Lange and possibly Douglas were sympathetic to the work of Keynes.

Minsky left copious bound class notes from courses he had with Lange and Knight—and these reinforce his claim that economics at Chicago in those days was taught as "part of the study of society, where economic history, political science, sociology, anthropology and economics were part of an integrated sequence aimed at understanding modern society," which he claimed to be "vastly superior to the usual practice of teaching economics in isolation in a specialized course. If I had my way the standard American course in economics would be introduced in the context of social sciences and history. The current American way of teaching economics leads to American economists who are well-trained but poorly educated."[5]

Although he served as Alvin Hansen's teaching assistant at Harvard, he later remarked that the "mechanistic" approach of mainstream Keynesians did not appeal to him. J. M. Keynes clearly influenced Minsky, but he did not have much affinity with the postwar American "Keynesians"—Paul Samuelson, Robert Solow, and James Tobin[6]—who Joan Robinson called "bastard Keynesians" (she said that we know the mother was neoclassical economics, but the father is unknown—certainly not Keynes).

Since Harvard was known to be "Keynesian" at the time, while the University of Chicago came to be known as the home of Milton Friedman's "monetarism," it is surprising that Minsky took away more from his early training at Chicago. However, as he insisted, Minsky's Chicago was nothing like today's bastion of free-market ideology. What he learned at Chicago was an appreciation for the need to develop a detailed understanding of real-world institutions and behavior, as well as of economic history. His notes from courses reveal that Chicago's economics was a far cry from the esoteric mathematical models taught today to graduate students.

From his earliest work, Minsky was interested in studying the dynamic, evolutionary change of an economy operating with institutional constraints. Indeed, in one of his first papers, he took Paul Samuelson's famous linear-accelerator model and added institutional "ceilings and floors." We address this work in more detail later, but the basic idea is that the modern capitalist economy is naturally unstable, with forces that cause it to move from boom to bust.

That is what Minsky borrowed from Samuelson's model. However, Minsky argued that a variety of institutions—some private, some public—constrain that instability. This is what he learned from the institutionalist tradition at Chicago. Combining the two, Minsky could explain that although there is a natural cyclical tendency in modern economies, runaway inflations and depressions are rare events because instability is attenuated by institutional constraints.

Minsky's approach to banking drew heavily on Jack Gurley and E. S. Shaw,[7] while adapting Schumpeter's theory of innovation to analysis of the financial sector. During the 1960s, he was involved in major studies of monetary policy formation and banking regulation, doing research for the Federal Reserve's Board of Governors and for the California state banking commission. Later, he served on the board of a Missouri bank holding company, which helped him to keep a finger on the pulse of finance. He also became a close friend to Martin Mayer, the most astute historian of American postwar financial institutions.

While at Berkeley, Minsky worked closely with labor economists to develop policy to reduce unemployment and poverty. Indeed, Minsky proposed an alternative to the Kennedy–Johnson War on Poverty, arguing that to be successful, an anti-poverty program would need to focus on job creation. Minsky integrated this proposal into his policy recommendations to promote economic stability.

All of this experience provided a deep understanding of real-world institutions and practices that influenced his writing and thinking. After he moved to the Levy Institute, he used Wall Street connections to establish a long-running research project titled "The Reconstitution of the Financial System," which led to the creation of the "Minsky Conference," held every year in April.[8] In recent years, his work on unemployment and poverty was also recovered, leading to a revival of interest in direct job creation as an important component of policy to promote full employment and economic stability.[9]

Minsky's Main Areas of Research

Minsky is best known for his development of the Financial Instability Hypothesis (FIH), but it was by no means his only contribution. This section also examines his work in three other areas: his analysis of money and banking; his "employer of last resort" proposal; and his views on the longer term evolution of the economy. Here we provide only a brief overview of his main research areas; in the chapters that follow, we go into more detail.

Money and Financial Institutions

Following Gurley and Shaw, Minsky took a broad approach to money creation, arguing that "everyone can create money; the problem is to get it accepted."[10] Money is really just an IOU denominated in the money of account, but there is a hierarchy of monies—some are more widely accepted than others—with the monetary IOUs issued by the treasury and the central bank sitting at the top of the money pyramid.

Minsky saw banking as essentially the business of "accepting" IOUs, making payments on behalf of customers, and holding their liabilities. Banks make payments in their own IOUs, which are then cleared using the central bank's reserves. Furthermore, "(b)ecause bankers live in the same expectational climate as businessmen, profit-seeking bankers will find ways of accommodating their customers; this behavior by bankers reinforces dis-equilibrating pressures. Symmetrically, the processes that decrease the prices of capital assets will also decrease the willingness of bankers to finance business."[11] In other words, the "money supply" expands and contracts as bankers accommodate the demands of their customers in a procyclical manner: when business is good, loans are easy to get; when prospects are bad, banks do not want to lend.

In one of his first publications,[12] Minsky analyzed the development of the "fed funds" market in the United States—the interbank market where banks lend reserves to one another to meet clearing drains as well as legally required reserve ratios. At the time, this was a relatively new financial innovation. Most people thought that the quantity of reserves constrains bank lending, since they would need to accumulate reserves *before* lending in order to be sure they would not be caught short.

Minsky, however, argued that banks use the fed funds market to economize on reserves—no bank would need to hold any extra reserves (called excess reserves) since they could lend them at interest to other banks that needed them. This would make it difficult for the Federal Reserve (Fed) to influence lending activity or "money creation" by trying to constrain reserves. According to Minsky, bank lending would not be determined by the quantity of reserves they held, but rather by the willingness of banks to lend, and of their customers to borrow. If they then needed reserves for clearing or to meet legal reserve requirements, they would simply go to the fed funds market and borrow them.

The implication is that if the central bank wants to influence bank lending, it must affect the decision of banks to lend and borrowers to borrow. For example, it can raise required underwriting standards (in which banks determine creditworthiness of borrowers)—forcing banks to require more collateral and better credit histories. Central banks can also raise interest rates to try to reduce lending; they do not really use the quantity of reserves to do so. Instead, they operate with interest rate targets, not reserve quantity targets.

Stemming from his research conducted for the Fed in the 1960s, Minsky came to the conclusion that reserves should be provided mostly at the discount window—forcing banks to borrow them directly from the central bank, rather than obtaining them from other banks or through open market purchases by the central bank. Minsky favored pushing banks to the discount window and forcing them to open their "books" (show the Fed their assets) when they wanted to borrow reserves.

By choosing which assets are eligible for "discounting," a bank submits assets that the Fed "discounts"—that is, lends reserves against. This method would allow the central bank to more closely supervise banks and to favor safer bank activities by choosing what could serve as collateral against loans of reserves.

Unfortunately, the Fed went the other way, gradually abandoning the discount window in favor of open market operations. In this, the Fed actually followed the recommendations of the monetarists like Milton Friedman, who wanted the Fed to control the *quantity* of reserves but let the market determine the allocation of reserves among banks as well as the "market price" (the interest rate) of reserves. In the early 1980s, the Fed even adopted a Friedman-type rule, which was to have reserves and the money supply grow at a constant rate. All of this was more consistent with the "free-market" views of Friedman.

That policy is now recognized as a complete failure. Minsky would be pleased to see that all modern central banks now operate with an overnight interest rate target (as he preferred), although they still persist in a "hands-off" policy of providing reserves largely through open market operations rather than at the discount window as he recommended. This method reduces their ability to supervise the banks, as Minsky wanted them to do.

If the Fed had been watching bank balance sheets closely in the early to mid-2000s, it would have seen all the trashy assets they were accumulating. Lending at the discount window would have provided the Fed with a clearer view of bank balance sheets. If it had followed Minsky's recommendation, it might have constrained the runaway speculative bubble driven by excessive bank lending without proper underwriting.

Financial Instability Hypothesis

The procyclical behavior of bank lending amplifies the business cycle, increasing the thrust toward instability. For Minsky, the modern business cycle *is* a financial cycle. Rising spending and asset purchases require finance. So long as banks are willing to meet the demand for finance, output and asset prices grow. This growth can increase the demand for credit as well as bank willingness to lend.

As Citigroup's CEO Chuck Prince famously explained, "as long as the music is playing, you've got to get up and dance." If everyone else is lending, your bank has to lend. But when the music stops, you suddenly find that your bank is holding assets it does not want and cannot sell. Lending and spending and asset prices collapse. Without this procyclical behavior of finance, we might still have business cycles, but they would be much attenuated and debt deflation would be impossible. We can think of the financial sector as an accelerator of the cycle—in both directions.

Minsky's theory can be summarized as "an investment theory of the cycle and a financial theory of investment." The first is the usual Keynesian view, which sees fluctuations of investment spending as driving the business cycle. When firms are optimistic, investment in plant and equipment grows, creating jobs and income. When expectations turn around, spending and employment fall.

Minsky's extension was to add the financial theory of investment, stressing that modern investment is expensive and must be financed—and it is the financing that generates structural fragility. During an upswing, profit-seeking firms and banks become more optimistic, taking on riskier financial structures. Firms commit larger portions of expected revenues to debt service. Lenders accept smaller down payments and lower quality collateral.

In the boom, financial institutions innovate new products and finesse rules and regulations imposed by supervisory authorities. Borrowers use more external finance (borrowing rather than using savings or retained earnings) and increasingly issue short-term debt that is potentially volatile (it must be "rolled over," or renewed, so there is risk that lenders might refuse to do so). As the economy heats up, the central bank hikes its interest rate to cool things down—but with greater use of short-term finance, borrowers face higher debt service costs (with short-term finance they cannot "lock in" rates).

Minsky developed a famous classification for fragility of financing positions. The safest is called "hedge" finance (note that this term is not related to so-called hedge funds). In a hedge position, expected income is sufficient to make all payments as they come due, including both interest and principal. A "speculative" position is one in which expected income is sufficient to make interest payments, but principal must be rolled over. It is "speculative" in the sense that income must increase, continued access to refinancing must be expected, or an asset must be sold to cover the principal payment.

Finally, a "Ponzi" position (named after a famous fraudster, Charles Ponzi, who ran a pyramid scheme—much like Bernie Madoff's more recent fraud) is one in which even interest payments cannot be met, so the debtor must borrow to pay interest (the outstanding loan balance grows by the interest due). Speculative positions turn into Ponzi positions if income falls or if interest rates rise. As the recent crisis showed, Ponzi finance also may emerge from the underwriting practices of the financial industry. Many households started from Ponzi finance positions in the early to mid-2000s because they took out mortgages they could not service.

Ponzi positions are inherently problematic as default is avoided only so long as the lender allows the loan balance to grow. Beyond some point, the lender will cut losses by forcing default.

Over the business cycle, fragility rises, exposing the system to the possibility of a crisis coming from a variety of directions: income flows turn out to be lower than expected, interest rates rise, lenders curtail lending, or a prominent firm or bank defaults on payment commitments. Just as finance accelerates the boom, it fuels the collapse as debtors need to cut back spending and sell assets to make contractual payments.

As spending falls, income and employment fall; as assets are sold, their prices fall. In the extreme, debt-deflation dynamics that Irving Fisher saw in the Great Depression can be generated—asset values plummet, wealth is wiped out, and widespread bankruptcies occur. That causes people and firms to cut back spending, so output and employment collapse.

However, following his early training in Chicago, Minsky recognized that institutional "ceilings and floors" can help to attenuate the cycle. The most obvious ones come from government, although there are also private institutional constraints, such as stock market rules that suspend trading when prices fall too far, helping to slow the deflation process.

The two most important constraining institutions are the "Big Government" (national treasury) and the "Big Bank" (central bank). The first helps to stabilize the economy through a countercyclical budget—spending falls and taxes rise in a boom, while spending rises and taxes fall in a bust—so budget surpluses in expansion and deficits in recession constrain the cycle. For Minsky, there is nothing wrong with a rising government budget deficit in recession—indeed, this deficit is necessary to prevent recessions from morphing into depressions.

The central bank can try to constrain lending in a boom (although Minsky was skeptical since profit-seeking banks innovate around constraints—the creation of the fed funds market is an example of one of those innovations). But more importantly, the central bank can act as lender of last resort when a financial crisis hits. The central bank should lend reserves to any banks that need them to meet withdrawals. Indeed, Minsky advocated extending discount window lending to a broad range of financial institutions, including "nonbank banks" (now called shadow banks). This lending prevents a run on financial institutions, which reduces pressure on banks to engage in fire sales of assets to meet withdrawals.

Minsky would have argued that the reason the GFC did not turn into a 1930s-style Great Depression is because the Big Government's budget moved sharply to large deficits (up to a trillion dollars) and the Big Bank (Fed) lent reserves on an unprecedented scale. Minsky probably would have argued that the deficit should have been even bigger and that the Fed's response should have been quicker and more decisive. He probably also would have criticized Washington (as well as London, Tokyo, and the European Monetary Union) for removing fiscal stimulus far too early, before sustained recovery got under way. However, he no doubt would have pointed to Big Governments and Big Banks as the main institutional factors that prevented a full-scale depression from engulfing the globe after 2008.

Employer of Last Resort

While Minsky's work on poverty and unemployment is not well known, from the 1960s through the mid-1970s he wrote almost as much on this topic as he did on financial instability. Although it might not be obvious, the two are linked. Minsky believed that reducing unemployment, poverty, and inequality would help to promote financial stability.

At Berkeley, he worked with labor economists to formulate an antipoverty strategy focusing on employment rather than welfare. Minsky criticized the Kennedy–Johnson War on Poverty, warning that without a significant job creation component it would fail to reduce poverty even as it created a welfare-dependent and marginalized class. He showed that offering one full-time job per low-income household instead–even at the minimum wage— would raise two-thirds of all poor families above the poverty line.[13] Furthermore, he estimated that the output created by putting people to work would more than provide for the extra consumption needed by the new workers by increasing gross domestic product (GDP) by a multiple of the extra wages.

Minsky argued that a legislated minimum wage is "effective" only with an "employer of last resort" (ELR) for otherwise the true minimum wage is zero for all those who cannot find a job. Hence, he proposed that the national government stand ready to fund a job for anyone ready and willing to work at the minimum wage. Only the national government can afford to offer an "infinitely elastic" supply of jobs at the minimum wage.

What he meant is that the national government would set the program wage, then hire all of those ready and willing to work at that wage. He called this an "employer of last resort program" in the sense that anyone with a better offer—either in the private sector or in regular government jobs—would take it. You could also think of the program as providing a "reserve army of the employed" since employers could recruit out of the program by paying slightly higher compensation. In Minsky's view, that is much better than Marx's "reserve army of the unemployed"— because the unemployed lose skills and develop bad habits while waiting for a job.

The government as employer of last resort (ELR) serves as a bookend to the central bank as lender of last resort—just as the lender of last resort sets a floor to asset prices (by lending so that banks do not have to engage in fire sales), the employer of last resort sets a floor to wages (anyone willing to work can get the minimum wage) and thus also to aggregate demand and consumption. In this manner, countercyclical fiscal policy is enhanced (government spending on job creation rises in recession and falls in expansion when workers are hired away by the private sector) and supplements countercyclical monetary policy interventions.

Minsky insisted that workers in the ELR program would do useful things and would gain skills on the job. He modeled his proposal on the various New Deal jobs programs. He actually had personal experience with them because he had worked in one as an assistant to Professor Paul Douglas (who later became a U.S. Senator), estimating Cobb–Douglas production functions!

Minsky was not advocating "make-work" projects, as that would be demoralizing for the workers and politically unpalatable. Like Keynes, Minsky was certain that there is plenty for such workers to do: improvements in parks and on school grounds, environmental enhancement (cleanup, reforestation, retrofitting buildings to improve energy efficiency), and a wide range of public services (including such work as Meals on Wheels for the aged and playground monitors for children).

Minsky saw the ELR program as a stabilizing alternative to the typical 1960s Keynesian approach that relied on a combination of "pump-priming" policy to encourage investment, plus welfare for those who fall behind. In Minsky's view, that approach would entail a "stop–go," destabilizing policy—with government ramping up demand to lower unemployment, then cutting spending and raising taxes to fight the inflation caused by pump priming. By promoting investment to get a boom going, government would also increase financial instability because part of the investment would be financed by private debt; then when government attempted to cool the economy, firms (and households) would have difficulty making payments on that debt run-up in good times. Hence, Minsky saw his proposal as preferable to the Keynesian approach.

Long-Term Evolution of the Economy

Whereas Minsky's FIH is usually interpreted as a theory of the business cycle, he also developed a theory of the long-term transformation of the economy, focusing especially on the changes since World War II. Here we quickly summarize Minsky's views; a more detailed treatment is provided later.

According to Minsky, capitalism has evolved through several stages, each marked by a different financial structure. The nineteenth century saw "commercial capitalism," where commercial banking dominated—banks made short-term commercial loans (for example, to allow firms to hire labor and buy raw materials) and issued deposits. Firms repaid these loans once they finished production and sold goods and services. Investment was mostly financed out of retained profits. Banking was relatively safe, except when a run on deposits developed—which governments learned to forestall by having the central bank act as lender of last resort.

This system was replaced by the beginning of the twentieth century, with "finance capitalism," a term coined by Rudolf Hilferding, where investment banks ruled. The distinguishing characteristic of this stage was the use by firms of long-term external finance to purchase expensive capital assets. The financial structure was riskier because the long-term finance could be repaid only over time and only if the investment project proved to be wise. This phase of capitalism collapsed into the Great Depression—which Minsky saw as the failure of finance capitalism.

We emerged from World War II with a new form of capitalism—"managerial welfare-state capitalism"—in which financial institutions were constrained by New Deal reforms, and with large oligopolistic corporations that financed investment out of retained earnings.[14] Private sector debt was small, but government debt left over from war finance was large—providing safe assets for households, firms, and banks. Unemployment was low, and government had put in place a social safety net to take care of the poor and the elderly. This system was financially robust and unlikely to experience deep recession because of the Big Government and Big Bank constraints discussed above.

However, the relatively stable prosperity of the first few decades after World War II generated a large pool of savings and encouraged ever-greater risk-taking, leading to "money manager capitalism." In this form of capitalism, the dominant financial players are "managed money"—lightly regulated "shadow banks," such as pension funds, hedge funds, sovereign wealth funds, and university endowments—with huge pools of funds in search of the highest returns. Innovations by financial engineers encouraged growth of private debt relative to income and increased reliance on volatile short-term finance.

Many others have also noticed some of these developments, with a variety of terms used to describe the new form of capitalism: critics have called it financialization and casino capitalism, whereas supporters called it the ownership society and neoliberalism. It was accompanied by the increasing domination of "finance" over "industry," the rising concentration of income and wealth at the top (the "1 percent"), reduction of government regulation in favor of "self-supervision" of the biggest financial institutions, rising debt ratios and increased layering of debt on debt, and dismantling of barriers to international trade and capital movement.

As a result of these changes, cracks in the financial system began to appear. The first U.S. postwar financial crisis occurred in 1966 (in the municipal bond market), but it was quickly resolved by swift government intervention. This set a pattern: crises came more frequently in the 1970s and 1980s, but government saved the day each time. As a result, ever more risky financial arrangements were "validated" by government intervention, leading to more experimentation. The crises became more severe, requiring greater rescue efforts by governments. Finally, the entire global financial system crashed in 2007—with many calling it the "Minsky Moment" or "Minsky crisis." Unfortunately, most analyses relied on his FIH rather than on his "stages" approach. As such, they did not understand that this was a crash of the entire financial system—not a garden-variety crisis.

If, as Minsky believed, the financial system had experienced a long-term transformation toward fragility then recovery without major reform would only presage an even bigger collapse—on a scale such as the 1929 crash that ended the finance capitalism stage. The only way to really cure the problem is fundamental—New Deal style—reforms. Anything less would just set the economy up for another crash.

What crashed in 2007 was "money manager capitalism." In important ways that Minsky identified, this stage was similar to the "finance capitalism" that crashed in 1929. Of course, the Great Depression followed that crash, leading to the development of a New Deal that substantially reformed the economy and especially the financial system.

This time, we got a very serious downturn and a terrible financial crisis, yet we did not sink to the depths of the 1930s depression, when unemployment reached 25 percent, the nation's output fell by half, and stock prices fell by up to 85 percent.

Why the difference? Minsky's answer was Big Government and Big Bank. The first referred to the federal government's share of the economy, which grew from around 3 percent of GDP to above 20 percent. A big government with a big budget is able to cushion the downturn through countercyclical spending. The Big Bank is the Fed, which intervenes to prop up financial institutions and markets.

Although the Fed had existed since 1913, it saw its role as very limited when the "Great Crash" of 1929 hit. Half of all banks failed over the following decade (most of them very quickly). However, after 2007 the Fed took a very broad view of its role—it saved not only banks and other financial institutions, but even intervened directly into financial markets, buying assets the markets did not want.

The Fed lent a cumulative total of $29 trillion over the next few years to rescue the financial system—an amount equal to double the annual GDP.[15] Whether or not that was good policy, this unprecedented intervention prevented or at least postponed a bigger collapse. Moreover, the "Big Government's" budget deficit rose above a trillion dollars annually. That helped to prop up aggregate demand. Together these interventions have prevented another Great Depression—so far.

What Minsky's analysis leads us to worry about, however, is that to the degree that these policies help to return the economy to stability, they are destabilizing! Financial market participants will adjust their expectations to include government bailouts should anything go wrong. So ironically, the success of the interventions encourages more risk-taking.

In the aftermath of the Great Depression, market participants were very careful, avoiding risk for decades—until memories of the debacle faded. This time around, certain kinds of risk-taking returned fairly quickly, although other behaviors that had led to big losses did not. Still, by 2012 many indicators of financial fragility (including debt ratios and stock prices relative to sales revenue) had returned to 2007 levels (or even higher!). Some of the dangerous financial practices that prevailed before the GFC are once again flourishing. Covenant-lite loans (loans made with fewer restrictions, such as collateral and income requirements), "payment-in-kind" securities, junk bonds, high-yield collateralized debt obligations, and the belief that efficient market pricing makes underwriting redundant are all on the rise.

Will we have another big financial crisis? We cannot be sure, but Minsky's theory tells us that it is probable. Furthermore, his theory provides some guidance for restructuring the financial system and for putting in place economic stabilizers that together could reduce the likelihood of a repeat performance in the near future.

Following his institutionalist roots, Minsky argued that there are "57 varieties" of capitalism, so the death of money manager capitalism might be replaced with a new, more stable form. However, as he insisted, there is no final once-and-for-all solution for the inherent tendency to instability of capitalism.

For that reason, Minsky still matters. In the final section of this chapter, we turn to Minsky's policy recommendations.

Reforming Capitalism

Minsky provided a number of general proposals to reform capitalism, to make it more stable as well as more equitable. Here is a summary of his main policy proposals. We save for later more specific proposals to deal with the problem of money manager capitalism and excessive financialization of our economy.

BIG GOVERNMENT (SIZE, SPENDING, TAXING)

According to Minsky, government must be large enough so that the swings of its budget are sufficient to offset swings of private investment. This definition dictates that government spending should be approximately "the same order of magnitude as or larger than investment".[16] Following Keynes, Minsky believed that the most volatile component of private spending is investment in plant and equipment; if the government is big enough, and if its budget swings countercyclically, that can offset fluctuation of investment and hence stabilize aggregate demand. By this measure, the U.S. federal government—at about a fifth of GDP—is more than large enough (as it is substantially larger than investment).

Minsky made this proposal when U.S. trade with foreign nations was essentially balanced and when consumption by households was fairly stable (passively adjusting to changes of household income). However, international trade has become more important, and swings of the trade deficit introduce more instability for the U.S. economy.[17] Furthermore, consumption also has become less stable as households rely increasingly on credit to finance spending, which Minsky started to recognize in the early 1990s. In a downturn, consumers cut back on borrowing and spending, making matters worse.

For these reasons, our Big Government's budget probably needs to be larger than investment spending. This means, for example, that at full employment the budget should be about 20 percent of GDP; below full employment, spending would be somewhat more than this while tax revenues would be less; above full employment, tax revenues would exceed 20 percent of GDP while spending might be less. The countercyclical swing of the budget would take demand out of the economy in a boom and add demand in a slump. This situation would help to offset swings of private spending.

With regard to taxes, Minsky believed that most taxes are inflationary because they add to costs; in particular, he argued that the portion of the Social Security tax paid by employers as well as the corporate income tax are costs passed along in prices (Minsky, *Stabilizing*, 1986, p. 305). In addition, Minsky feared that the payroll tax encourages substitution of capital for labor (more machines, fewer workers). He thus advocated elimination of the corporate income tax as well as the employer portion of the payroll tax.

He supported a broad-based value-added tax as an alternative (these are sales taxes on consumption and are common in Europe). He also supported greater use of excise and "sin" taxes to influence behavior; in particular, he advocated a much larger tax on petroleum to reduce its use.

EMPLOYMENT STRATEGY AND INFLATION

Minsky wanted to reorder spending priorities toward employment programs, child allowances, and public infrastructure investment, and away from defense and non-Old Age, Survivors, Disability, and Hospital Insurance (OASDHI) transfers (Minsky, *Stabilizing*, 1986, p. 308). He believed that an employment program could substitute for most transfers other than those aimed at the aged, which would allow substantial cuts in non-defense spending.

Finally, he wanted to dispense with automatic cost-of-living adjustments in transfer payments so that inflation would move the government's budget toward balance (by increasing tax revenues through "bracket creep" while avoiding automatic increases of social spending). This would help to attenuate the thrust to inflation when the economy operates at full employment.

Part of the reason Minsky wanted to reduce transfers (e.g., "welfare," food stamps, and unemployment compensation) is because he was convinced that these transfers impart an inflationary bias to the economy (Minsky, *Stabilizing*, 1986, p. 313). In his view, the level of aggregate demand determines the markup of prices at the aggregate level over aggregate costs of production (primarily wages). As social spending generates income and adds to aggregate demand without contributing much to aggregate supply, the markup over costs is higher. As transfer payments rise relative to output, prices rise.

If government spending could be shifted away from policies to raise aggregate demand without increasing production to those that would increase both aggregate demand as well as aggregate supply, then prices would be lower. In particular, public infrastructure development as well as job creation through an employer of last resort program (rather than welfare) would reduce inflation by increasing capacity to supply along with increasing demand.

CORPORATE REFORM

While the corporate form is necessary in an economy with extremely expensive capital assets, according to Minsky this sort of institutional arrangement "facilitates the divorce of financing from the ownership and acquisition of particular assets. . . . Consequently, the corporation, initially a device for extending hedge financing to long-lasting capital assets, can be a vehicle for speculative finance—and because it facilitates both capital intensive modes of production and speculative financing, a destabilizing influence" (Minsky, *Stabilizing*, 1986, p. 316). What Minsky is saying is that the creation of corporations helped to provide funds for investment since firms could sell stocks; however, the modern stock market is used mostly for speculation—not for financing new capital stock.

He believed that policies could reduce the "instability-enhancing power of corporations." Some of the policies he advanced were elimination of the corporate income tax, which leads to a bias in favor of debt financing over equity financing, as well as to leveraged buyouts that increase indebtedness of the takeover targets (since interest receives favorable tax treatment, borrowing is encouraged). He also pushed for policies that would favor employment of labor over investment in physical capital (such as elimination of the payroll tax on employers). High employment is stabilizing as it induces growth based on consumption rather than on investment.

MARKET POWER

Countercyclical government deficits maintain profit flows, allowing firms to meet their debt commitments. Minsky saw no alternative to such policy on an aggregate level (Minsky, *Stabilizing*, 1986, p. 332)—Big Government's budget needs to help stabilize the economy. However, it is essential that individual firms and banks are allowed to fail; otherwise, there is no market discipline.

In Minsky's view, the primary incentive to obtaining market power is the ability to set prices at a sufficient level to service debt. In the small government form of capitalism (that is, the kind of capitalism we had before World War II), collusion and government policy may be warranted to try to maintain prices in conditions of low demand. However, in Big Government capitalism, where government deficits maintain profits, "there is no need for policy to foster market power that protects profits" (Minsky, *Stabilizing*, 1986, p. 318).

Indeed, Minsky feared that conditions favoring large monopolies could be detrimental because they would lead to firms that are "too big to fail." Thus, he favored policies that would reduce the incentives to "bigness"; in particular, he believed that policies that favor medium size banks would also favor medium size firms, as bank size determines, to a large extent, the size of customers—big banks serve big customers, while medium size banks serve medium size customers. "A decentralized banking system with many small and independent banks is conducive to an industrial structure made up of mainly small and medium-size firms" (Minsky, *Stabilizing*, 1986, p. 319).[18]

Policies that would promote such a system include elimination of much of the segmentation of activities such as commercial banking and investment (for small-to-medium size banks so they could provide a wide range of services to their small-to-medium size customers), uniform and high capital-to-asset ratios (this would favor smaller banks as these typically have higher ratios), and freer entry.

Minsky also argued that industrial policy should not only favor smaller firms but could also favor employment over capital-intensive production techniques. Smaller firms tend to use more labor-intensive techniques because their ability to finance purchase of long-lived and expensive capital assets is lower.

He also favored regulation and government intervention into specific markets wherever this would promote competition. Though he agreed with orthodoxy that "competitive markets are devices to promote efficiency," he went on to note that, "The market is an adequate regulator of products and processes except when market power or externalities exist; once they exist—whether caused by the government or by market processes—regulation can be necessary to constrain the exercise of power" (Minsky, *Stabilizing*, 1986, p. 329). Thus, "An industrial policy that takes the form of promoting competitive industry, facilitating financing and aiding and abetting the develop of a labor force that is trained and productive, is highly desirable" (Minsky, *Stabilizing*, 1986, p. 329). Note, by the way, that he credited his Chicago teacher, Henry Simons, for this insight.

He also saw industrial policy as a viable alternative to antitrust prosecution, which he believed to be a failure because it cannot create the conditions required to permit smaller firms to prosper.

2

∎

Where Did We Go Wrong? Macroeconomics and the Road Not Taken

Just as there never really was a Keynesian revolution
in economic theory, there also never really was one in
policy. . . . All that was assimilated from Keynes by the policy
establishment and its clients was the analysis of an economy
in deep depression and a policy tool of deficit financing.
—*Minsky, 1986, p. 291*[1]

We first examine mainstream economics to help us understand why it failed to see the crisis coming. We then discuss how mainstream economics deviated from Keynes's own economics—which had represented a revolution in thought. In important respects, that revolution failed; however, it strongly influenced Minsky. For that reason, it is worthwhile to see how Keynes's own economics provides the basis for understanding how orthodoxy gets it wrong.

The Mainstream Theory That Dominated Economics until the GFC

Before we delve deeply into Minsky's approach, it is useful to quickly review the mainstream economics that he rejected. As

we said earlier, Minsky moved from the University of Chicago—
which at that time was a home to institutional economics (only later
did it become a bastion of Milton Friedman's monetarism)—to
Harvard University for his graduate studies, which became one
of the foremost centers for Keynesian economics.

At Harvard, Minsky was assigned to be Alvin Hansen's
teaching assistant. Hansen could be called the father of American Keynesianism as he played a role in refining and propagat-
ing the main "Keynesian"[2] model that began to appear in all
macroeconomic textbooks—the famous ISLM model (often
called the Hicks–Hansen model, this is misleadingly presented
in mainstream macroeconomics courses as *Keynes's* model[3]).
Minsky found Hansen's approach to Keynes "too mechanical,"
and he also faulted the "Keynesians" for "lack of nerve" because
they failed to embrace income redistribution (from rich to poor)
as a means to increase aggregate demand (since the poor spend
more and save less than do the rich, redistribution would have
increased consumer demand). So while Keynes's own theory
was extremely important for Minsky's own approach, he rejected the version propagated by "Keynesians."

Like Minsky, many others have also questioned the degree to
which "Keynesian" theory and policy actually followed Keynes's
General Theory (GT).[4] Immediately after World War II, mac-
roeconomists set out to "marry" the "Keynesian" ISLM model
with the old pre-Keynesian microeconomic theory based on
individual rational utility and profit maximization—in other
words, the neoclassical approach to the behavior of firms and
consumers.[5] Paul Samuelson called it the "neoclassical synthesis," and it became the foundation for macroeconomics taught
in classrooms.[6]

Macro theory continued to develop through the 1960s as
James Tobin's portfolio balance approach, Don Patinkin's real
balance effect (which made the labor market dominate), and

the Phillips curve (unemployment–inflation trade-off) were added to Hicks's ISLM model.[7] Likewise, "Keynesian" policy based on this synthesis gradually developed over the postwar period, finally taking hold in the administration of President Kennedy.

Beginning in the 1950s, Milton Friedman developed monetarism as a "laissez-faire" opposition to Keynesian policy, which relied on government intervention.[8] For two decades, the "Keynesian" and the "monetarist" approaches dominated economic debate. While Keynesians favored discretionary fine-tuning of fiscal policy, the monetarists preferred rules-based monetary policy.

Still, even the monetarist approach was easily integrated within the neoclassical synthesis so that the "great debate" between "Keynesians" and monetarists was reduced to differences over parameters (interest rate elasticity of investment and income elasticity of money demand) and policy prescriptions (discretionary interest rate targets or money growth rules).

In both of these theoretical approaches, money and financial institutions play only a tangential role, with "real" variables dominating in the long run where money is "neutral," determining only the price level. In the short run, money might be nonneutral (affecting decisions) as workers and firms could mistake a nominal price rise for a real or relative price increase.

For example, if your hourly wage rises by 10 percent but prices of everything you buy also rise by 10 percent, the "real" or relative prices have not changed, and you *should not* change your behavior. You would be willing to work more hours because of the higher nominal wage only if you had been "fooled" because you ignored inflation of prices. Surprisingly, the degree to which people are "fooled" in this manner became perhaps the single biggest controversy to separate rival mainstream approaches to economics after the 1960s.

The debate concerned whether an increase of the money supply would simply cause prices to rise (without changing behavior) or would increase spending and income in *real terms*. Symmetrically, if the central bank reduces the money supply—which should lower prices—would workers accept a reduction of nominal wages, or would they work fewer hours because they mistook a lower nominal wage (and also lower prices) for a lower real wage?

Whether or not policy "matters" came down to the "fooling" question—monetarists argued that it is hard to fool workers and firms, while Keynesians argued that it is rather easy.

Mainstream Keynesian theory essentially reduced Keynes to a case of sticky wages and prices—where a stubborn refusal by workers to accept nominal wage decreases is the main cause of unemployment. The Keynesian solution to unemployment was to stimulate aggregate demand (through more government spending plus tax cuts or by an increase of money supply, although "Keynesians" thought that method could be less effective), causing inflation that would fool workers into thinking their real wages had gone up so that they'd work more even as employers were fooled into believing that rising prices indicated a shift of demand toward their own products so that they would employ more workers.

So, the trade-off was one of more employment but also higher prices. Policy makers had to choose the right trade-off of unemployment versus inflation.

Monetarists argued that this method could work only temporarily because, as President Lincoln supposedly remarked, "you can fool all the people some of the time and some of the people all the time, but you cannot fool all the people all the time"—hence a policy that tried to cause inflation in order to reduce unemployment would eventually just cause inflation. They thus preferred to constrain fiscal policy and to impose a rule on money growth in order to keep inflation low.

The stagflation of the late 1970s ended the great debate between "Keynesians" and "monetarists" in favor of Milton Friedman's rules. This is because the Keynesians had no answer to a problem of high inflation and high unemployment at the same time—policy should stimulate demand to fight unemployment but should slow demand to fight inflation. They had no answer for stagflation. Policy adopted the monetarist recommendation of focusing on controlling money growth by sticking to a rule.

Yet, monetarism itself suffered a defeat in the early 1980s when the Fed under Chairman Volcker tried to hit money growth targets (in line with Friedman's prescription) but repeatedly failed to hit them. So not only did "Keynesian" theory and policy fall out of favor, but monetarism also lost sway.

This then set the stage for the rise of a succession of increasingly radical theories rooted in pre-Keynesian thought—most notably the rational expectations–new classical economics of Robert Lucas and the real business cycle theory of Charles Plosser and others.

As Lord Robert Skidelsky (Keynes's biographer) argues, "Rarely in history can such powerful minds have devoted themselves to such strange ideas."[9] Let's see what he means by "strange ideas."

First, new classical theory restored the most extreme version of neoclassical economics with continual market clearing (including continuous full employment) and "rational expectations theory," which ensures that economic agents do not make persistent errors. This restoration makes it impossible to fool rational actors even in the manner that Friedman's monetarism supposed, since expectation formation is forward-looking and is based on the correct model of the economy.

This also means that nonrandom policy has no effect at all because agents immediately figure out what policy makers are doing (if policy is not random, it is predictable) and adjust their own behavior in an optimal manner. Money matters only temporarily, while agents gather the information necessary to distinguish real from nominal prices. Fiscal policy does not matter at all—for example, deficit spending is completely crowded out because taxpayers know they will have to pay down government's debt later and so begin saving immediately in an amount equal to the deficit (this is called Ricardian equivalence).

Still, new classical theory's explanation of the business cycle depended on short-run non-neutrality caused by random changes to the money supply (generating the misperception of rising nominal prices as rising relative prices).

Real business cycle theory took the final step to eliminate any effect of money by making the business cycle a function only of real variables. The most important is random and large fluctuations of productivity. In this way, the Great Depression was explained not as a fault of insufficient demand (the Keynesian argument) or of errant monetary policy (Friedman's story) but rather as a negative productivity shock. Because workers were suddenly less productive, their real wage fell. At the lower real wages, they decided to take more leisure. Hence, involuntary unemployment did not rise during the Great Depression—rather, people took long vacations because shocks to technology had suddenly made them less productive and therefore deserving of lower wages. At those lower real wages, they preferred leisure over work.

In this approach, all behavior is always optimal, all markets always clear—indeed, the observed business cycle is not a cycle at all; rather, the economy follows a "random walk with drift." (The economy follows a constant growth rate trend until it is shocked so that it instantly adapts to a new trend rate of growth determined by "real" factors like productivity growth.) Government should not do anything about what we have called recessions or depressions because these are actually optimal responses to random shocks.

You can see why Lord Skidelsky labels these theories "strange"—the suffering of the unemployed in the Great Depression was an "optimal" response because workers preferred standing in bread lines over working at lower real wages. Those who developed these theories actually got Nobels for this work.

Developments in finance theory mirrored the evolution of mainstream economic theory in the sense that just as the new neoclassical theories made money neutral, finance also became irrelevant.[10] So long as markets are efficient, all forms of finance are supposedly equivalent—whether you use your own funds, sell stock, or borrow makes no difference. Financial institutions are seen as intermediaries that come between savers and investors, efficiently allocating savings to highest use projects. Evolution of financial practices continually reduces the "wedge" between the interest rate received by savers and that paid by investors—encouraging more saving and investment.

Domestic financial market deregulation (under way since the mid-1960s in the United States) as well as globalization of international financial markets play key roles in enhancing these efficiencies, and hence, in promoting growth. Furthermore, markets discipline financial institutions; hence, self-regulation is enough because it will align incentives to produce safe practices. This theory was the main justification for "freeing" the financial sector from regulation and supervision at the end of the 1990s.

In recent years, a "new" neoclassical synthesis (often called the "new monetary consensus") was developed, adopting most of the "strange ideas" but obtaining "Keynesian" style results by reviving sticky wages and prices. Again, Lord Skidelsky nicely skewers the new orthodoxy: "Having swallowed the elephant of rational expectations, they strained at the gnat of the continuous full employment implied by it, and developed theories of market failure to allow a role for government."[11] Sticky wages and other market imperfections slow the movement to full employment, opening some room for policy.

Unlike the early postwar "Keynesian policy" that advocated use of fiscal policy to fine-tune the economy, this version elevated monetary policy to that role. By this time, however, mainstream economists had given up on attempts by central banks to control the money supply—Friedman's preferred target—and replaced that with control over the interest rate.

Yet the goal was the same. Following a strategy known as the Taylor rule, the central bank would adjust its interest rate target based on deviation of actual inflation rates from targets as well as the output gap (differential between potential output and actual output). For example, if inflation is higher than desired and if actual output exceeds potential output, then the central bank raises interest rates to cool the economy. This is really just a slightly updated Phillips curve notion—if the unemployment rate gets too low, inflation results—but with far more concern shown for inflation than unemployment.

Some advocates go a bit further, actually proposing specific inflation rate targets (policy makers are to completely ignore unemployment outcomes)—with several central banks around the world explicitly adopting such targets. In any event, the belief is that all government really needs to do is to keep inflation low—by itself, that will promote robust growth that will keep the economy close to full employment. There is also the belief that monetary policy is highly potent—central banks *can* keep inflation on target (say, 1–2 percent per year), which by itself will fine-tune the economy as market forces are unleashed to move it quickly back to full employment equilibrium. The argument went a bit further toward the end of the 1990s and early 2000s, with proponents of inflation targeting (like Bernanke) arguing that price stability not only promotes robust growth but also financial stability. The central bank can kill three birds (price instability, output instability, and financial instability) with one stone (interest rate target)! Quite a feat!

Mainstream economists thought it all worked splendidly through 2007. Central bankers around the world congratulated themselves for keeping inflation low. Fed Chairman Alan Greenspan was known as the "Maestro" and was proclaimed to be not only the greatest central banker ever but also the most powerful policy maker on Earth.

When he retired, the chairmanship mantle was handed over to Ben Bernanke, who promoted the idea of the "Great Moderation" and the crucial role that the Fed played in contributing to this moderation.[12] By keeping inflation low, the world's central bankers had promoted economic stability (the "moderation"). Since everyone in the economy knew that central bankers were committed to stability, all expected stability, and hence, we would have stability.

All that was now necessary was to manage expectations. Markets knew that the central banks would keep inflation low and knew that if there were any economic hiccups, the central banks would quickly act to restore stability. That, itself, provided confidence—it was known as the "Greenspan put" and then as the "Bernanke put," the idea that the chairman of the Fed would prevent anything bad from happening. Real estate prices boomed, commodities prices bubbled, stock markets rose, and Wall Street's financial institutions recorded terrific profits.

Well, the theory and policy worked until they didn't—more precisely, they failed spectacularly beginning in spring 2007 as the world's economy slipped into the worst crisis since the 1930s (only a few nations escaped—notably, China—which had not allowed unfettered financial markets). The major central banks moved to reassure markets that they were in charge. Yet, it became apparent that lowering interest rates—essentially to zero— had no effect. The crisis grew worse, with rising unemployment, falling retail sales, the worst collapse of real estate markets since the Great Depression, and with one financial institution after another falling into trouble.

So much for "maestros" and "great moderations." The global crisis exposed the problems with conventional economics.

To be sure, we have been here before. The Great Depression had also exploded the reigning orthodoxy—which similarly relied on laissez-faire policy. Keynes offered a revolution in thought. Unfortunately, that revolution was aborted, or at least, co-opted by "synthesizers" like Paul Samuelson, who borrowed only the less revolutionary aspects of his theory and then integrated these into the old neoclassical approach.

In Minsky's view, many important aspects of Keynes's GT were absent from postwar macroeconomics theory. For example, the synthesis version of Keynes never incorporated true uncertainty or "unknowledge" and thus deviated substantially from Keynes's treatment of expectations. This absence of uncertainty in mainstream theory was important for its belief in the economy's own inherent tendency to always move back to an equilibrium with full employment.

Minsky wanted to emphasize what should be recovered from Keynes and to update Keynes's theory to make it relevant for the world in which we actually live. What else was important? An important role to be played by money, financial institutions, and instability and a positive role to be played by government.

Keynes's Revolution in Theory

The central proposition of the Keynes's General Theory (1936) can be simply stated as follows: Entrepreneurs produce what they expect to sell, and there is no reason to presume that the sum of these production decisions is consistent with the full employment level of output either in the short run or in the long run.

Moreover, this proposition holds even in conditions of perfect competition and flexible wages, even if expectations are always fulfilled, and even in a stable economic environment. In other words, Keynes did not rely on sticky wages, monopoly power, disappointed expectations, or economic instability (caused, for example, by "exogenous" shocks or random policy) to explain unemployment. Though each of these conditions could certainly make matters worse, he wanted to explain the possibility of equilibrium with unemployment even under the conditions most favorable to the neoclassical model.

Keynes's approach begins with a focus on the entrepreneurial decision—each firm produces what it expects to sell—rather than on the consumer who maximizes utility through time. That entrepreneurial decision is based on a comparison between the costs incurred to produce now against the proceeds expected to be received in the future. A decision to produce is simultaneously a decision to employ and to provide incomes to workers. It probably also commits the firm to a stream of payments over some time period (since firms usually borrow to finance at least some production costs).

Production will not be undertaken unless the expected proceeds exceed by a sufficient margin the costs incurred today and into the future. Both the costs and the revenues accrue in the form of money. If the comparison of estimated costs and expected revenues is deemed unfavorable, production is not undertaken and income is not generated. Unemployment results when expected effective demand is insufficient.

In addition, downward flexibility of the wage rate does not promote more employment because the income effect (the decline in revenues induced by lower spending from wage earners) more than offsets the substitution effect (the decline in labor cost that provides an incentive to hire). Lower wages negatively affect profits and so demand by firms for labor. This crucial point made by Keynes has been lost in debates of the past forty years over the flexibility or inflexibility of the labor market.

Note also that because production begins and ends with money, Keynes rejects the notion of neutrality of money—in an important sense, the purpose of production *is* money (Keynes called this a monetary theory of production; Marx designated this "M–C–M'": the entrepreneur begins with money, produces commodities, and hopes to end up with more money).[13]

We can say that recession and unemployment are caused by a decision to "not spend"—that is, to save in the form of money. When firms see sales going down, they lay off workers. This move compounds the problem. For Keynes, the most important decision is the one made by entrepreneurs to invest because this decision is by its very nature forward-looking toward an unknowable future. As worries about future prospects rise, investment falls—which then means lower employment and lower sales to consumers. More workers lose their jobs and we are off to recession.

This dynamic is why Minsky called Keynes's theory of boom and bust "an investment theory of the cycle"—in contrast to mainstream theories that saw cycles as the result of bad policy, fooling, or technology shocks. Importantly, Keynes had an "endogenous" theory of the cycle—it is in the nature of capitalism to cycle due to "whirlwinds" of optimism and pessimism. The cycle is thus related to the investment decision, which depends on expectations about an inherently uncertain future.

It is the uncertainty that generates a preference for liquid assets and thus a barrier to achieving full employment. Again, firms produce only what they expect to sell at profit, and it is not necessary for them to have been disappointed or to be subject to unstable economic forces in order for the sum of their individual production decisions to leave some labor resources unused. If the future looks problematic, firms decide not to invest, and wealth holders decide to seek liquid assets—often called "hoarding money" or a "run to quality"—that is, to assets with relatively low risk, such as government bonds or even currency.

Keynes famously remarked that no one in a neoclassical world would hold money because there could be no value to holding a riskless (hence, low return) asset. This was later confirmed by Frank Hahn, who lamented that there is no room for money in the rigorous orthodox model.[14] This is because such models ignore uncertainty and bankruptcy.

Charles Goodhart[15] insists that the possibility of default is central to any analysis of a money-using economy. As decisions about production made today commit entrepreneurs to payments in the future, there is the possibility that they will not be able to meet contractual terms. However, the most rigorous orthodox models explicitly rule out default, implying that all IOUs are risk-free, thereby eliminating any need for the monitoring services provided by financial institutions. Not only is there no room for money in these models; there is also no need for banks or other financial intermediaries.

Financial instability is also ruled out because absence of the possibility of default requires perfect foresight or complete and perfect markets so that all outcomes can be hedged.

Thus, these mainstream macro models cannot incorporate the real-world features that Keynes included: animal spirits and degree of confidence, market psychology, and liquidity preference. By contrast, Keynes's basic model is easily extended to account for heterogeneous credit ratings, to allow default to affect expectations, and to include "contagions" and other repercussions set off by default of one large economic entity on its commitments. The best example of such extensions is the work of Minsky.

In conclusion, most economists "didn't see it coming" because their approach to economics denies that "it" could happen. The neoclassical approach that provides the foundation for mainstream macroeconomics is applicable only to an imaginary world, an economy focused on market exchange based on a barter paradigm. Money and finance are added to the model as an afterthought—they really do not matter. Because an invisible hand supposedly guides rational individuals who have perfect foresight toward an equilibrium in which all resources are efficiently allocated, there is little role for government to play.

The current crisis has shown this approach to be irrelevant for analysis of the economy in which we live. By contrast, the Keynesian revolution that began with the GT offered an alternative that does allow us to understand the world around us. Keynes's different methodological approach allowed him to develop a theory that was at the same time "general" but also "specific" in the sense that it incorporated those features of the capitalist (entrepreneurial) economy that cause it to move toward crisis.

Economists working in that tradition did see "it" coming, and they have offered policy advice that would help to get the economy back on track and to reform it so that it would not only be more stable, but also so that it would operate in the interest of most of the population.

Let us turn to the revolution in policy introduced by Keynes.

Toward a Keynesian Policy Revolution

Keynes had long rejected the notion of laissez-faire , writing a pamphlet titled "The End of Laissez-Faire" in 1926.[16] Not only did he argue against the claim that some "invisible hand" could guide self-interested individuals to behave in the public interest; he also denied that these individuals even know their own self-interest.

He went further, arguing that the notion of laissez-faire had never really been embraced by economists. Rather it was adopted by ideologues. To be sure, in that 1926 piece, Keynes did not provide a convincing rebuttal to the laissez-faire doctrine, nor did he provide a policy solution. His theory of effective demand had to wait another decade. It was only with his 1936 publication of the General Theory (GT) that Keynes made it clear why the invisible hand would fail and why government had to play a positive role in the economy.

Keynes's effect on postwar policy was at least as great as his effect on theory, but it is questionable whether much of the policy that was called Keynesian really had strong roots in Keynes's GT. Still, the influences of Keynes's work on domestic fiscal and monetary policy, on the international financial system, and on development policy—especially in Latin America—cannot be denied.

If we take the central message of the GT as the proposition that entrepreneurial production decisions cannot be expected to generate equilibrium at full employment, then the obvious policy response is to use government to try to raise production beyond the level "ground out" by market forces. Unfortunately, "Keynesian" policy was eventually reduced to overly simplistic metaphors such as "pump priming" and "fine-tuning" that would keep aggregate demand at just the right level to maintain full employment. It is now commonplace to claim that Keynesian policy was tried but failed.[17]

In practice, postwar policy usually consisted of measures to promote saving and investment. The first was wholly inconsistent with Keynes, based instead on the neoclassical loanable funds view that saving "finances" investment; the second was based on the spending multiplier view,[18] that though somewhat consistent with Keynes's explication of the determination of the equilibrium level of output, relied on overly simplistic views of entrepreneurial expectation formation while ignoring important stability questions.

Minsky rejected such policies for a number of reasons.

The Capacity Effect of Investment

First, there is no reason to believe that the demand (or multiplier) effect of investment is sufficient to absorb the additional capacity generated by the supply (or capacity) effect of investment. There are a number of related avenues of research—ranging from Alvin Hansen's stagnation thesis (modern capitalism tends to stagnate because of lack of investment opportunities),[19] to the Harold Vatter and John Walker view that sustaining adequate rates of growth through time would require continuous growth of the government sector relative to growth of the private sector in order to ensure that aggregate demand would be sufficient to absorb the new capacity.

The Problem with Inequality

Second, attempting to maintain full employment by stimulating private investment would shift the distribution of income toward owners of capital, worsening inequality and thereby lowering the society's propensity to consume—one of the problems addressed by Keynes in chapter 24 of the GT. In addition, a high investment strategy tends to favor capital-intensive industries, shifting the distribution of income toward higher paid and unionized workers. (These effects are taken up in more detail later.)

The Sectoral Balance Problem

The sectoral balances approach implicitly adopted by Minsky in his earliest work, and developed in detail by Minsky's colleague at the Levy Institute, Wynne Godley, examines the implications for financial balances implied by spending growth.[20] As we'll see later, Godley developed this approach based on the macroeconomic identity, according to which the sum of the balances of the domestic private sector, the domestic government sector, and the foreign sector must equal zero. Whereas any one of these sectors can run a deficit or a surplus, for every sector in deficit, there must be at least one other sector in surplus.

Generally, the domestic private sector (firms and households) needs to be in surplus (spending less than its income) in order to accumulate savings and financial wealth. But that means that either the nation's government must run a budget deficit or the nation must run a current account surplus (i.e., export more than it imports).

Minsky argued that an expansion led by private sector deficit spending (with firms borrowing to finance investment in excess of internal income flows) implies that private debt might grow faster than private sector income. Indeed, this is exactly what happened in the decade after 1996 in the United States (and in some other nations), helping to create the over-indebtedness of our private sector that led to the Global Financial Crisis (GFC). This is another reason Minsky rejected the "Keynesian" mainstream's belief that government ought to stimulate growth by favoring investment.

Financial Instability

Fourth, Minsky's financial instability hypothesis raises related concerns. Over the course of an economic boom that is led by investment spending, private firms stretch liquidity (borrowing more so that income flows are leveraged by debt, and the ratio of safe assets to liabilities falls), leading to increasingly fragile financial positions.

Combining the financial instability hypothesis with the Godley sectoral balances approach, it is apparent that the government budget plays an important role in cooling a boom: rapid growth of income moves the government budget toward balance and even to a surplus. The mostly unrecognized flip side to a government sector surplus is a private sector deficit (holding the foreign balance constant), so "improvement" of government balances must mean by identity that nongovernment balances become more precarious.

From Goldilocks to Crash

Followers of the work of Minsky and Godley were thus amused by positive reactions to the Clinton-era budget surpluses and the predictions that all federal government debt would be eliminated over the coming decade and a half. It was no surprise to the followers of Minsky that the Clinton surpluses killed the boom and morphed into budget deficits, since the budget automatically moves toward larger deficits in a slump, maintaining profit flows and strengthening private balance sheets that accumulate net wealth in the form of safe government bonds.

Hence, Minsky's approach that follows Keynes is skeptical that the private sector can be a reliable engine of growth. It is also skeptical of a "pump-priming" approach to government policy. Rather, policy making must be targeted and specific, with well-formulated regulations to constrain private firms and with well-targeted government spending. The wholesale abandonment of regulation and supervision of the financial sector has proven to be a tremendous mistake. Left to supervise itself, Wall Street created complex and exceedingly risky financial instruments that allowed it to burden households and nonfinancial firms (as well as state and local governments) with debt. As we will see later, relying on such an approach helped increase fragility that contributed to the GFC.

Wall Street also shifted the distribution of income toward the financial sector and toward the top 1 percent of income earners and wealth holders. The nation's firms and households were saddled with debt they could not afford to service. Yet growth required ever more borrowing. The situation was unsustainable—and as Minsky frequently remarked, that which is unsustainable won't be sustained.

Policy Lessons after the Crash

Minsky had always believed that we need to promote policy that would create jobs and raise living standards. If Minsky did not believe that "fine-tuning" is possible, what can be done? Policy should address the obvious areas that have been neglected for more than three decades, as well as new problems that have emerged. America's public infrastructure is entirely inadequate—with problems ranging from collapsing bridges and levees, to overcrowded urban highways and airports, an outdated electrical grid, and lack of a high-speed rail network.

Like Keynes, Minsky advocated targeted spending rather than pump priming (as discussed earlier). If policy is trying to reduce unemployment, the best way to do that is to create jobs and hire workers. The best way to improve infrastructure is to direct those workers toward projects that accomplish that goal.

Global warming raises new problems that need to be addressed: moving to cleaner energy production, expanding public transportation, retrofitting buildings to make them energy efficient, and reforestation. In all of these areas, government must increase its spending—either taking on the projects directly or subsidizing private spending. Because this spending will help to make America more productive, the spending will be more effective than general pump priming and will not suffer from the drawbacks discussed above.

Still, it is likely that even if all of these projects are undertaken, millions of workers will be left behind. First, there is no reason to believe that the additional demand for labor will be sufficient to create enough jobs; second, there can be a skills mismatch, problems of discrimination (against ethnic groups, by gender, against people with disabilities, and against people with low educational attainment or criminal records), and geographic mismatch (jobs need to be created where the unemployed live). A point that Keynes again made when he noted that, as an economy improves, a rightly distributed demand is a more pressing issue than a rise in aggregate demand.[21] For these reasons, Minsky called for an "employer of last resort."[22] We examine his proposal in more detail in a later chapter.

All of this could require more government spending (although it is possible that reducing spending in areas that do not generate jobs and that do not enhance U.S. production and living standards would offset much of the additional spending). Though orthodoxy fears budget deficits (with many arguing that they only "crowd out" private spending), that fear conflates government budgets with household budgets.

A sovereign government's budget is not like the budget of a household or firm. Government issues the currency, whereas households and firms are users of that currency. As the chartalist, or modern money approach, explains, modern governments actually spend by crediting bank accounts.[23] It really just amounts to a keystroke, pushing a key on a computer that generates an entry on someone's balance sheet. Government can never run out of these keystrokes.

Minsky put it this way:

> For fiat money to be generally acceptable and valuable there must be a set of payments units must make for which this money will do. Taxes are such payments, thus fiat money really should not be introduced without introducing a government with taxes and expenditures. Symmetrically money as a liability of a fractional reserve bank acquires value in the market because there exist units, the debtors to the banks, which have payments to make for which this credit money will be acceptable. The acceptability and value of a money depends upon the existence of payments denominated in that money: thus fiat money without a government that taxes and spends and credit money without debtors under constraint to meet payments commitments are quite meaningless concepts. (p. 23)[24]

A "fiat" money (essentially keystroked onto balance sheets) is valuable because taxes must be paid in that money. People accept it because they need to pay taxes. The issuer of "keystroked" fiat money cannot run out of it and ensures that it is in demand by accepting it in payments that must be paid.

Remarkably, even the Chairman of the Fed, Ben Bernanke, testified to Congress that the Fed spends through simple keystrokes and hence could afford to buy as many assets as necessary to bail out Wall Street's banks. All that is necessary is to recognize that the Treasury spends the same way, and then Washington's policy makers could stop worrying about "affordability" of the types of programs that everyone recognizes to be necessary: public infrastructure investment, "green" investments to reduce global warming, and job creation.

To be sure, this is not a call for "the sky is the limit" spending by government. Too much spending is inflationary and could cause currency depreciation. Government spending must be well targeted and must not be too large. How big is too large? Once productive capacity is fully used and the labor force is fully employed, additional spending would be inflationary.

This is also called the "functional finance" approach to policy, developed by Abba Lerner,[25] Minsky's close friend. Policy should be directed to resolving problems, raising living standards, and achieving the public purpose as defined by the democratic process. There should be no preconceived budgetary outcome—such as a balanced government budget over a year or over the cycle.

In other words, the goal should be to use the government's "purse" to achieve the public purpose—not to mandate any specific dollar amount for government's total spending or for its deficit. This does not mean that government spending on programs should not be constrained by a budget—Congress needs to approve the budgets for individual programs and then hold program administrators accountable for meeting the budgets. The purpose of budgeting is not to ensure that the overall federal government budget balances but rather to reduce waste, graft, and corruption.

Budgeting is one means of controlling projects to help ensure that they serve the public interest. Unlike the case of a household or firm, the sovereign government can always "afford" to spend more on a program—but that does not mean that it should spend more than necessary.

When the crisis hit, there was an instinctive turn back to Keynes, as many governments (including first the second Bush administration and then the Obama team) adopted fiscal stimulus packages. However, the generation of large government deficits (President Obama's deficit reached a trillion dollars, mostly because of the depth of the recession that reduced tax revenue, although part of the deficit increase was caused by discretionary increases of spending as well as tax relief) raised fears of governmental insolvency. As a result, policy makers lost their resolve and cut back on the stimulus. Some nations even went the opposite direction, imposing fiscal austerity in the hope that austerity might reduce deficits.

As of early 2015, there is little sign of a robust recovery and indeed many U.S. households are still suffering without jobs or with stagnant wages along with debt loads that are almost as high as they were in 2007! Euroland as a whole is barely growing, and some nations are still in severe crisis. Even China and other developing nations seem to be slowing down. Another slowdown looks possible, perhaps even likely.

It is time to look at Minsky's approach to cycles. He accepted Keynes's "investment theory of the cycle"; what he added was a "financial theory of investment." In his early work, it was precisely the financial aspects of the investment decision that led to instability. As we will see, this explanation gets us part of the way to understanding what is wrong with the mainstream view, and also what is wrong with our economy.

We then investigate Minsky's approach to financial institutions as well as his suggestions for policy reform. We'll see that he had long warned of the problems with the path that evolution of financial institutions and practices had taken over the past three decades, leading to what he called "money manager capitalism." Minsky's proffered reforms would attenuate the thrust to financial fragility that we've lived with for several decades and would reduce the substantial uncertainty and precarious situation under which too many Americans have been forced to live.

3

■

Minsky's Early Contributions: The Financial Instability Hypothesis

The financial structure is a cause of both the adaptability and the instability of capitalism.

—Minsky, 1986, p. 175[1]

In this framework, crises are not due to the special characteristics of any institution; crisis-prone situations emerge out of the normal profit-seeking activities of borrowers and lenders. The shift in the financial posture of units from hedge to speculative (rollover) and Ponzi (capitalizing of interest) characterizes the evolution from a robust financial structure, where most failures are due to idiosyncratic attributes, to a fragile one, where systemic conditions are responsible for a large number of failures.

—Campbell and Minsky, 1987, p. 25[2]

It is not surprising that Minsky would have been concerned about business cycles, since he had come of age during the Great Depression. Whereas most modern macroeconomics sees cycles as resulting from "shocks" or policy mistakes, Minsky believed that they are created by the internal dynamics of the economic system.

To put it another way, mainstream economists believe that market forces are naturally stabilizing. There is some disagreement over the quickness with which markets can restore equilibrium, but there is the notion that if we waited long enough, free markets would eventually get the economy to full employment after some external shock causes a recession.

In Minsky's view, this is precisely wrong: market forces are destabilizing and must be constrained to create stability. However, there is no permanent solution to the problem of cycles because "stability is destabilizing"! Markets will subvert the constraints and create instability that eventually results in yet another recession.

For Minsky, the greatest threat to stability is the boom—because it encourages the risky behavior that ultimately leads to the crash. As he put it, the biggest danger is not a tendency to stagnation but rather the tendency to explosive growth that eventually crashes.

Minsky's Earliest Contributions

In his publications in the 1950s through the mid-1960s, Minsky gradually developed his analysis of the cycles that seem to perennially afflict the economy. He argued that institutions, and in particular financial institutions, matter. This was a reaction against the growing dominance of a particular version of Keynesian economics best represented in the ISLM model.[3] That model was "high theory," eschewing analysis of real-world institutions in favor of simple math models.

Although Minsky had studied with Alvin Hansen at Harvard, he preferred the institutional detail of Henry Simons at Chicago. The overly simplistic Harvard approach to macroeconomics buried finance behind the LM curve; furthermore, because the ISLM analysis only concerned the unique point of equilibrium, it could say nothing about the dynamics of a real-world economy.

For these reasons, Minsky was more interested in the multiplier-accelerator model (developed by fellow Harvard student Paul Samuelson), which allowed for the possibility of explosive growth. Whereas that model at least allowed for instability, the problem was that it was *too* unstable: gross domestic product (GDP) could shoot off toward infinity or toward zero, depending on assumptions.

Minsky knew that the real world is unstable, but it is constrained by institutions—what he later would call "circuit breakers." For example, on Wall Street, trading in stocks is suspended if prices fall too far in one day. Or another example is that when there is a run on banks, the central bank lends reserves to stop the run as depositors realize that they can safely wait because the bank is backstopped by the government. The first of these is a privately imposed circuit breaker, and the second is a government intervention to protect banks from market "irrationality."

Recognizing that such institutions constrain inherent market dynamics, in his work in the late 1950s, Minsky added institutional ceilings and floors to the multiplier-accelerator model to constrain the explosions and crashes.

He ultimately came back to these models in some of his last papers written in the 1990s at the Levy Economics Institute. It is clear, however, that the results of his work in the 1950s played a role in his frequent argument that the New Deal and postwar institutional arrangements constrained the inherent instability of modern capitalism, producing the semblance of stability. Minsky noted that the period from World War II to the mid-1960s was probably the most stable in U.S. history—with no significant financial crises. He attributed this to the institutional constraints inherited largely from the New Deal period, with additional stabilizing institutions added in the early postwar period.

Many of these institutions constrained the financial system (in the United States, this included Regulation Q, which limited interest payments on deposits; the Federal Deposit Insurance Corporation, which protected deposits; and the Glass–Steagall Act's separation of commercial banking from riskier investment banking), although Minsky also included the creation of Social Security and the later adoption of Aid to Families with Dependent Children as important income stabilizers. Furthermore, he pointed to the countervailing power of unions (with some government support to protect workers' rights) as well as minimum wage legislation to prevent the sort of downward spiral of wage cuts in recession that could generate another Great Depression.

Finally, the two most important developments in his view were the strengthening of the commitments of the "Big Bank" (Federal Reserve) and "Big Government" (federal government) to economic stabilization. Together, these postwar institutions constrained instability, particularly downside risks.

In his early writing, Minsky also examined financial innovation, arguing that normal profit seeking by financial institutions continually subverts attempts by the authorities to constrain money supply growth. This is one of the main reasons why he rejected the LM curve's presumption of a fixed money supply (supposedly controlled by the central bank). Indeed, central bank restraint would induce innovations to ensure that it could never follow a growth rate rule, such as that propagated for decades by Milton Friedman.[4] These innovations would also stretch liquidity in ways that would make the system more vulnerable to disruption. If the central bank intervened as lender of last resort, it would validate the innovation, ensuring that it would persist.

For these reasons, Minsky never accepted the proposal made by Milton Friedman that monetary policy should be governed by a rule, such as Friedman's famous recommendation for the central bank to have the money supply grow at a constant rate. Minsky's response was, "The only universal rule for Federal Reserve policy is that it cannot be dictated by any universal rule" (p. 152).[5] A rule would inevitably cause behavior to change, which would make the rule inapplicable. Policy must always adapt.

Minsky's first important paper in 1957[6] examined the creation of the fed funds market, showing how it allowed the banking system to economize on reserves in a way that would endogenize the money supply. What this meant is that innovations would allow banks to get around attempts by the central bank to constrain their lending and money creation. Minsky hypothesized that these innovations would gradually increase systemic fragility; however, if a financial crisis occurred, he thought that the central bank would resolve the crisis by acting as lender of last resort.

The first serious test of the strength of the financial system came in 1966 in the municipal bond market, and the second in 1970 with a run on commercial paper. Additional tests came afterward (commercial paper in 1970, Franklin National in 1974, and so on), but each was resolved through prompt central bank action. Thus, although the early postwar period was a good example of a "conditionally coherent" financial system, with little private debt and a huge inherited stock of federal debt (from World War II), profit-seeking innovations would gradually render the institutional constraints less binding. Financial crises would become more frequent and more severe, challenging the ability of the authorities to prevent "it" (another Great Crash) from happening again. The apparent stability would promote instability.

In other words, all of those postwar institutions that helped to stabilize the economy would ultimately generate greater risk-taking. It is far easier to put in place a "floor" to support the private sector than it is to impose a "ceiling" that would limit speculative excess. By reducing downside risks, government actually encourages more risk-taking with greater upside possibilities. Financial institutions would continually innovate to get around any of the "ceilings."

For this reason, Minsky argued that it would be critically important to continually change the regulatory and supervisory response to the private sector's innovation. Unfortunately, over the postwar period, the policy response was generally in the opposite direction: as institutions found ways around rules and regulations, the response was often to deregulate—de facto accepting the innovations.

As we will see, that had disastrous consequences.

Extensions of the Early Work

With his 1975 book,[7] Minsky provided an alternative analysis of Keynes's theory, with his most detailed presentation of the "financial theory of investment and investment theory of the cycle." The two key building blocks are the "two price system," which he borrows from Keynes, and the "lender's and borrower's risk," also derived from Keynes. These concepts are a bit complex but worth understanding because they underlie his theory of financial instability.

Briefly, Minsky distinguished between a price system for current output (the goods and services produced and included in GDP) and one for asset prices (prices for both financial assets, such as stocks and bonds, and real assets, such as plant and equipment). Current output prices can be taken as determined by "cost plus markup," set at a level that generates profits. In other words, firms typically set a price that covers the production costs, then "mark up" over that to ensure that they can pay overhead, taxes, and interest while leaving profits for owners. This price system covers consumer goods and services, investment goods, and even goods and services purchased by government.

In the case of investment goods, the current output price is effectively a supply price of capital—the price just sufficient to induce a supplier to provide new capital assets (plant and equipment). However, this simple analysis can be applied only to purchases of capital that can be financed out of internal funds (typically, revenues from sales of output). If the firm must borrow external funds (from banks, other financial institutions, or financial markets), then the supply price of capital also includes explicit finance costs—including of course the interest rate, but also all other fees and costs. In that case, the supply price increases because of "lender's risk"—the additional costs associated with borrowing funds from a lender.[8]

There is a second price system: that for assets that can be held through time—again, both financial assets and real assets. Except for money (the most liquid asset), these assets are expected to generate a stream of income and possibly capital gains. Here, Minsky follows Keynes's treatment in chapter 17 (the most important chapter of *The General Theory of Employment, Interest, and Money* (1936), according to Minsky), which is a rather difficult read. The important point is that the prospective income stream cannot be known with certainty and thus is subject to expectations.

These expectations are uncertain, depending on the degree of optimism and pessimism. All else being equal, one prefers highly liquid assets that can be sold quickly and with little loss of value. One holds less liquid and risky assets only if the expected return is higher. Capital assets, in particular, are not only risky but are also relatively illiquid—factories can be hard to sell, and the machines are usually designed to produce specific products. In some cases, the value of capital assets to others is no more than "scrap" value.

We obtain a demand price for capital assets from this asset price system: how much would one pay for the asset, given expectations concerning the net revenues that it can generate? The lower and the more uncertain the returns, the less the buyer is willing to pay. We can call that the demand price. Again, however, that is too simplistic because it ignores the financing arrangements. Minsky argued that the amount one is willing to pay depends on the amount of external finance required—greater borrowing exposes the buyer to higher risk of insolvency and bankruptcy. This is why "borrower's risk" must also be incorporated into demand prices. All else being equal, the greater the reliance on borrowed funds, the less one is willing to pay for capital assets.

We can think of adding "borrower's risk" and "lender's risk" to the analysis as a way of including uncertainty over the prospects of success. These adjustments add a margin of safety in case the future turns out to be worse than we expect. However, as Minsky would say, success breeds greater confidence so that over the course of a period of good times, the margins of safety are reduced.

Investment can proceed only if the demand price exceeds supply price of capital assets. Recall that the demand price comes out of the asset price system, and the supply price comes out of the current output price system. For that reason, demand prices and supply prices can move independently—they are in some sense separately determined. Because these prices include margins of safety, they are affected by expectations concerning unknowable outcomes that determine how big the margin of safety is.

Optimism and reduced uncertainty would tend to raise the demand price for capital assets. At the same time, optimism would lower both lender's risk and borrower's risk—further reinforcing the demand price while actually lowering the supply price. That could encourage lots of investment in capital assets since the demand price is high and the supply price is low. Pessimism and rising uncertainty work in the opposite direction: lower expected income plus higher borrower's risk mean low demand prices, and greater perceived lender's risk leads to higher supply prices so that little new investment is undertaken. In Minsky's theory, both lenders and borrowers operate with margins of safety. If a firm must commit $1,000 in monthly payments to finance purchase of a new machine, then it will want to generate income of, say, $1,500 monthly from operating the machine. The $500 is a margin of safety—if costs turn out to be higher or revenues are lower than expected, the margin of safety helps to ensure a cushion.

In a recovery from a severe downturn, margins are kept large because expectations are muted; over time, if an expansion exceeds pessimistic projections, these margins prove to be larger than necessary. Thus, margins are reduced over time to the degree that projects are generally successful.

Minsky created a famous distinction among three financing profiles to account for the margins of safety. The safest is called hedge, where prospective income flows are expected to cover all interest and principal payments. A riskier profile is called speculative, where near-term income flows cover only interest so that principal cannot be covered, but it is expected that income will eventually rise sufficiently to pay down principal.

Finally, there is Ponzi—named after Charles Ponzi who ran a pyramid scheme (today's counterpart would be Bernie Madoff in terms of notoriety)—where near-term receipts are insufficient to cover even interest payments so that debt increases as interest is "capitalized" into the principal. (Essentially, a Ponzi unit is borrowing to pay interest. Unless interest rates fall or income flows rise, this is an unsustainable situation.[9])

Over the course of an expansion, the financial stance of firms and even households evolves from largely hedge to include ever-rising proportions of speculative and even Ponzi positions. The riskier financial structure is much more vulnerable to either a rise of interest rates or a shortfall of income.

Adding the Kalecki Investment-Profit Relations

Even in his early work, Minsky recognized that desires to raise leverage and to move to more speculative positions could be frustrated: if results turned out to be more favorable than expected, an attempt to engage in speculative finance could remain a hedge position because incomes realized turn out to be greater than anticipated. Thus, while Minsky did not incorporate the now well-known Kalecki relation[10] (in the simple model, investment determines aggregate profit so that rising spending on capital assets actually increases the flow of income to firms), he did recognize that an investment boom could raise aggregate demand and spending (through the Keynesian spending multiplier) and thus generate more sales than projected. Indeed, in his view, that made the dynamics even worse: if the expectations of borrowing firms about profits were systematically exceeded, they would make increasingly crazy bets—generating a runaway speculative boom.

Later, he explicitly incorporated the Kaleckian result that in the simplest model, aggregate profits equal investment plus the government's deficit. Thus, in an investment boom, profits would be increasing along with investment, helping to validate expectations and encouraging even more investment. This result added weight to his proposition that the fundamental instability in the capitalist economy is upward—toward a speculative frenzy. Furthermore, since the government's budget deficit would grow in a downturn, this growth would help to prop up profits—reducing downside risks, as discussed earlier.

In addition, in the early 1960s he argued that effects on private sector balance sheets would depend on the stance of the government's balance sheet. A government-spending-led expansion would allow the private sector to expand without creating fragile balance sheets—indeed, government deficits would boost profits and add safe treasury debt to private portfolios.

However, a robust private sector-led expansion would tend to cause tax revenues to grow faster than private sector income (with a progressive tax system and with transfer spending falling in a boom) so that the government budget would "improve" (move toward surplus) while the private sector balance would deteriorate (move toward deficit). For that reason, Minsky argued that private sector-led expansions tend to be more unsustainable than government-led expansions because private deficits and debt are more dangerous than government deficits and debt.

Once he added the Kalecki equation to his exposition, he could explain how the countercyclical movement of the government's budget would automatically stabilize profits—limiting both the upside in a boom and the downside in a slump. This change added strength to his argument that Big Government is a stabilizing force.

With the Kalecki view of profits incorporated within his investment theory of the cycle, Minsky argued that investment is forthcoming today only if investment is expected in the future—since investment in the future will determine profits in the future (in the skeletal Kaleckian model). Furthermore, because investment today validates the decisions undertaken "yesterday" (those investment decisions taken in the past), expectations about "tomorrow" (which determine investment today) affect ability to meet previous commitments undertaken when financing the capital assets in place today.

There is thus a complex and dynamic temporal relation involved in Minsky's approach to investment that could be easily disturbed. As Minsky put it,

> The peculiar circularity of a capitalist economy—that sufficient investment to assure the economy does well now will be forthcoming only as it is believed that sufficient investment to assure the economy does well will be forthcoming in the future—has a banking and financial-system corollary. Not only must the banking and financial system maintain favorable asset prices and conditions for investment financing now, but the banking and financing system also must be expected to maintain favorable asset prices and conditions for investment financing in the future. Because such normal functioning of the banking and financial system is a necessary condition for the satisfactory operation of a capitalist economy, disruption of the system will lead to malfunctioning of the economy.
>
> —*Minsky, 1986, p. 227*[11]

Once this circularity is linked to the "two price" approach, it becomes apparent that anything that lowers expected future profitability can push today's demand price of capital below the supply price, reducing investment and today's profits below the level necessary to validate past expectations on which demand prices were based when previous capital projects were begun.

If investment is reduced, the margins of safety that had been included in borrower's and lender's risk in the past prove to be inadequate, leading to revisions of desired margins of safety going forward. This reduction of investment and the upward revision of margins of safety hinder investment and hence fuel a downturn as aggregate demand falls.

Minsky continually developed his financial instability hypothesis to incorporate the extensions made to his investment theory over the course of the 1960s, 1970s, and 1980s. The Kalecki equation was added; the two-price system was incorporated; and a more complex treatment of sectoral balances was included.

Minsky's Early Extensions to His Theory of Monetary Policy

Minsky also continued to improve his approach to banks, recognizing the futility of Fed attempts to control the money supply. He argued that whereas the Fed had been created to act as lender of last resort, making business debts more liquid, the Fed no longer relied on the discount window. Indeed, most reserves supplied by the Fed come through open market operations (buying government bonds), which greatly restricts the Fed's ability to ensure safety and soundness of the system by deciding which collateral to accept.

The Fed no longer had the opportunity to take a close look at balance sheets of borrowing banks or to assess ability to generate cash inflows to cover expenses. Instead, the Fed had come to rely on Friedman's simplistic monetarist view that the primary role of the Fed is to "control" the money supply by restricting the supply of reserves created in open market purchases. In Friedman's view, this view allows the Fed to control the economy as a whole simply by controlling the creation of money by banks.

In Minsky's view, the central bank really cannot control the money supply. The problem is that attempts to constrain reserves only induce bank innovations that ultimately require lender of last resort interventions and even bailouts that validate riskier practices. Together with countercyclical deficits to maintain demand, this approach not only prevents deep recession but also creates a chronic inflation bias. To fight inflation, fiscal policy would be skewed toward austerity while monetary policy would maintain high interest rates.

All of this came to a head at the end of the 1970s, when the economy was suffering from stagflation—high unemployment and high inflation at the same time. Fed Chairman Paul Volcker announced a plan to implement a strict version of monetarism—an experiment that consisted of extremely high interest rates to fight the inflation, with an announced money growth rule so that no one would be surprised. This was supposed to eliminate price pressures without causing unemployment (through "fooling" discussed earlier—the idea is that no one would be fooled if the policy was widely known).

It didn't work. The United States went into the deepest recession (at the time) since the Great Depression. The policy also devastated the entire U.S. "thrift" sector (the savings and loan system) because thrifts were stuck with relatively low interest fixed-rate mortgage loans but had to pay high rates on their own shorter term liabilities. A severe financial crisis added to the nation's woes. In Minsky's view, this crisis created unnecessary suffering and also showed that the monetarist theory and policy were flawed. The lesson to be learned was that the central bank cannot control the money supply and that money growth by itself is not a good predictor of either income growth or of inflation.

Using Minsky to Understand the Transformation of the Financial System after 1970

A better approach would be to follow Minsky by taking account of the evolution of the financial system and ultimately the erosion of the institutional ceilings and floors that for some time had stabilized the economy. According to Minsky, the economy emerged from World War II with a robust financial system— less private debt (some had been wiped out in the Great Depression) and lots of safe and liquid federal government debt (due to deficit spending during World War II). This situation allowed relatively rapid economic growth without borrowing by households and firms.

Various New Deal and postwar reforms also made the economy stable: a safety net that stabilized consumption (Social Security, unemployment compensation, welfare, and food stamps); strict financial regulation; minimum wage laws and support of unions; and low-cost mortgage loans and student loans. In addition, memories of the Great Depression discouraged risky behavior.

Gradually all that changed—the memories faded, financial institutions got around regulations, the movement to downsize government replaced regulation with deregulation, unions lost power and government support, globalization introduced low-wage competition and increased uncertainties, and the safety net was chronically underfunded. [12]

To be sure, Minsky believed that the transformation might have occurred even without those changes, as profit-seeking firms and financial institutions would take on greater risks with more precarious financing schemes. Financial crises and recessions became more frequent and more severe, but the remaining New Deal institutions and reforms helped the economy to recover relatively quickly from each crisis. Thus, debts built up and fragility grew on trend over the entire postwar period. This made "it" (another Great Crash like the one that occurred in 1929) possible again.

Minsky died in 1996, but the GFC unfolded in a manner consistent with his projections. Indeed, many have called this a "Minsky crisis," and his name has become almost a household word—at least among those who are studying the crisis that began in 2007.[13] In other words, Minsky did "see it coming" because unlike mainstream economists, his theory included the possibility that the economy would evolve toward instability.

Furthermore, finance and money matter in his theory—as in Keynes, money is never neutral. He takes Keynes further by adding a detailed analysis of financial operations. Keynes had addressed stability issues when he argued that if wages are flexible, then market forces set off by unemployment will lower wages and move the economy further from full employment because of effects on aggregate demand, profits, and expectations. This process is why Keynes had argued that one condition for stability is a degree of wage stickiness in terms of money. (Incredibly, this argument has been misinterpreted to mean that sticky wages cause unemployment—a point almost directly opposite to Keynes's conclusion.)[14]

Minsky extended Keynes by arguing that if the economy ever were to achieve full employment, this would generate destabilizing forces restoring unemployment. As discussed, Minsky believed that the main instability experienced in a modern capitalist economy is a tendency toward explosive euphoria. High aggregate demand and high profits associated with full employment raise expectations and encourage increasingly risky ventures based on commitments of future revenues that are too optimistic. When the expected revenues are not realized, a snowball of defaults then leads to debt deflation (debtors default on their debts, which are assets of creditors) and high unemployment unless there are "circuit breakers" that intervene to stop the market forces, including most importantly intervention by Big Government and the Big Bank.[15]

In the next chapter, we examine in more detail Minsky's analysis of the financial system.

4

∎

Minsky's Views on Money and Banking

A bank is not a money lender that first acquires and then places funds. . . . a bank first lends or invests and then "finds" the cash to cover whatever cash drains arise.
—*Minsky, 1975, p. 154*[1]

It cannot be assumed that the amount and the rate of change of reserve money is either exogenously determined or the result of a policy decision.
—*Minsky, 1967, p. 266*[2]

Money matters most of the time, at some rare but important times it is all that matters, and sometimes money hardly matters at all.
—*Minsky, 1969, p. 228*[3]

Above we very briefly mentioned the role played by lenders in financing investment in Minsky's approach to the investment decision. Furthermore, we discussed the evolution of financial positions from the safest (hedge) through speculative and finally to Ponzi positions. But it is worthwhile to go into Minsky's views on money and banking in more detail as they underlie his general approach to the economy.

As he always argued, we can analyze every economic unit (firm, household, or government) as if it were a bank that issues liabilities and takes positions in assets. Because his approach—and especially his terminology—is not familiar to most people (including economists operating outside Wall Street), it is useful to lay it out simply and clearly.

When I was Minsky's student, he would always warn me, "discipline your analysis with balance sheets." He insisted that every economic unit (firm, household, or government) has a balance sheet and if we begin with assets, liabilities, and net worth of each, we have a better chance of getting the analysis correct. Unfortunately, most people—including economists—do not think in terms of balance sheets. Economists often begin with the assumption that "money is dropped from helicopters"—it falls into your hands as an asset.

But that doesn't happen in the real world. In the real world, all the "money" you have is someone's liability. In the United States, coins are the Treasury's debt, paper notes are the Fed's liability, and demand deposits are the liabilities of banks. Normally, you get that "money" either by earning it or by issuing your own liability to obtain it. In today's world, almost all of this is handled electronically—as entries on electronic balance sheets.

Minsky's heterodox views on banking are quite different from those of mainstream economists. As discussed in the introduction of this book, the mainstream Keynesian Paul Krugman tried to reread Minsky in the aftermath of the GFC. He criticized Minsky's heterodox approach and went on to argue that heterodoxy fundamentally misunderstands banking:

> As I read various stuff on banking . . . I often see the view that banks can create credit out of thin air. There are vehement denials of the proposition that banks' lending is

limited by their deposits, or that the monetary base plays any important role; banks, we're told, hold hardly any reserves (which is true), so the Fed's creation or destruction of reserves has no effect. This is all wrong, and if you think about how the people in your story are assumed to behave—as opposed to getting bogged down in abstract algebra—it should be obvious that it's all wrong.

First of all, any individual bank does, in fact, have to lend out the money it receives in deposits. Bank loan officers can't just issue checks out of thin air; like employees of any financial intermediary, they must buy assets with funds they have on hand. I hope this isn't controversial, although given what usually happens when we discuss banks, I assume that even this proposition will spur outrage.[4]

Those who have studied a bit of economics may recognize that the position Krugman is taking here is the typical presentation in money and banking textbooks: individual banks cannot create money. They must first accept a deposit but then can loan a portion of that because we have a fractional reserve system (they must keep on reserve only a fraction of the deposit). The textbook goes on to explain that the banking system as a whole can expand the money supply through the "deposit multiplier" by a multiple of the excess reserves created when a deposit is made.

In this chapter, we'll look at Minsky's alternative view. It has the advantage of being correct!

What Do Banks Do?

We begin with Minsky's approach to the nature of banking: what is it that banks do?

Minsky always argued that "anyone can create money" but "the problem lies in getting it accepted." He insisted that banking is not "money lending"—a money lender must first obtain money before making a loan (that is Krugman's view of banks). Whereas most people think that banks sit around and wait for deposits to flow in so that they can make loans, Minsky argued that that is the "money lender's" business, not banking business. Banks, instead, create money as they make loans. That makes a big difference. Let us see how that works.

But before proceeding, look at it this way. A bank deposit is the IOU ("I owe you") of the bank, showing up on the liability side of the bank's balance sheet. Banks have trillions and trillions of dollars of these IOUs on their balance sheets (in the United States we have two banks, each of which alone has issued $2 trillion in IOUs, and several others are not that much smaller). The IOUs are "contingent liabilities" in the sense that the bank's creditors can insist on "payment" or "conversion to cash" either on demand ("demand deposit") or after some waiting period ("time deposit").

Minsky said that where most people go wrong is that they think banks operate like "money lenders" who stand on street corners in Chicago—taking in deposits of currency and then lending them out at a higher (usurious) interest rate.[5]

Banks supposedly then hold some of the deposited cash as reserves to meet withdrawal of deposits. Since the Fed (Federal Reserve Bank) limits the quantity of cash, bank lending is limited.

But how could that be so? In the first place, the math won't work. The total amount of cash in existence is less than a trillion dollars—and estimates put well over half of that outside the United States, while much of the total is used to evade taxes and to finance illegal activities in black markets such as gun running and drug smuggling. So, only a small fraction of the total cash is available for banks to receive in deposits in order to make loans. And yet they've got trillions and trillions of loans on their balance sheets and have issued just as many IOUs, including deposits.

Think about the last time you went to a bank. Did you take a wheelbarrow of cash in for deposit, so that your friendly banker could make some mortgage loans?

Actually, what we see is that most people go to the bank to *take cash out!*[6] Banks mostly *supply* cash; they do not wait around to receive it in order to make loans. So how do things really work?

Whenever banks need cash to meet withdrawal, they do not turn to depositors; rather, they call up the Fed. The Fed trucks cash to the banks to stock the automatic teller machines (ATMs). In turn, the Fed debits bank reserves held at the Fed (these are just the private banking system's "checking account" held at the Fed). Over time, the outstanding amount of cash (including that held outside the United States) tends to grow on trend because banks pay out more cash than they receive. (All U.S. dollars—cash—in existence were paid out by banks at the teller's window or ATMs.)

What if a bank is short reserves—will the Fed refuse to send the cash? No. The Fed lends reserves to cover the cash needs. Otherwise, the bank would have to close its doors—refusing to meet demands for cash—which would scare other depositors and lead to runs on banks. Except for occasional hiccups, you do not find the ATMs shut down or bank doors closed because of cash shortages. Indeed, all money and banking textbooks insist that the nonbank public determines the supply of cash— since banks promise to supply it on demand, the Fed provides banks with all they need to meet withdrawals.

It is the Fed that brings the wheelbarrows of cash to the banks—not depositors. And the Fed supplies cash not so that banks can make loans. Rather, the cash is to cover withdrawals from deposits.

When the Fed sends cash to banks, it debits their reserve account at the Fed—which is essentially the bank's demand deposit account. Where did the banks get those deposits? From Fed keystrokes to their accounts.

Where does the Fed get the reserves it credits to bank "checking accounts" at the Fed? It creates them out of "thin air"—either by printing notes or, mostly, through keystrokes that credit bank reserves.[7] In fact, the vast majority of bank reserves are nothing but electronic entries. Reserves are always entered on two balance sheets, first as the liability of the central bank and second as the asset of the bank receiving the credit.

Where does the Fed get the banknotes it trucks to the ATMs? Also out of thin air—keystrokes instruct the printing press (at the U.S. Treasury) to print more. If banks do not have the reserves to debit when the Fed sends them banknotes, the Fed lends reserves and records an entry, "borrowed reserves" as the Fed's asset and the bank's liability. Again, this is "keystrokes."

We can also ask, "Where do banks get the deposits they credit to the accounts of their customers?" Again, they create them out of "thin air": the deposit is entered on the bank's balance sheet as a liability and on the customer's balance sheet as an asset.

Is there a pattern? Money is *always created out of "thin air."* Except for actual cash, money exists only as an entry on a balance sheet—actually two entries: the IOU of the issuer and the asset of the creditor. In the case of cash, it is an asset of the holder (whether a bank or an individual) and a liability of the issuer (Treasury coins or Federal Reserve notes). The cash is really just a record of the liability that happens to be printed on metal or paper, unlike the keystroke entry that is an electronic record.

So most people—including Krugman and many other economists—have the banking business all wrong. Whenever you make deposits into banks, they are usually deposits of bank IOUs—that is, a check drawn on another bank or an electronic deposit, which is also a claim on another bank. It is (mostly) all about bank money. Where did it come from? From banks. Where did they get it? They created it. How? They mostly created deposits through keystroke credits to accounts.

This is not as mysterious as it first seems. Say that you write an IOU to your neighbor: "I owe you five dollars." It is your financial liability and your neighbor's financial asset. Where did it come from? Thin air. You might record it on paper or wood or a chalkboard or in a computer file. Memories are faulty and may not be accepted in evidence should you need to go to court. You can think of the method of recording the IOU as determined by law, tradition, and technology—but it does not change the nature of the monetary IOU.

Did you have to get cash first to write the IOU? No. Do you have to have $5 in cash in your pocket to write the IOU? No. While having cash on hand—or easy access to cash—might enhance the acceptability of your IOU, you can write IOUs without it.

You do have to "redeem" your debt at some point. Your neighbor presents your IOU to you for redemption and you must come up with the cash, or you write a check on your bank deposit, or you provide something else of value that is mutually acceptable. When you satisfactorily redeem yourself, your neighbor hands back your IOU, and you tear it up.

In this process, you "created money" out of "thin air"; the "money" was your IOU denominated in dollars. (The money you created is destroyed when you repay your debt.) This is what Minsky means when he says "anyone can create money."[8] One might object: "But how can that be money? It was just my debt held by my neighbor. It didn't circulate. The neighbor could not buy anything with it." Yes, all of that could be true.

On the other hand, it is conceivable that you are well known and trusted across your entire neighborhood. In that case, the neighbor holding your IOU might be able to pass it in redemption of her own IOU to another neighbor (a "third party"). In that case, this other neighbor can present it to you for redemption. Or, your neighbor might hire a local kid to mow the lawn—and then the kid presents it to you for redemption. So, at least in theory, your IOU *could* circulate to pay debts or to buy services—if your neighbors deemed it "acceptable."

As Minsky always said, "anyone can create money," but "the problem lies in getting it accepted." Both banks and money market mutual funds "create money" in the sense that they issue money-denominated liabilities. Both have to "get them accepted." Banks are more special than other financial institutions because government gives them special protection. When times are good, this might not matter much—the "money" created by other types of financial institutions is "just about as good as" the deposits created by banks. In bad times, that reverses, and the liabilities created by shadow banks are about as desired as a fork in the eye. PIMCO's Paul McCulley put it this way shortly after the shadow banks crashed in 2008:

> Over the last three decades or so, the growth of "banking" outside formal, sovereign-regulated banking has exploded, and it was a great gig so long as the public bought the notion that such funding instruments were "just as good" as bank deposits. Keynes provides the essential—and existential— answer as to why the shadow banking system became so large, the unraveling of which lies at the root of the current global financial system crisis. It was a belief in a convention, undergirded by the length of time that belief held: shadow bank liabilities were viewed as "just as good" as conventional bank deposits not because they are, but because they

had been. . . . Maybe, just maybe, there was and is something special about a real bank, as opposed to a shadow bank! And indeed that is unambiguously the case, as evidenced by the ongoing partial re-intermediation of the shadow banking system back into the sovereign-supported conventional banking system, as well as the mad scramble by remaining shadow banks to convert themselves into conventional banks, so as to eat at the same sovereign-subsidized capital and liquidity cafeteria as their former stodgy brethren.[9]

But that does not make "shadow banks" or "commercial banks" mere intermediaries that take in deposits and then lend them out. Both "finance" positions in assets by issuing liabilities. Their liabilities are variously called deposits or "NOW" accounts or MMMF[10] shares. Ultimately, however, only insured deposits are guaranteed to never "break the buck."[11] For that reason, banks are special. This has nothing to do with them being "money creators" versus "intermediaries"—it has to do with sovereign government backing. If a bank suffers a clearing drain to other banks, it goes to the fed funds market to borrow reserves, or to the Fed's discount window. If it suffers a cash drain to withdrawals through the ATM, the Fed sends an armored truck to replenish cash (and debits the bank's reserves).

What we are getting at is the degree of "moneyness." Minsky made no claim that your IOU is as good as a bank's IOU—clearly that is not the case. Banks are special—except for government's own currency, nothing fulfills money's functions as well as bank deposit IOUs. Yet the dividing lines have always been blurred and are much more fluid today with all the innovations by banks and shadow banks. For example, except in crisis, money market mutual funds—issued by shadow banks—are almost equivalent to bank deposits. The holder can write checks on MMMFs, and until the 2007 crisis, no MMMF had broken the buck (the value of a credit in an MMMF had never previously fallen below parity).

In crisis, however, the government backstop provided to banks in the form of Federal Deposit Insurance Corporation (FDIC) insurance and Fed lender of last resort promises makes bank IOUs much safer than shadow bank IOUs. (When the crisis hit, the MMMF institutions faced runs by their creditors, who feared that "the buck" would be "broken." The run was stopped only by temporary extension of the U.S. government's guarantee to include these shadow banks.) So, unless you have Uncle Sam standing behind you, your IOUs will be "less liquid" and thus inferior money in comparison to bank deposits. (To be sure, there are other reasons banks are special, including their specialization in underwriting—determining creditworthiness, although underwriting standards fell considerably in the speculative boom of the mid-2000s—a topic for a later chapter.)

As usual, Minsky was ahead of his time. What he was advancing in the late 1950s was the view that money is "endogenously" created by banks. This was a rejection of the simple monetarist view that the central bank "exogenously" controls money creation through its control over the quantity of bank reserves. This also meant that Minsky rejected the simplistic "deposit multiplier" view still presented in textbooks (and, as discussed earlier, still accepted by Paul Krugman). Instead, Minsky argued, if a bank is approached by a good customer, it makes a loan by creating a demand deposit. If the bank later needs reserves, it will borrow them in the fed funds market or at the discount window.

Over the past couple of decades, an entire literature developed that carried these views forward—so that today among economists as well as policy makers the "endogenous money" view is dominant. It is easy to find quotes by economists at the Fed, the BIS (Bank for International Settlements), and the other international agencies involved in money and banking to back this up. The endogenous money approach is consistent with Minsky's view: banks "create money" by issuing their own IOUs. If there is a willing bank and a willing borrower, deposits will be created through "keystroke" entries to the borrower's deposit account. The corresponding entry is on the bank's asset side, as a loan is recorded.

What this means is that today a bank loan is created "out of thin air" and leads to four simultaneous entries on two balance sheets: the borrower's balance sheet records an increase of deposits as an asset and the borrower's IOU (the loan) as her liability; on the bank's balance sheet, the deposit is a liability and the loan is the asset.

Because the borrower takes out a loan[12] in order to spend, the borrower's demand deposit will be debited and a seller's demand deposit will be credited. Unless the seller happens to use the same bank, the borrower's check will be deposited by the seller in another bank. The two banks must "clear" accounts. Much of the clearing takes the form of a debit of the borrower's bank's reserves and a credit to the seller's bank's reserves.

Although some people used to believe that banks would need excess reserves before they could make a loan because they would need the reserves for net clearing, we now know that banks do not really operate that way. Instead, they obtain the reserves when and if they need them; they create deposits first by granting advances and look for reserves after. Minsky had already argued this in his 1957 publication about the developing "fed funds" market: a bank that needs reserves for clearing can borrow them short-term in the fed funds market at the overnight fed funds rate.

The Fed targets the fed funds rate (its main policy variable), and if there is pressure on the rate (excess demand for reserves for clearing pushes it up; excess supply of reserves pushes it below the target), the Fed intervenes by buying bonds (to relieve upward pressure on the rate) or selling bonds (to relieve downward pressure on the rate since open market sales reduce bank reserves).[13] As Basil Moore argues,[14] these open market operations are defensive, as the Fed accommodates the demand for reserves to keep the fed funds rate on target.

All of these details are now well understood and validate Minsky's early beliefs on money and banking. Let us turn to his analysis of current institutions.

Minsky's Views on Financial Institutions Today

Let us turn to a more detailed summary of Minsky's view of the way the financial institutions and the financial system work today. In many of his writings, he emphasized six main points:

1. A capitalist economy is a financial system;
2. Neoclassical (mainstream) economics is not useful because it denies that the financial system matters;
3. The financial structure has become much more fragile;
4. This fragility makes it likely that stagnation or even a deep depression is possible;
5. A stagnant capitalist economy does not promote capital development;
6. However, this fragility can be avoided by apt reform of the financial structure in conjunction with apt use of fiscal powers of the government.

Here we focus on Minsky's general approach to financial institutions and policy, and we briefly contrast that to the orthodox approach, the topic of the first two points above. In chapter 6, we look in detail at the long-term transformation of the financial system toward what Minsky called money manager capitalism, and in the final chapter, we look at specific recommendations for policy reform.

According to Minsky, "A capitalist economy can be described by a set of interrelated balance sheets and income statements."[15] The assets on a balance sheet are either financial or real; they are held to yield income flows or to be sold or pledged as collateral against loans. The liabilities represent a prior commitment to make payments on demand, on a specified date, or when some contingency occurs. Assets and liabilities are denominated in the money of account (the dollar in the United States), and the excess of the value of assets over the value of liabilities is counted as nominal net worth.

Indeed, as discussed earlier, all economic units—e.g., households, firms, financial institutions, and governments—can be analyzed as "banks" since all have balance sheets, and they all can take positions in assets by issuing liabilities, with margins of safety maintained for protection.

One margin of safety is the excess of income expected to be generated by ownership of assets over the payment commitments promised due to the liabilities. This is a "cash flow" cushion, which is the difference between cash flow income and cash flow outgo. For banks, the inflows are largely interest on loans and securities plus fees, while the outflows are interest paid on liabilities plus the costs of running a bank (wages, rent, computers, ATMs, and so on). They want to operate with a margin of safety, which allows them to add to their loan loss reserves and net worth (capital).

Another margin of safety is net worth—for a given expected income stream, the greater the value of assets relative to liabilities, the greater the margin of safety. This one is a "stock" (equity) cushion. In the event of a shortfall of income, the unit can sell assets to meet payment commitments.

And still another is the liquidity of the position—the liquidity cushion: if assets can be sold quickly or pledged as collateral in a loan, the margin of safety is bigger. All three of these types of cushions can be important in protecting an institution (whether financial, nonfinancial, business, or household).

If the time duration (maturity) of assets exceeds that of liabilities for any unit, then positions must be continually refinanced because liabilities are due before the assets mature. A good example is a thrift institution that purchases thirty-year mortgages as assets but issues savings deposits that can be liquidated in no more than thirty days.[16] This arrangement requires, as Minsky put it, "the normal functioning of various markets, including dependable fall-back markets in case the usual refinancing channels break down or become 'too' expensive."[17]

If financial disruption occurs, economic units that require continual access to refinancing try to "make position" by "selling out position"—selling assets to meet cash commitments. Since financial assets and liabilities net to zero[18] for the economy as a whole, the dynamic of a generalized sell-off is to drive asset prices down—and in the extreme toward zero—what Irving Fisher called a debt deflation process. The greater the pressure to sell, the greater the deflation pressure on asset prices. This is why the net worth stock cushion (that can absorb losses) and the liquidity cushion (that postpones "fire sales") are important when the cash flow cushion is eroded.

Specialist financial institutions can try to protect markets by standing ready to purchase or lend against assets, preventing prices from falling. However, they can be overwhelmed by a contagion when many institutions are trying to sell the same assets and thus will close up shop and refuse to provide finance in a crisis.

Dealers are an example of such institutions—they stand ready to buy, but when sales volumes are too large, they stop answering the phones. For this reason, central bank interventions are required to protect at least some financial institutions by temporarily providing finance through lender of last resort facilities. As the creator of the high-powered money, only the government—central bank plus treasury—can purchase or lend against assets without limit, providing an infinitely elastic supply of high-powered money.

These are general statements applicable to all kinds of economic units. This is what Minsky meant when he said that any unit can be analyzed as if it were a "bank," taking positions by issuing debt.

Yet financial institutions are "special" in that they operate with very high leverage ratios: for every hundred dollars of assets, they might issue $95 of liabilities and have only $5 of capital. If we take a very simplified bank balance sheet, it would hold approximately $99 of loans and bonds as assets plus $1 of reserve deposits and cash in the ATM. Its liabilities would consist of as much as $95 of deposits (demand deposits plus saving deposits), leaving $5 of capital or net worth.

Bank positions in assets really *are* "financed" positions. They issue liabilities as they buy assets. The liabilities they issue become "other people's money." Very little of the bank's own net worth is at risk. This situation implies that losses must be rare because the equity cushion is small.

Furthermore, some kinds of financial institutions specialize in taking positions in longer term financial assets while issuing short-term liabilities—that is, they intentionally put themselves in the position of continually requiring refinancing. We can call that an illiquid position.

An extreme example would be an early 1980s-era bank or thrift institution that holds thirty-year fixed-rate mortgages while issuing demand deposits.[19] Such an institution requires continuing access to refinancing on favorable terms because the interest rate it earns is fixed and because it cannot easily sell assets. This situation can be described as an illiquid position, which requires access to a source of liquidity; in the case of thrift institutions, that was the Federal Home Loan Banks, and for banks, it is the Fed.

Still other kinds of financial institutions—investment banks—specialize in arranging finance by placing equities or debt into portfolios using markets. They typically rely on fee income rather than interest for revenue. In normal circumstances, they would not hold these assets directly, but if markets become disorderly, investment banks can get stuck with assets they cannot sell (at prices they have promised) and thus will need access to financing of their inventories of stocks and bonds.[20] Some banks might hold and trade assets for their own account, earning income and capital gains, or might do so for clients.

Types of Banks

There are many kinds of financial institutions. Minsky distinguished among traditional commercial banking, investment banking, universal banking, and public holding company models.

A traditional commercial bank makes only short-term loans that are collateralized by goods in production and distribution.[21] The loans can be repaid as soon as the goods are sold—this is the model the old real bills doctrine had in mind. The idea is that if banks only lend against goods that have already been produced, their lending is safe and won't be inflationary (there cannot be "too much money chasing too few goods" if the goods already exist). The bank's loan portfolio is financed through the issue of short-term liabilities, such as demand and savings deposits (or, in the nineteenth century, banknotes).

With the traditional bank model, the connections among the bank, the "money supply," and real production are close—the sort of relation that Milton Friedman's quantity theory of money supposed. In truth, bank lending was never strictly constrained in this manner, so the "traditional" bank following "real bills doctrine" was more of a nineteenth and early twentieth century ideal rather than a reality.

In practice, commercial banks made short-term loans to finance the production process. Essentially, the firm borrows to pay wages and raw materials, and the bank advances demand deposits that the borrowing firm uses to pay workers and suppliers. When the finished goods are sold, firms are able to repay loans. Banks charge higher interest on loans than they pay on deposits—the net interest margin supplies bank profits.

As we have noted, these commercial banks do not sit and wait for deposits in order to lend. The process is precisely the reverse: the bank accepts the IOU of the firm that needs to pay for wages and raw materials, then creates a deposit (or in the old days, a banknote) that the firm uses for its purchases. As endogenous money proponents say, "loans create deposits"—not in some metaphysical sense but in the sense that the bank "buys" the IOU of the firm (the "note" that represents the promise to repay the loan) by issuing its own deposit IOUs. It "finances" its position in the firm's IOU by issuing its own deposit IOU.

Once the firm finishes production and sells the output, it receives deposits and uses these to retire the short-term loan. Following our earlier discussion, the firm "redeems" itself by bringing back to the bank the bank's own IOUs; repayment of the loan "redeems" or retires the bank deposits (the loans and deposits on the bank's balance sheet are simultaneously debited when the firm writes a check on its bank account to pay down its loan balance).

However, it is likely that many of the sales the firm makes are to consumers who bank at some other bank, so the firm receives bank checks (or, in the old days, banknotes) drawn on other banks and submits these to its own bank. In modern financial systems, the checks are cleared (either through the central bank or a private interbank settlement system) at par. So it is not necessary for the firm to return to its bank that bank's own IOUs—the IOUs of any bank will suffice.

If deposits are to maintain parity (with each other and with cash), losses on assets must be small because the commercial bank's equity must absorb all losses on assets. It is the duty of the commercial banker to be skeptical; as Minsky loved to say, a banker's cliché is, "I've never seen a *pro forma* I didn't like"— borrowers always present a favorable view of their prospects in the *pro forma*. This is why careful underwriting is essential—the bank must be skeptical of the borrower's plans. The commercial banker must always wonder, "How will I be repaid?"

Although it is true that loans can be made against collateral (for example, the goods in the process of production and distribution), a successful bank would almost never be forced to take the collateral. A bank should not operate like a pawn shop. As Minsky's good friend Martin Mayer writes, banking has always been a business where profits come over time as borrowers pay principal and interest.[22] He alludes to the morality of a loan officer, whose success depends on the success of the borrower.

The banker holds the key—he or she is the "ephor of capitalism,"[23] as Minsky's original dissertation advisor, Joseph Schumpeter,[24] put it—because not only do entrepreneurs have to be sufficiently optimistic to invest, but they must also find a banker willing to advance the wage bill to produce investment output. Like Schumpeter, Minsky believed that investment in innovative processes is important for what Minsky called the "capital development" of the nation.

Even though traditional commercial banks do not finance purchases of investment goods, they still play a role in the investment process since investment goods must be produced before they can be sold. By financing the wage bill of workers in the investment goods sector, commercial banks are promoting the capital development of the economy even if they do not actually provide finance for position taking in investment goods. Hence, we can separate the issue of producing capital goods (which can be financed by commercial banks) from financing ownership of them (which is the proper purview of investment banks, not commercial banks).[25]

Minsky argued that by the last quarter of the nineteenth century, commercial banking alone was not sufficient to finance the "capital development" of the country. Investment goods had become far too expensive with the rise of railroads and modern factories for even rich "robber barons" to purchase out of their own family savings. Specialized investment banks would be needed to provide external finance (note how this links up with Minsky's "financial theory of investment" discussed earlier).

While commercial banks could provide the finance for the production of investment goods, investment banks were necessary to provide the funding for purchases of the finished investment goods. The late nineteenth century saw the rising dominance of the investment banks—the Goldman Sachs and J.P. Morgan banks—and the rise of what Rudolf Hilferding[26] had called "finance capitalism," a topic to which we return in chapter 6. Investment banks became important because expensive capital assets required long-term funding.

There are two basic models of investment bank: the first acts as an intermediary, placing the corporation's liabilities (bonds) or equities into markets where investors can buy them; the second actually holds the bonds and equities and issues its own liabilities to finance its purchases. In the first case, the investment bank charges fees for its services, and in the second, its revenue depends on the performance of the firms purchasing the investment goods. In practice, investment banks typically combine these two models.

The important point is that the investment banker finances the long-term positions in capital assets either directly or indirectly. This is a quite different activity from commercial banking. Investment banks allow savers to choose between holding liquid (financial) assets (the liabilities of banks) or positions in real assets (either directly by owning a firm, or indirectly through ownership of shares).

It was always recognized that investment banking is more risky, and as was discovered in the 1920s, investment banks can more easily dupe their customers. Whereas commercial banks offer deposits (or in the nineteenth century, banknotes) that they promise to convert on demand to cash, investment banks sell stocks and bonds (as well as more complex and opaque products) that have uncertain prospects. Furthermore, because investment banks work closely with the firms requiring finance, they may have long-term relations with—and inside information on—these firms that they find convenient to withhold from the general public that buys stocks and bonds.

To make a long story short, the investment banks had engaged in underhanded tactics in the 1920s that contributed to the "Great Crash" of 1929.[27] As Minsky would later argue, 1929 marked the end of "finance capitalism" as stock and bond prices collapsed and as half of all banks failed. The New Deal reforms put in place a number of prohibitions and restrictions (recall the earlier discussion of institutional "ceilings and floors") that severely constrained investment banking.

Furthermore, new legislation in the United States, known as the Glass–Steagall Act, created a clear separation of the investment banking and commercial banking functions. The idea was that commercial banks would be closely regulated to protect customers, and though investment banks would be allowed much greater latitude, they would not be able to offer lending and deposit-making services to the general public. To put it bluntly, they would not be allowed to dupe customers in the manner they had during the roaring 1920s.

This separation remained on the books for the next six decades. However, over time the real-world separation was gradually eroded through a combination of innovation by banks to subvert the intentions of the law and also by deregulation, desupervision, and finally repeal of the legislation.

Minsky pointed out that lines were blurred when we first allowed bank holding companies to own both types of banks (and, indeed, eventually to hold the full range of financial services companies) and then gutted and finally repealed Glass–Steagall in 1999. As the separation was gradually removed, the same sorts of abuses we had seen in the 1920s returned. And, as we'll see in chapter 6, we got the same result: a financial collapse in 2007.[28]

Conclusions

We'll examine the transformation of the financial system that led up to the crisis later. For now, let's recap the main points of Minsky's alternative views on banking.

1. Banking should not be described as a process of accepting deposits in order to make loans.
2. Rather, banks accept the IOUs of borrowers then create bank deposit IOUs that the borrowers can spend.
3. Indeed, often the bank simply accepts the IOU of the borrower and then makes the payment for the borrower—

cutting a check in the name of the car dealer, for example. This system is why Minsky argued that banking is not money lending, rather the business of banking is "acceptance" of IOUs and making payments for the bank's debtors.

4. Like all economic units, banks finance positions in their assets (including IOUs of borrowers) by issuing their own IOUs (including demand deposits). But banks and other financial institutions are unusual because little of their own equity is at risk relative to the size of their portfolios; for every $5 to $10 of the bank's "own money" (equity), they have issued $90 to $95 of liabilities that represent "other people's money" to buy $100 of assets.

5. Banks use reserves for clearing with other banks (and with the government—a topic not covered in this chapter). Banks also use reserves to meet cash withdrawals by customers. Bank reserves at the central bank are debited when they need cash for withdrawal or clearing with other banks.

6. In some systems, including the United States, the central bank sets a required reserve ratio. However, this ratio does not provide the central bank with any quantitative controls over bank loans and deposits. Rather, the central bank supplies reserves on demand but sets the "price" (interest rate charged) at which it supplies reserves when it targets the overnight interest rate. In the United States, the main target is the fed funds rate. Fed control over banks is all about "price" (the cost of fed funds), not quantity, of reserves.

That gets us up to a twentieth century understanding of banking. In the next chapter, we turn to a quite different area of Minsky's research interests: unemployment and poverty. Then we return to the role of financial institutions in the economy.

5

∎

Minsky's Approach to Poverty and Unemployment

The liberals' War on Poverty was born out of neo-classical theory in which it is the poor—not the economy—that is to blame for poverty. The War on Poverty tried to change the poor, not the economy.

—*Minsky, 1971, p. 20*[1]

A necessary ingredient of any war against poverty is a program of job creation; and it has never been shown that a thorough program of job creation, taking people as they are, will not by itself, eliminate a large part of the poverty that exists.

—*Minsky, 1975, p. 20*[2]

A full-employment economy, where full employment is guaranteed by government employment programs for both youth and adults, in the context of competitive markets and stable money wages, is a possible offset to the inflationary pressures which follow from the way threats of a deep depression are offset.

—*Minsky, 1983, p. 276*[3]

When I was his student, I found Professor Minsky's attitude toward welfare perplexing. Unlike most progressive economists, he opposed Aid to Families with Dependent Children (AFDC, known as "welfare") as well as the Food Stamp program. Instead, he advocated removing barriers to work, including provisions of Social Security that discourage retirees from seeking jobs (such as taxing benefit payments). To me, he sounded a bit like then-President Reagan, who argued for work, not handouts.

Gradually I came to understand; his argument was that we should create New Deal–style jobs programs so that anyone willing to work could find gainful employment rather than welfare. Minsky called his preferred policy "employer of last resort"—in the same way that the Fed should be "lender of last resort" to the financial system, the Treasury should provide public sector jobs to those who could not find them in the private sector.

Still, it was only much later, as I went through Minsky's papers,[4] that I discovered the active role he had played in the 1960s in promoting job creation as an alternative to welfare—to fight the main cause of poverty, unemployment. By then he was a professor at the University of California, Berkeley, where he worked with a prominent team of labor economists to formulate a plan to fight poverty and unemployment.

It is important to recognize that poverty had become a burning issue in America with the election of John F. Kennedy, and equally important was the exposé written by Michael Harrington, *The Other America*,[5] which revealed rampant poverty and hunger in the midst of America's postwar plenty. Indeed, the Kennedy–Johnson administrations declared a "War on Poverty," and after Kennedy's assassination in 1963, President Johnson launched that war.

At that time, Minsky argued that the War on Poverty would fail in its mission because it did not contain a significant job creation program. Unless policy were directed toward eliminating involuntary unemployment, he insisted, it would not resolve the poverty problem. Over the subsequent decade, Minsky wrote many articles, letters, and manuscripts on the problems of poverty and unemployment, many of which recommended the employer of last resort (ELR) approach to job creation.

Indeed, he probably wrote just about as much on those topics as he did on the financial system during those years. It is remarkable that his work in this area is virtually unknown. For Minsky, eliminating poverty and joblessness is essential to "stabilizing an unstable economy" (the title of his 1986 book). Focusing only on the financial system while ignoring all of the instability and insecurity associated with poverty and unemployment would be a mistake. Indeed, Minsky argued that "Keynesian" policy of the United States in the 1960s—which had relied on the War on Poverty plus demand stimulus—actually fuels financial instability. By contrast, a jobs program would enhance stability.

In this chapter, we first look at Minsky's views on the War on Poverty and his ELR alternative. We then turn to his more general views on "Keynesian" approaches to unemployment—particularly those reflected in the so-called Phillips curve employment–inflation trade-off—and "Keynesian" policies to deal with unemployment. We finally examine why he believed that the ELR approach would achieve full employment while improving stability.

The War on Poverty[6]

Minsky characterized the original War on Poverty as an attempt to "upgrade workers," and any number of programs have been created since 1964 to improve education, skills, and incentives of the jobless to make them more appealing to private sector employers. As Hyman Minsky remarked barely one year into the battle, the War on Poverty "can spread poverty more fairly. . . . However, this approach, standing by itself, cannot end poverty."[7]

His argument was that simply increasing the "employability" of the poor by providing training without increasing the supply of jobs would just redistribute unemployment and poverty. For every better trained worker who got a job, a worker with less training would become unemployed. Minsky was not arguing against better education and training—he was arguing that to reduce unemployment and poverty we need more jobs, too.

Today in the United States there are more people living in poverty than before the War on Poverty began. That poverty is highly concentrated among families with children. Indeed, with the exception of poverty rates among the aged—which fell because of Social Security, not because of the War on Poverty— U.S. poverty rates have barely moved since the early 1960s. If we want to assess the success of the War on Poverty by that measure, we'd have to say that Minsky was right: it failed to lift the poor out of poverty.

Furthermore, we must remember that it was not just President Reagan who sought to end "handouts" to the poor, even as he unfairly portrayed them as "welfare queens" who drive Cadillacs.[8] For it was President Clinton who ended "welfare as we know it" by pushing Congress to end the AFDC program. His justification was that we need to change our view of the poor— from dependents who rely on the generosity of the government to workers who deserve help.

Hence, Clinton's welfare reform included lifetime limits and strong incentives to work. In some respects, Clinton's argument about eliminating welfare dependency was similar to Minsky's. However, unlike Minsky's ELR proposal, Clinton's proposal did not provide the jobs. The idea was that if the economy grows at a sufficiently robust pace, the jobs will magically appear.

In truth, this was also the Kennedy–Johnson approach that was developed by the orthodox Keynesian economists[9] who advised the presidents (one of the components of the War on Poverty was the creation of the Council of Economic Advisers (CEA)—which was originally dominated by Keynesians) in those years.

Typically, "Keynesian" policies to raise aggregate demand in order to stimulate private sector employment have been adopted on the belief that economic growth would raise the demand for labor and thereby "lift the boats" of the poor.[10] The idea was that the War on Poverty would prepare those who could work, upgrading their skills, and it would provide welfare and food stamps to those who could not, would not, or should not work. Finally, it would rely on the private sector to create jobs for the new workers seeking them.

Still, unemployment rates (and especially jobless rates) have trended upward since the 1960s, long-term joblessness has become increasingly concentrated among the labor force's disadvantaged, poverty rates have remained rigid, real wages for most workers have declined since the early 1970s, and labor markets and residential neighborhoods have become increasingly segregated as the "haves" construct gated communities and the "have-nots" are left behind in the crumbling urban core.

In other words, the War on Poverty not only failed to reduce poverty, but it also failed to provide jobs on a sustained basis to those who wanted them.

Minsky predicted these outcomes. His argument was that the economic theories on which the War on Poverty was based misunderstand the nature of poverty. The notion that economic growth together with supply-side policies to upgrade workers and provide proper work incentives would be enough to eliminate poverty was recognized by Minsky at the time to be fallacious.

Indeed, evidence suggests that economic growth mildly favors the "haves" over the "have-nots"—increasing inequality—and that jobs do not simply trickle down, at least at the levels of growth usually experienced in the postwar period.[11] Furthermore, most of the early success at eliminating poverty had to do with expansion of Social Security for the aged and those with disabilities; it had little to do with either more rapid growth or with the War on Poverty programs. This is why poverty rates for those under age sixty-five did not improve.[12]

The Theory behind the War on Poverty

In his first State of the Union address on January 8, 1964, President Johnson declared an "unconditional War on Poverty," and its centerpiece, the Economic Opportunity Act was submitted to Congress later that year. According to Johnson, the plan was designed to deal with the causes of poverty, rather than simply trying to ameliorate its consequences. By expanding educational and training opportunities for the poor, Johnson believed that it would be possible to end poverty forever.

Johnson declared "a total commitment . . . to pursue victory over the most ancient of mankind's enemies."[13] In Minsky's assessment, because the act focused on preparing workers for jobs that might not exist, it would fail in its mission. Only a targeted jobs program, paying decent wages, would successfully fight poverty among the nonaged in a politically acceptable manner.

Why had the War on Poverty downplayed job creation? The answer is that both Kennedy and Johnson relied on their economists at the CEA. As Judith Russell[14] documents, the CEA's belief was that (a) poverty is not inextricably linked to unemployment, (b) unemployment could in any case be sufficiently reduced through aggregate fiscal policies (such as Kennedy's tax cut of 1963), and (c) millions of Americans would have to be maintained as an unemployed buffer stock to keep inflation in check. These views still hold sway among economists.

The CEA was able to turn the president and policy against the dominant "structuralist" views of unemployment held by many economists, most policy makers, and even most of Congress—and by Kennedy's close advisor, John Kenneth Galbraith—all of whom believed that unemployment above 2 percent is unacceptable.

One of the main bastions of the structuralist view was Berkeley, so it is not surprising that Minsky made the structuralist argument that demand stimulus alone could never generate jobs where they were most needed—by low-skilled workers and by African-Americans. Furthermore, given that the CEA was prepared to accept 4 percent (or more) unemployment as "full employment," and as black unemployment rates ran two to three times higher than the overall unemployment rates, a War on Poverty formulated by the CEA could never have made much of a dent in African-American poverty.

It was the CEA's version of Keynesianism—based on "priming the pump" to raise demand—that played the major role in convincing the President that a jobs program was not a necessary element in the fight against poverty. Another culprit was the widespread belief that the poor had to be changed before poverty could be eliminated. Minsky rejected these views and argued that without a jobs program that takes the poor as they are, the War on Poverty would not be successful. His argument is that you provide the jobs first, and then you boost skills through on-the-job training. Furthermore, he warned that the "Keynesian" approach would also be unsustainable because it would promote instability.

Minsky's Contemporary Assessment
of the War on Poverty

Minsky considered the War on Poverty "a conservative rebuttal to an ancient challenge of the radicals, that capitalism necessarily generates 'poverty in the midst of plenty'"[15] (p. 175). As he saw it, Johnson's version of this "conservative rebuttal" was fundamentally flawed. Instead of providing the impoverished with an opportunity to work, it provided them with the opportunity to learn how to work.

Minsky blamed most of American poverty on unemployment. And, since he blamed unemployment on our economic system rather than on the shortcomings of its workers, he rejected supply-side "solutions" such as workfare, training, education, and so-called "incentives to work."

Minsky also rejected the kind of demand stimulus policies that have been called upon to stimulate employment since World War II. A decade into the War on Poverty (WOP), he argued in 1975, "We have to reverse the thrust of policy of the past 40 years and move towards a system in which labor force attachment is encouraged. But to do that we must make jobs available; any policy strategy which does not take job creation as its first and primary objective is but a continuation of the impoverishing strategy of the past decade"[16] (p. 20). Since the postwar antipoverty strategy had proven ineffectual, Minsky believed that policy makers should return to the kind of strategy that characterized policy making before World War II, namely programs to provide public employment.

One could see the War on Poverty as a victory for the "Age of Keynes" but a defeat for a real antipoverty strategy, in the sense that it brought with it a belief in the importance of maintaining aggregate demand in order to promote economic growth, but it neglected the importance of jobs in reducing poverty.

Minsky emphasized that joblessness, insufficient hours of work, and low pay combine to create poverty among the able-bodied. He went on to argue that it is obvious that "expanded, improved, and modernized programs of transfer payments and income in kind for the aged, the infirm, the disabled, and needy children are necessary. As I see it, this has little to do with the WOP; it has mainly to do with our national conscience and affection for man" (Minsky, 1965, pp. 176–77). In other words, he was willing to grant that a system of welfare would be required to deal with those who could not, or should not, work. However, he insisted that a comprehensive jobs program together with an effective and adequate minimum wage would go a long way toward eliminating poverty among those willing and able to work.

Significantly, he called for a "tight full employment" goal of a measured 2.5 percent unemployment rate. Compared with the expected 5.2 percent unemployment rate in 1965, he calculated that this would have increased GNP by $34 billion to $53 billion.[17] Minsky pointed out that this is far above the estimated $11 or $12 billion it would take to raise the incomes of all living in poverty above the poverty line for that year. In other words, putting people to work would generate from three to almost five times as much output as would be required to bring all Americans above the poverty line.

Hence, while a comprehensive employment strategy might not resolve all poverty problems, it would certainly generate more than enough GNP that could be redistributed to eliminate poverty.

At that time, structuralists tended to emphasize job mismatch: even at cyclical peaks when the aggregate number of jobs might be sufficient, the skills, education, and other characteristics of a substantial set of the unemployed would leave them without jobs. Such views were dominant among policy makers, and similar views were also favored at the end of the 1990s as the "new economy" boom left low-skilled workers behind (see Pigeon and Wray, 2000).

However, the structuralists like Minsky went further because they argued that technological and other structural changes to job markets would outstrip any ability to educate and retrain displaced workers for the types of jobs that would exist. In other words, they were highly skeptical that "supply-side" policies alone would be sufficient to resolve the growing unemployment problem. What was needed was a combination of "active labor market" policies and direct job creation programs for the structurally displaced.

Minsky pointed out that even if the economy were not dynamically creating structurally displaced workers, labor market supply-side programs would have little effect for up to twenty years—what Minsky termed the "gestation" period required to produce a worker:

> We are learning that what happens to a child between the ages of three to five is of vital importance in determining the capabilities of the adult. Thus, preschool training is necessary to break the vicious circle of poverty. But if this view is true, then it takes 18 to 20 years to realize the benefits from such programs.
> —*Minsky, 1965, p. 195*

In a dynamic society that is always raising the skills goalposts, that long gestation period almost guarantees that many individuals achieving the age of labor force entry will not be prepared for the jobs that then exist. Thus, there would always be a mismatch between labor "supply" and "demand." For that reason, jobs would need to be created to resolve the mismatch.

Was Minsky Right about the War on Poverty?

Let's look at the data to see if Minsky got it right. U.S. "official" poverty rates had been declining sharply in the postwar period even before the War on Poverty, to 15 percent in 1965 when the War on Poverty began. For both whites and blacks, there is a decline of poverty rates in the mid-1960s, but no improvement subsequently—at least until the Clinton expansion of the mid-1990s, when African-American poverty rates improved. Overall, poverty rates finished the millennium back at 12 percent, the level they had reached in 1968. From these data, it is hard to discern any positive effect from the War on Poverty.

How much of the problem is due to joblessness? In research I did with Stephanie Bell (Kelton) on the fortieth anniversary of the War on Poverty in 2004, we found that just about 10 percent of all families fell below the poverty line.[18] About a quarter of families with no workers lived below the poverty line, as did a quarter of families with at least one part-time or part-year worker. On the other hand, families with at least one full-time, year-round worker had a poverty rate of only 3.5 percent.

If employment is so important to poverty reduction, it is instructive to look at employment trends for the least advantaged since implementation of the War on Poverty and "Keynesian" policies. In 1965, the employment rate for high school dropouts aged twenty-five to sixty-four was 62 percent; by 1994, this had fallen to 51 percent. This situation is consistent with Minsky's structuralist belief that a successful War on Poverty would need jobs targeted to "workers as they are"—especially to high school dropouts.

The probability of gaining employment without a high school degree has fallen considerably—with barely half of dropouts working. Note that these figures are for the noninstitutionalized population—if incarcerated "prime age" (eighteen to forty-four years old), high school dropout males are included, things look much worse. As our previous research (Pigeon and Wray, 2000) has shown, the 1999 employment rate for prime age, high school dropout males falls from 68 percent to 62 percent if we include the incarcerated population. For similarly situated African-American males, the employment rate falls from 46 percent to 33 percent if the incarcerated population is included as part of the population without jobs. That should be shocking: only one-third of prime age African-American high school dropouts were employed in 1999—the peak of the Clinton boom.

In sum, the War on Poverty had little long-term success at significantly raising employment and reducing poverty rates—at least for those under age sixty-five—especially for the least advantaged males without a high school degree. The War on Poverty had little to do with direct job creation, and as Minsky had warned, the War on Poverty would only redistribute poverty among the less fortunate unless it created jobs.

The "Keynesians" who formulated the Kennedy–Johnson strategy relied on economic growth to create the jobs that would reduce poverty rates. In the next section, we examine Minsky's skepticism about the ability of growth to reduce poverty.

Minsky's Views on the Growth through Private Investment Strategy

As we mentioned earlier, the CEA pushed the notion of pump priming to generate growth. In the postwar era, with the exception of defense spending, "the preferred instrument for generating fiscal expansion has been some type of tax cut or loophole, i.e., the shifting of resources to private consumption and investment" (Minsky, 1971, p. 15). These "Keynesian" policies to promote full employment relied on a favorable business environment to stimulate investment spending, which was supposed to induce consumption through the spending multiplier. Various tax incentives, including accelerated depreciation and investment tax credits, were a common feature of the postwar investment strategy. Policy makers also tried to increase the certainty of capital income, through the use of government contracts with guaranteed profits, such as those granted to defense, transportation, and housing industries.

However, Minsky (1973)[19] argued that there are four problems with the high investment strategy. First, tax incentives to shift income to capital exacerbate inequality between ordinary workers and those who have income to invest—who reap the rewards when policy promotes investment. Second, high capital incomes lead to opulent consumption by the rich and emulative consumption by the less affluent, creating the potential for demand-pull inflation (not to mention debt-financed consumption by those with lower income who try to "keep up with the Joneses"—or the Kardashians!).

Third, government contracts granted to sophisticated high-tech industries generate demand for skilled, high-wage labor, thereby exacerbating income inequality within the labor force. Finally, by targeting the size and surety of capital income, tax-cut programs would increase business confidence and debt financing, and borrowers' margins of safety would decline. Thus, a private investment strategy can lead to a debt-financed investment boom, thereby undermining the stability of the financial system.

As discussed earlier, Minsky had earlier argued that an expansion led by the private sector tends to increase private indebtedness and financial fragility as debt-service payments rise relative to prospective business revenues. In contrast, an expansion led by public sector spending could actually enhance stability by providing safe assets (government bonds issued as the budget moved to deficit).

This analysis is interesting in light of the problems created during the Clinton boom of the 1990s—an expansion led by private sector borrowing, with a federal budget that moved to large surpluses. As we now know in retrospect, the decade of debt-fueled consumption growth from 1996 to 2006 ultimately contributed to the collapse in 2007. Indeed, it is impossible to understand the Global Financial Crisis without recognizing the importance played by household borrowing to fuel home purchases as well as consumption.

In sum, the postwar era was characterized by a preference for private investment strategies to promote private spending and economic growth. Even as the War on Poverty got under way, the Johnson administration demonstrated its preference for private sector spending strategies, passing tax cuts in 1964 and again in 1965 and 1966. By encouraging private sector spending (especially investment), policy makers aimed to stimulate growth in total income.

But these strategies did little to improve the conditions of lower-middle-income workers (e.g., factory workers), whose real incomes declined by 2.5 percent over the period 1965–1970 (Minsky, 2013, p. 114). Things were even worse after that, as blue collar wages stagnated over the decades following 1970. Furthermore, the private investment strategies tended to exacerbate income inequality, generate inflation, and undermine financial stability.

Even though the Kennedy and Johnson administrations succeeded in generating postwar growth that temporarily reduced unemployment rates in the mid-1960s (often called the "golden age" of the U.S. economy), policy makers failed to understand that "policy weapons which are sufficient to move an economy from slack to sustained full employment are not sufficient to sustain full employment" (Minsky, 2013, p. 122). Though demand stimulus might get the economy near to full employment, the position would be unsustainable because it would encourage risky behavior leading to financial fragility and inflation.

As long as policy makers continued to favor private investment strategies, there would be no sustained strides made in the war against poverty across the business cycle. Rather, according to Minsky, this "Keynesian" approach would have to resort to a "stop–go" policy that would stimulate investment and thus growth until inflation picked up, then would use policy to slow growth to fight inflation. Hence, although unemployment would fall in the boom, it would return in the slump.

Meanwhile, financial fragility would grow on trend and repeated financial crises would stress the system. If government intervened to fight a crisis, that would simply encourage even more risk-taking. In other words, such a policy strategy would be biased toward promotion of inflation as well as financial instability.

Public Employment Strategy: The ELR Proposal

Minsky argued that consumption is the most stable component of aggregate demand—since households consume a fairly high and stable fraction of income. So long as consumption is financed out of income rather than debt, a high consumption economy would be more stable. For that reason, Minsky's alternative would stress policy that favors high consumption (rather than high investment)[20] fueled by policies that would increase wages and incomes at the bottom of the distribution.

Furthermore, government spending—especially on wages—should play a major role in generating growth. This is because a sovereign government can increase its spending—even if that results in a budget deficit—without increasing risk of insolvency and default. In contrast, if private spending leads the way, it will tend to outpace income of households and firms, meaning that private indebtedness will grow. That is risky and ultimately unsustainable.

Hence, Minsky's policies would favor both greater equality and greater stability. To permanently improve the lot of the poor, Minsky believed that policy makers needed to address the question of income distribution: "The questions that need answering if, someday, a serious WAR ON POVERTY is to be mounted relate to the distribution of income and the available policy tools which can affect the distribution of income in the relatively short run" (1968, p. 328).

"How," he asked "can the distribution of income be improved?" (Minsky, 1972, p. 5). He answered, "First of all by full employment." By this, Minsky meant that it was necessary to achieve and sustain "tight full employment," which he defined as "[the situation that] exists when over a broad cross section of occupations, industries, and locations, employers, at going wages and salaries, would prefer to employ more workers than they in fact do" (1965, p. 177). That would be the case where job vacancies normally exceed the number of job seekers.

This would require a "bolder, more imaginative, and more consistent use of expansionary monetary and fiscal policy to create jobs than we have witnessed to date" (1965, p. 175). "The achievement and sustaining of tight full employment could do almost all of the job of eliminating poverty" (1968, p. 329). Here, Minsky's position is consistent with his notion that "a large portion of those living in poverty and an even larger portion of those living close to poverty do so because of the meager income they receive from work"—a point we have also emphasized earlier (Minsky, 1968, p. 328).

Minsky believed that "A suggestion of real merit is that the government become an employer of last resort" (p. 338).[21] The employer of last resort (ELR) proposal, which in recent years has been taken up by a number of analysts,[22] calls upon the federal government to institute a job guarantee program similar to the New Deal's Works Progress Administration (WPA), Civilian Conservation Corps (CCC), and National Youth Administration (NYA) programs.[23] The federal government would fund a job guarantee program, setting the wage of (unskilled) labor and adjusting the number of jobs to the number in need of work.

Minsky argued that only the federal government can offer an infinitely elastic demand for workers—hiring anyone ready and willing to work—at a decent wage. This is because government employment is not undertaken to make a profit. All private firms must be profitable to survive, so they only employ the number of workers required to produce what they can sell at a profit.

Minsky saw clear advantages to this proposal. First, he expected it to eliminate the kind of poverty that is due to joblessness. Whereas the investment strategy begins with demand increases for specialized labor, hoping for the trickle-down creation of jobs for those with less education and training, the employment strategy "takes the unemployed as they are and tailor makes jobs to their skills" (Minsky, 1972, p. 6). The ELR program then upgrades their skills through on-the-job training.

Second, if the existence of tight labor markets draws additional workers into the labor force, the number of workers per family will increase, moving some families who are in or near poverty away from it. Third, a tight labor market strategy should improve the distribution of income among workers, setting the program wage at a decent level and then raising the wages of low-income workers faster than the wages of high-income workers.

Fourth, by discontinuing the preferential treatment of capital income (the investment-led strategy favors investors), Minsky believed that it was possible to "decrease [labor–profit] inequality by decreasing capital's share of income" (1973, p. 94). In other words, by creating jobs for those at the bottom, wages would rise relative to profits. Fifth, Minsky believed that by de-emphasizing investment-led growth, the likelihood of financial fragility would decrease.

Finally, a public employment strategy frees policy makers from the overriding need to induce investment through tax incentives—since it creates jobs directly rather than hoping that jobs trickle down from investment-led growth.

An employer of last resort program is much more ambitious than demand-stimulus programs because it offers a job to all who are ready and willing to work. Many of those who will accept employment are currently counted as out of the labor force because they are not actively seeking jobs. Hence, the increase of employment will be larger than what is indicated by a decline of unemployment by some number of percentage points.

Furthermore, the measured unemployment rate would probably fall below the 2.5 percent that Minsky had used in his calculations—perhaps below the 2 percent usually used as an estimate of frictional and structural unemployment.

In research I conducted with Marc-Andre Pigeon[24], we calculated how many "potentially employable" individuals had been left behind by the Clinton rising tide—coming up with a figure of more than 14 million employable workers aged twenty-five to sixty-four for 1999. At that time, the number of officially unemployed individuals in this age group was under 4 million—or less than one-third the number of potentially employable. The official unemployment numbers always vastly understate the number of people who would take jobs if they were available. Minsky's ELR proposal provides a paying job to anyone who wants one, at the program wage.

Barriers to Attaining and Sustaining Tight Full Employment

Minsky anticipated the "pie-in-the-sky" objections that might be raised, cautioning that "irrational prejudices . . . against spending, deficits and easy money" must be ignored (1965, p. 176). But he recognized that legitimate barriers must be taken into account: "Economic forces can frustrate programs if either the policy objective is inconsistent with such forces or if the program is so poorly conceived that it quite unnecessarily runs afoul of a barrier, even though the objective is, in principle, attainable" (Minsky, 2013, p. 45).

One such frustrating force is inflation. "The policy problem," he argued, is to achieve and sustain tight full employment "without an inflationary rise in prices and wages" (Minsky, 1972, p. 5). But Minsky's antipoverty campaign called for "a rapid increase of those wages that are close to or below the poverty line" (Minsky, 1965, p. 183). He recognized that there might be an inflationary bias in a policy of this sort, particularly if the productivity (output per hour) of the low-wage workers failed to keep pace with their wage increases.

In order to keep the overall price level fairly stable, prices of other goods and services would have to be constrained. Minsky suggested that in the high-wage industries, wages "would have to rise by less than the increases in the productivity of their workers" (1965, p. 183). To prevent firms from simply increasing their profits, it was necessary to ensure that "management in these often oligopolistic industries would have to pass this decline in unit costs on to their customers" (1965, p. 183). Thus, he argued that "effective profit and price constraints would have to accompany tight full employment" (Minsky, 1972, p. 6). If inflationary pressures were not contained, Minsky feared that the "political popularity of full employment" would be undermined (Minsky, 2013, p. 69).

However, the inflation constraint is much less of a concern in today's global economy.

First, deflationary pressures around the globe are substantial as many nations keep domestic demand depressed in order to run trade surpluses, looking to the United States to provide demand for the world's "excess" output. Most importantly, many of the global exporters have very low wages, which keeps global prices down. This means that U.S. firms face substantial price competition so that even relatively rapid growth—such as that experienced in the Clinton expansion and again in the years before the Global Financial Crisis—does not produce significant inflationary pressures.

Second, technological advances and removal of trade restrictions have increased wage competition from abroad, reducing the likelihood that low unemployment could generate a wage-price spiral.

Finally, much of the 1970s' and 1980s' concern with low productivity growth disappeared during the Clinton boom, when productivity growth returned to more normal long-run averages.[25] Indeed, since the mid-1970s, the problem has been that average wages have grown much more slowly than labor productivity—in part because of globalization of production. To the extent that such competitive pressures keep wage growth in line with productivity growth, price pressures will remain moderate.

The final institutional barrier discussed by Minsky concerns the exchange rate regime. Most of Minsky's papers on antipoverty policy were written in the 1960s or early 1970s, when U.S.

policy was constrained by the international monetary system with fixed exchange rates. Because the integrity of the Bretton Woods System rested on dollar convertibility to gold, policy makers had to restrict their fiscal and monetary operations to those that would not adversely affect the balance of payments. In Minsky's words,

> To a considerable extent, ever since 1958 the needs of the dollar standard have acted as a constraint upon domestic income. We have not had tight labor markets because of the peculiar bind that the dollar is in internationally. It is apparently appropriate to allude to William Jennings Bryan by saying that, in part, the cross that the American poor bear is made of gold . . . The solution to the gold standard barrier is simple: get rid of the gold standard.
>
> —*1965, pp. 192–93*

Today, the dollar is a floating currency so that policy is not constrained by the need to protect foreign currency and gold reserves. Thus, the primary barrier to attaining and sustaining tight full employment is political will—not the exchange rate regime.

Conclusion on Minsky's Alternative to the War on Poverty

Private investment strategies and policies to "improve" the characteristics of poor people dominated the postwar approach to poverty. And, though the 1950s and 1960s are commonly referred to as the "golden age" of U.S. capitalism, important barriers prevented the American economy from sustaining what Minsky characterized as tight full employment.

Minsky's fundamental argument is simple: (1) poverty is largely an employment problem; (2) tight full employment improves income at the bottom of the wage spectrum; and (3) a program of direct job creation is necessary to sustain tight full employment.

Thus, he argued that a program of direct job creation is "a necessary ingredient of any war against poverty" (Minsky, 1965, p. 175). As Minsky put it, "The New Deal, with its WPA, NYA, and CCC took workers as they were and generated jobs for them. . . . The resurrection of WPA and allied projects should be a major weapon of the WOP" (Minsky, 1965, p. 195).

Unfortunately, Johnson's Economic Opportunity Act did not provide for significant job creation. Instead, the War on Poverty aimed to improve the skills and knowledge of the impoverished, hoping to "end poverty forever" by offering education and training to those living in or near poverty.

But, as Minsky argued, "education and training have to start at virtually the cradle. . . . All the poor who missed prekindergarten or other special training are, except for the lucky or the gifted, doomed to a life of poverty—a dead end life" (Minsky, 2013, pp. 115–16). Improving the educational and skill sets of the workforce is certainly desirable, but Minsky believed that a reordering of policy objectives is required: "Once tight full employment is achieved, the second step is to generate programs to upgrade workers. I am afraid that in the poverty campaign we have taken the second step without the first; and perhaps this is analogous to the great error-producing sin of infields— throwing the ball before you have it" (Minsky, 1965, p. 200).

Putting it somewhat differently, Minsky viewed full employment as the "horse" and skill- and educational-enhancement programs as the cart. And he strongly believed that a successful antipoverty campaign required the "cart" to follow the horse.

Updating Minsky's Employer
of Last Resort Proposal

In this concluding section, we lay out a concrete proposal based on Minsky's ideas. Let's begin with a relevant quote from Keynes:

> The Conservative belief that there is some law of nature which prevents men [*sic*] from being employed, that it is "rash" to employ men, and that it is financially "sound" to maintain a tenth of the population in idleness for an indefinite period, is crazily improbable—the sort of thing which no man could believe who had not had his head fuddled with nonsense for years and years. . . . We shall try to show him that if new forms of employment are offered more men will be employed, . . . that to set unemployed men to work on useful tasks does what it appears to do, namely, increases the national wealth; and that the notion, that we shall, for intricate reasons, ruin ourselves financially if we use this means to increase our well-being, is what it looks like—a bogy.
> —*John Maynard Keynes, "Essays in Persuasion,"*
> *The Collected Writings of John Maynard Keynes,*
> *vol. 9, Donald Moggridge, ed., (London and Basingstoke:*
> *Macmillan/St. Martin's Press, 1972), pp. 90–92*

Whereas the Employment Act of 1946 committed the U.S. government to achieving high employment—amended by the Humphrey–Hawkins Act to set a goal of a measured unemployment rate of 3 percent—we have continued to act as if achievement of anything close to full employment would "ruin ourselves financially," would destroy the value of our currency through inflation and depreciation, and would destroy the labor discipline that high unemployment maintains through enforced destitution. Through the thick and thin of the business cycle, we leave tens of millions of men and women idle in the "crazily improbable" belief that this makes political, economic, and social sense. It doesn't. Recognized benefits of full employment include the following:

- Production of goods, services, and income;
- On-the-job training and skill development;
- Poverty alleviation;
- Community building and social networking;
- Intergenerational stability;
- Social, political, and economic stability; and
- Social multipliers (Positive feedback and reinforcing dynamics create a virtuous cycle of socioeconomic benefits. The total effect exceeds the sum of the individual benefits).

There are few economic policies that are more important than ensuring that anyone who wants to work has access to a job. And yet decades of experience provide ample evidence that though the private sector plays an invaluable and dynamic force in providing jobs, it cannot by itself ensure full employment.

There is an alternative: a job guarantee through a government-provided employer of last resort program offering a job to anyone who is ready and willing to work at the federal minimum wage[26] plus legislated benefits. The program would be universal, with no time limits or income, gender, education, or experience requirements

The program operates like an employment buffer stock: in a boom, employers will recruit workers out of the program; in a slump, the safety net allows those who lost their jobs to continue to work to preserve good habits, keeping them ready for work.

It will also take those whose education, training, or job experience is initially inadequate to obtain work outside the program, enhancing their employability through on-the-job training. Work records will be maintained for all program participants, available for potential employers. The program will be a better source of potential employees than are the unemployed or those who have left the labor force after giving up hope of ever finding a job. Unemployment offices will be converted to employment offices, to match workers with jobs in the program and to help private and public employers to recruit workers out of the program.

Program wages and benefits will be federally funded; the wage will be periodically adjusted to reflect inflation and rising average labor productivity to prevent erosion of purchasing power and to allow workers to share in rising national productivity so that real living standards will rise. We should strive for a "living wage" for anyone who works.

Program administration and operation will be decentralized. All state and local governments and registered not-for-profit organizations can propose projects for approval by responsible offices designated within each of the states and U.S. territories, as well as the District of Columbia. Upon approval, the proposals will be submitted to the program's federal office for final approval and funding. The U.S. Department of Labor will maintain a website providing details on all projects submitted, all projects approved, and all projects started. Upon completion, a final report will be prepared and kept on the website.

Project proposals will be evaluated on the following criteria: value to the community; value to the participants; likelihood of successful implementation of project; and contribution to preparing workers for nonprogram employment.

All program participants would obtain a Social Security number and maintain a bank account in an FDIC-insured bank. Wages will be paid weekly directly to the participant's account.[27] The federal government will also provide funding on approved expenses of each project up to a maximum of 25 percent of wages paid for a project.[28] Approved uses include administrative expenses; materials costs; and tools, machines, and equipment used in the project.

Workers in the program will be subject to all usual work rules, including those dealing with worker safety, discipline, and grievance procedures. Workers will be dismissed for cause. An individual who is dismissed three times in a twelve-month period will be ineligible to participate in the program for twelve months upon the third dismissal. Workers will be allowed to organize through labor unions.

The program will "take workers as they are" and will "take workers where they are." The jobs will be designed so that they can be performed by workers with the education and training they already have, but the designers will strive to improve the education and skills of all workers as they participate in the program. Proposals will be solicited from every community in America to employ workers in every community. Project proposals should include provisions for part-time work and other flexible arrangements for workers who need them, including but not restricted to flexible arrangements for parents of young children.

In most cases, project output will be provided to communities free of charge. However, the program should encourage experimentation with alternative arrangements on a limited, trial basis, including some production for sale. For example, workers might form labor cooperatives with wages and benefits, plus 10 percent overhead and materials expenses paid by the federal government for a limited period, with workers selling output to recover costs and to share net revenues. Government support would be phased out as the cooperative proves successful; if it doesn't, the cooperative would close and workers would return to the regular ELR program.

Program spending will be exempt from requirements of balanced budget acts. No new taxes will be imposed to fund the program. Spending will be treated as deriving from general revenue. Estimated spending is 1–3 percent of GDP, with economic, social, and political benefits several times larger.

This is the sort of alternative that Minsky had proposed back in the 1960s. A half century later, unemployment and poverty remain with us—just as he had argued they would. Until we get serious about jobs, we will not significantly reduce unemployment and poverty. To paraphrase President Clinton's well-known phrase ("It's the economy, stupid"), "It's the jobs, stupid."

6

■

Minsky and the Global Financial Crisis

At the annual banking structure and competition conference of the Federal Reserve Bank of Chicago in May 1987, the buzzword heard in the corridors and used by many of the speakers was "that which can be securitized, will be securitized."

—Minsky, 1987[1]

There is a symbiotic relation between the globalization of the world's financial structure and the securitization of financial instruments. Globalization requires the conformity of institutions across national lines and in particular the ability of creditors to capture assets that underlie the securities.

—Minsky, 1987[2]

Securitization reflects a change in the weight of market and bank funding capabilities: market funding capabilities have increased relative to the funding abilities of banks and depository financial intermediaries. It is in part a lagged response to monetarism. The fighting of inflation by constraining monetary growth opened opportunities for nonbanking financing techniques.

—Minsky, 1987[3]

The emergence of money manager capitalism means that
the financing of the capital development of the economy has
taken a back seat to the quest for short run total returns.
—*Minsky, 1992, p. 32*[4]

When the GFC (Global Financial Crisis) struck, many commentators called it the "Minsky crisis" or "Minsky moment," recognizing the work of Minsky who—as discussed earlier—had developed the "financial instability hypothesis" that described the transformation of an economy from a "robust" financial structure to a "fragile" one. A "run of good times" would encourage ever-greater risk-taking, and growing instability would be encouraged if financial crises were resolved by swift government intervention.

As Minsky insisted "stability is destabilizing"[5]—and this seemed to perfectly describe the last few decades of U.S. experience, during which financial crises became more frequent and increasingly severe. We could list, for example, the savings and loan crisis of the 1980s, the stock market crash of 1987, the developing country debt crises (1980s to early 1990s), the Long Term Capital Markets (1998) and Enron (2001) fiascoes, and the dot-com collapse (2000–2001) as precursors to the final "great crash" in 2007.[6]

Each of these crises led to U.S. government intervention that prevented a downward spiral of financial markets or of the economy (although in some cases, recessions followed the crises); indeed, after the dot-com crisis, the belief was that a new Great Moderation[7] had taken hold in the United States, making serious downturns impossible. This notion encouraged more risk, more financial layering, and more leveraging (debt issued against debt, with little net worth backing it up). All of this dangerous financial structure fits Minsky's arguments about growing financial instability.

So, though it is completely appropriate to give credit to Minsky's foresight, we also need to look at Minsky's later writings, which developed a "stages" approach to the longer term transformation of the financial system. This approach went well beyond the "financial theory of investment and investment theory of the cycle" that Minsky had begun to develop in the 1950s.

Minsky's Stages Approach: Finance Capitalism and Managerial Welfare-State Capitalism

Minsky's later writing during the late 1980s and through the 1990s focused on the long-term transformation of the financial system since the late nineteenth century. In a sense, he was returning to the evolutionary approach of his dissertation advisor, Joseph Schumpeter. Let us briefly describe the main stages.

Commercial Capitalism. We can begin with the "commercial capitalism" stage that coincides with the dominance of "commercial banking," as described in chapter 4. In this stage, banks were important for financing the production process itself—lending to firms so that they could hire labor and purchase the materials needed for production.

Investment goods were mostly purchased with internal funds, provided by the firms' owners. However, as investment goods became increasingly expensive, owners had to look for external funds. This problem led to a demand for the services of a different type of financial institution, the investment bank. As discussed earlier, the investment bank would either provide long-term funding directly, or it would float the debts or equity of the investing firms.

Finance Capitalism.[8] In the early twentieth century, a new form of capitalism, named "finance capitalism" by Rudolf

Hilferding, took form, dominated by investment banks that provided the finance for corporations. This development made it possible to obtain external finance for the expensive projects undertaken by the steel and energy firms and railroads owned by the "robber barons."

To a substantial degree, finance became "globalized" as shares and bonds were sold in international markets. The investment banks played an important role in helping the "trusts" to consolidate power and oligopolize markets. Indeed, to obtain long-term external finance through the investment banks, the borrower really needed market power—for otherwise the lending was too risky. Borrowing firms needed to demonstrate that they had sufficient price-setting power to ensure that they could service the long-term debt issued to finance positions in complex and long-lived plant and equipment. The railroads are a perfect example: very expensive and long-lived infrastructure that was financed by floating bonds in global markets.

By the late 1920s, investment banks were largely devoting their efforts to financing speculation in financial assets, particularly in equities issued by subsidiary trusts of the investment banks themselves. In truth, these were little more than pyramid schemes—speculating in essentially worthless shares, much like the infamous schemes of Charles Ponzi or the modern-day Bernie Madoff.[9]

Managerial-Welfare State Capitalism.[10] In any event, in Minsky's view, the Great Depression ended the finance capitalism stage and ushered in a much more stable version, with the New Deal reforms of the financial sector plus a much bigger role for the federal government in managing the economy. Minsky called this "managerial-welfare state" capitalism, where the "Big Bank" (Fed) and "Big Government" (Treasury) promoted stable economic growth, high employment, and rising wages with falling inequality. The United States entered its economic "golden age," which lasted from the end of World War II through the early 1970s.

The problem is that "stability is destabilizing"—the absence of deep recessions and severe financial crises encouraged innovations that increased financial instability. Furthermore, for reasons we won't explore now, conservative politicians and economists were able to slowly chip away at the New Deal reforms that promoted growth while providing social protection. After 1974, median male earnings stopped growing and began to fall as workers lost effective representation by unions, the social safety net was gutted, and unemployment came to be seen as a desirable outcome—a tool used by policy makers to keep inflation down. Financial institutions were deregulated and desupervised, and their power grew in a self-reinforcing manner: as they were able to capture a greater share of profits, their political power increased, making it possible to further subvert or eliminate regulations so that they could gain an even larger share of profits.

The Long Transformation to Instability. There are many aspects to this transformation, and Minsky was certainly not the only one to notice it. Some called it the rise of "casino capitalism," and many identified it as "financialization."[11] In important respects, it was similar to Hilferding's "finance capitalism"— with what were called "nonbank banks," or later, "shadow banks" rising to challenge the investment banks and the commercial banks. This development also provided justification for dropping the New Deal reforms so that the banks could compete with the new intruders who were poaching business. This is a huge topic, but the important point is that even as shadow banks pushed financial practice to new frontiers, the commercial (and less regulated investment) banks insisted that they had to follow suit.

At the same time, the structure of incentives and rewards was changed such that risky bets, high leverage ratios, and

short-term profits were promoted over long-term firm survival
and returns to investors. Many if not most of the new practices
served no social purpose beyond making top management of
financial institutions incredibly rich. A good example of the
transformation was the conversion of the venerable investment
banks like Goldman Sachs from partnerships to publicly held
firms with hired and richly rewarded management.

While the structure and practices were somewhat different,
the results were similar to those that led up to the "Great Crash"
in 1929—"pump and dump" incentives were created, through
which top management would exercise stock options, "pump"
asset and equity prices, and then sell out ("dump") their own
stocks before the speculative boom collapsed.

What we see by the early 2000s is the coalescence of three
phenomena that made the biggest financial institutions extremely dangerous: the return of "pump and dump" strategies,
ripping off customers and shareholders; the move from partnerships to corporate form, which increases the agency problems
(institutions run in the interests of management, not owners);
and excessive executive compensation that was tied to short-
term performance (i.e., by rewarding them with stock options),
which increases the pressures to "cheat" or to do anything else
that justifies huge bonuses.

Money Manager Capitalism

Minsky called this new stage "money manager capitalism." This
name draws attention to a characteristic feature: huge pools
of funds under management by professionals—pension funds,
sovereign wealth funds, hedge funds, university endowments,
corporate treasuries, and so on.[12]

Every money manager had to beat the average return to retain
clients, something that is of course statistically impossible. But

with such incentives and with virtually no government regulation or oversight of shadow banking, this encouraged not only risky behavior but also ethically compromised actions.

In Minsky's view, the rise of these managed funds was caused by the success of the earlier managerial-welfare state capitalism: the absence of depressions and relatively good growth—plus policies that favored private pensions (such as tax exemptions)—allowed financial wealth to grow over the entire postwar period. Although financial crises came along and wiped out some wealth, each crisis was contained so that most wealth survived and quickly resumed growth in recovery.

What was really important was the dynamic created by the shift of power away from banks to the very lightly regulated "money managers" at the "shadow banks." To compete, banks needed to subvert regulations through innovations and then to have them legislatively eliminated. This dynamic allowed banks to increase leverage ratios, and thus risk, to keep pace with shadow banking practice.

There was a "Gresham's law"[13] in operation: those institutions that could reduce capital ratios and loss reserves[14] the most quickly were able to increase net earnings and thus rewards to management and investors.

Furthermore, there was a shift to maximization of share prices as one of the main goals of management—which supposedly aligned the interests of shareholders and top managers who received stock options in compensation. That in turn encouraged short-term focus on performance in equity markets, which—as we had already discovered in 1929—is accomplished through market manipulation (both legal and illegal). Again, top management was incentivized to engage in "pump and dump" once they exercised stock options. They could make tens of millions of dollars—and even much more—in this way.

The problem was that the sheer volume of financial wealth under management outstripped socially useful investments.

To keep returns high, money managers and bankers had to turn to increasingly esoteric financial speculation—in areas that not only did not serve the public purpose but actively subverted it.

An example would be the rise of index speculation in commodities markets that drives up global prices of energy and food, leading to hunger and even starvation around the world.[15] The dot-com bubble is another example—speculators drove up the prices of stocks of Internet companies with no business model or prospective profits. The inevitable crash wiped out hundreds of billions of dollars of wealth.

Another example of speculation against the public interest is the U.S. real estate boom that began before 2000 and finally collapsed in 2007, triggering the GFC. It was the biggest speculative boom in U.S. history and was driven by money managers who created complex securities and derivatives for speculative bets—with many of those bets actually paying off if the homeowners defaulted and lost their homes.

Shredding of the New Deal Reforms and the Rise of Insecurity

Minsky had linked rising economic insecurity to the money manager phase.[16] As discussed previously, in the 1960s he argued against the Kennedy–Johnson War on Poverty because it emphasized welfare and training over job creation. Furthermore, unlike most Keynesian economists, he opposed policy to promote investment and other business-friendly policies that seek to achieve full employment by "pumping" aggregate demand—such as "military Keynesianism," which would stimulate spending in the defense sector in the hope that spending by workers in this sector would create jobs in others.

Minsky never believed the "rising tide lifts all boats" story. Instead, he wanted targeted spending, New Deal-style government job creation (modeled after the Works Progress Administration, which created eight million jobs in the 1930s), and support for consumption by workers. His proposals were based on his theoretical approach.

First, he worried that the typical "Keynesian" policies would generate inflation long before they created full employment because they would create employment and output bottlenecks in the most advanced sectors (i.e., the defense industries, which are heavily unionized and oligopolistic). The inflation, in turn, would induce "stop–go" policy, with government purposely slowing growth and raising unemployment each time inflation increased.

Second, and related to this, the already well-off workers would see income gains fueled by Keynesian pump priming, increasing inequality among workers. General demand stimulus would likely benefit disproportionately the sectors and workers with economic power. Less skilled workers would be left behind.

Finally, he argued that offering only welfare and training, but no jobs, to the unemployed is unnecessarily defeatist, putting "the cart before the horse." It essentially tells the poor and unemployed that they must improve their skills, education, training, and even their character before they can get a job.[17] And it would train people for jobs that don't exist.

Time would prove him correct—inequality began to rise after 1970, along with trend increases to the unemployment rate—at least until the boom-and-bust cycle that began with President Clinton. Yet, after a decade with improvement of some social measures (between 1996 and 2006, unemployment trended somewhat lower, economic growth was a bit better, and poverty stopped rising), the GFC caused massive unemployment, increased poverty, and boosted inequality to record levels.

Minsky believed that the dynamics of money manager capitalism accelerated the rise of insecurity. The leveraged buyout is a good example because managed funds would buy "cash cows" (corporations with little debt) by issuing debt, then strip the best assets for sale and downsize the remaining hulk—slashing wages and benefits and laying off workers. As a result, Minsky worried, "workers at nearly all levels are insecure, as entire divisions are bought and sold and as corporate boards exhibit a chronic need to downsize overhead and to seek out the least expensive set of variable inputs." (Minsky and Whalen, 1996, p. 6).

With the demise of the paternalistic (or managerial-welfare) stage of capitalism, "Many families cannot distinguish recession from recovery" (Minsky and Whalen, 1996, p. 7). Even in "good times," wages barely rise and families fear for their jobs; more workers have to work several jobs to make ends meet, and most families need more than one wage earner to survive. Minsky quoted a *U.S. News and World Report* from 1994, which reported that "57 percent of those asked said the American Dream is out of reach for most families, while more than two thirds were worried that their children will not live as well as they do" (Minsky and Whalen, 1996. p. 8).

Minsky died shortly after he wrote these words. He had been hopeful when President Clinton took office in 1992; however, by 1996 Minsky worried that money manager capitalism had forced a "race to the bottom" by job- and wage-cutting. Ironically, a boom was just getting under way—the so-called Goldilocks economy (it was called the Goldilocks economy because it grew fast enough to create jobs but not so rapidly as to generate inflation), which appeared to have restored the kind of growth America had last seen in the 1960s.

But appearances can be deceiving! As we now know, Goldilocks was blowing bubbles, fueled by Wall Street's excesses. The economy stumbled in 2000 but then resumed growth in the mid-2000s—fueled by the real estate and commodities markets bubbles—before finally collapsing into the Global Financial Crisis. Let's see what went wrong.

Financial Bubbles, Goldilocks Growth, and Government Budgets

From the 1980s, the financial sector grew relative to the non-financial sectors (manufacturing, agriculture, and nonfinancial services, including government)—by the time of the GFC, the financial sector accounted for 20 percent of U.S. national value added and 40 percent of corporate profits. By itself, it was an autonomous source of growth and also of rising inequality because of high compensation in the sector. Up to half of the college graduates from the elite colleges went into the financial sector because rewards there could be far higher than in other sectors.[18] Compensation at the very top quite simply exploded.

This became fairly obvious by the time of the Clinton administration—with worker income lagging behind and with loss of U.S. manufacturing jobs, the financial sector played a big role in the Clinton recovery of the 1990s. Indeed, economic growth was sufficiently robust, and the boost to income at the very top caused federal government tax revenues to grow swiftly.

During Clinton's second term, the federal government's budget went into significant surplus for the first time since the late 1920s. Although most economists thought that was good and celebrated the President's projection that the surpluses would continue for at least fifteen years, allowing all federal debt to be retired, a few of us at the Levy Economics Institute (where Minsky was employed until his death in 1996) argued that the surplus would be short-lived—and that it would kill the boom and cause a deep recession.[19]

Here's why. Wynne Godley at the Levy Institute had developed a "three balances" approach to macroanalysis based on the accounting identity that the sum of the balances of the domestic private sector, the government sector, and the foreign sector must be zero. Although any one of these could run a surplus, at least one of the others would have to run a deficit.

In the case of the United States, by the late 1990s the government sector was running a surplus of about 2.5 percent of GDP, the foreign balance was 4 percent of GDP (meaning that the United States was running a trade deficit so the rest of the world had a surplus), and by identity the U.S. private sector (firms plus households) had a deficit of 6.5 percent (the sum of the other two). In other words, the private sector was spending $106.50 for every hundred dollars of income. Each year that the private sector spent more than its income, it went more deeply into debt.

This was the ugly side of money manager capitalism: the growth of financial assets under management was equal to the growth of financial liabilities of *somebody*. (For every financial asset, there is an equal financial liability.) At the Levy Institute, we believed that the private sector debt load would become too great, causing borrowing and spending to fall. Then the economy would slip into recession. That in turn would cause job losses and force defaults on some of the debt. We believed that would set off a severe financial crisis.

At the beginning of 2000, that appeared to be happening, but it turned out that the crisis was not as severe as we had expected. The dot-com bubble went bust and stock markets tanked. The private sector retrenched—spending less than its income—and the Clinton budget surpluses morphed into deficits. The Fed responded by lowering interest rates as the big budget deficits expanded—just as we had expected.

And then something amazing happened: the American consumer started borrowing again—at a pace even greater than during the Clinton boom. Much of that was to finance housing purchases and to buy big-ticket consumer items financed through "cash-out equity finance"—taking out second mortgages against homes.

In other words, the U.S. real estate boom had begun. From 1996 to 2006, U.S. households spent more than their incomes, with only the brief respite in the recession of 2000. Nothing like this had ever happened before.[20] And it was aided and abetted by the practices of the money managers, inducing homeowners to go deeply into risky mortgage debt, which was then securitized and sold into portfolios managed by money managers.

By 2007, the U.S. ratio of total debt to GDP reached an all-time peak of 500 percent, or five dollars of debt to service using each dollar of income.[21] Whereas much discussion in the early 2000s focused on the government debt ratio, the debt of the household sector, as well as nonfinancial business and financial business, were all much higher as a percentage of GDP.

Nonfinancial business debt was actually not a huge problem in spite of its size because much of this debt was caused by long-term finance of capital equipment—and after 2000, U.S. nonfinancial businesses actually did not borrow much. Household debt *was* a huge problem, of course, and still weighs heavily on consumers half a decade after the GFC, slowing recovery.

But what was particularly unusual, and had long been ignored, was the unprecedented rise of financial sector indebtedness, which reached 125 percent of GDP. As we discuss in the next section, that is one aspect of "financialization" of the economy, with financial institutions layering debt on debt as they issued liabilities to one another to finance purchases of a wide variety of esoteric and ultimately dangerously risky assets—including trashy securities but also various kinds of derivatives that were little more than gambling bets.

The biggest political problem created from the experience of the Clinton years is that the wrong lesson was learned. The Clinton administration and many Democrats continue to believe that the budget surpluses were good for the economy; indeed, they argue that the Goldilocks growth was *caused* by government budget surpluses. They point to the Bush deficits that followed the recession in 2000 as an example of mismanagement of the budget. And so when the GFC finally hit the economy, they joined with Republicans in keeping the fiscal response too small, arguing that budget deficits are dangerous when too large.

When the economic slowdown began to lower tax revenues after 2008, the new Obama administration saw the budget deficit explode to 10 percent of GDP—the highest since World War II. This explosion generated concern about deficits that made it difficult to get support for stimulus on the appropriate scale.[22] As a result, the economy would not recover robustly.

The correct lesson should have been the view propagated at the Levy Institute, following the work of Minsky and Godley: the Clinton budget surpluses were dangerous because they implied private sector deficits that were unsustainable. Economic growth was fueled by bubbles, especially in real estate, and these bubbles required growing debt throughout the private sector. When private debt became too big, consumers stopped borrowing and the bubble collapsed.

Far from being dangerous, the growing budget deficits of "Big Government" were necessary to prevent the GFC from deteriorating to another Great Depression. Still, even more fiscal stimulus was needed to proactively boost recovery. But that couldn't happen because economists and policy makers had learned the wrong lesson from the Clinton years—it was actually the robust growth that boosted tax revenues and resulted in unsustainable budget surpluses. The surpluses were unsustainable because they required deficits in the private sector that generated too much *private* debt.

Financialization, Layering, and Liquidity

We need to understand one final aspect of the rise of money manager capitalism. Earlier, we mentioned that the financial sector's debt reached 125 percent of GDP. This is the debt of one financial institution to another. Most of it was very short term, even overnight. This is the "financialization" and "layering" that many economists now recognize: debt on debt on debt. Let us see what this means.

What financial institutions had done was to shift the source of their finance from deposits (household checking accounts and saving deposits) to financing positions in assets by issuing mostly short-term, nondeposit liabilities held by other (mostly "shadow") financial institutions. In other words, rather than bank indebtedness to households (demand and time deposits), banks owed debt to other financial institutions—often shadow banks. The shadow banks in turn might also owe debts to other financial institutions, which finally offered "depositlike" liabilities to households. In that case, we would have two layers of financial institution indebtedness between the bank and the households.

In the old days, a bank would make a loan (such as a commercial loan to a firm or a mortgage loan to a home buyer) and issue a deposit (to a firm or household). In this case, the bank directly funds its position in the loan by issuing a deposit to a household or firm. There is no layering, that is, issuing liabilities to other financial institutions to fund positions in loans (assets). Though the loan might be risky, the deposit is not. Household bank deposits are insured by the government (FDIC insurance), and banks have essentially unrestricted access to the Fed should they need to cover withdrawals. As such, runs on bank deposits are virtually a thing of the past—they almost never happen in the United States any more. So bank deposits are a stable funding source for banks that make loans or buy mortgage-backed securities (MBSs) or other assets.

As an example of layering, a bank now purchases MBSs and other assets by issuing short-term nondeposit liabilities such as commercial paper that might be bought by a money market mutual fund (MMMF) that issues depositlike liabilities to firms and households. Since the bank's funding source is short term (often overnight), it would need to "roll over" the liabilities as they mature (i.e., the next morning). There is a chance that the MMMF might refuse rollover and insist on "cash." That is the modern equivalent to a "run"—no longer on deposits but rather on short-term nondeposit liabilities. (It is actually much more complicated than that because there can be several layers and much more complicated financial arrangements—including "insurance" with derivative bets.)

Here's the problem: When U.S. mortgage markets tanked and bad reports were coming out about crashing market values of MBSs, households did not need to worry about their insured deposits. But the MMMFs worried about the uninsured commercial paper issued by banks—if the MBS assets were bad, the banks were in trouble, so their commercial paper was risky, too. That led to a run out of commercial paper and all kinds of other nondeposit liabilities, meaning that banks had trouble refinancing their positions (in MBSs and other assets)—and they could not simply sell the MBSs because there was no longer any market for them (because no one could obtain the short-term finance to buy them).

The MMMFs in turn suffered losses on their assets—since fire sales drive down asset prices. That created concern that their liabilities might "break the buck," falling below par against cash. So, finally the holders of "deposits" in MMMFs *did* run out of them because they were not insured—in a crisis these no longer looked like traditional bank deposits.

Suddenly there was a "liquidity crisis"—a run into the most liquid and safe assets (insured deposits plus federal government debt) and a run out of almost everything else.

Since financial institutions relied so much on borrowing from each other and because they no longer trusted each other, the entire global financial system froze. Without government intervention, all financial institutions would have to "sell out position to make position," as Minsky put it, meaning sell their assets because they could no longer finance them.

And that situation would lead to a Fisher–Minsky type debt deflation dynamic because with no buyers, prices of financial assets would collapse. That is precisely what had happened in the 1930s. It began to happen again in 2007–2008.

Policy Response to the GFC

Minsky believed that the Big Bank and the Big Government are lasting legacies from the Great Depression that help to constrain the natural instability of our market economy. In a downturn, the budget moves toward deficit and the central bank acts as lender of last resort.

The first is more-or-less automatic since some kinds of spending (say, unemployment compensation) increase in response to rising unemployment, and taxes fall as incomes fall. The impact of Big Government can also be enhanced through discretionary spending increases or tax cuts—this is called a fiscal stimulus package. And when the GFC hit, the new administration of President Obama did rush through such a package that amounted to about $800 billion over two years.

In addition, the automatic stabilizers added much more to the budget deficit, which eventually reached almost $1 trillion a year at the peak. Though many observers argued that the fiscal stimulus package was too small, there's not much doubt that the downturn would have been worse without the countercyclical movement of the government's budget.

The Fed's response to a crisis is not so automatic, but lender of last resort operations are relatively routine. It has been recognized for well over a century that the central bank must intervene as "lender of last resort" in a crisis. Walter Bagehot[23] explained this as a policy of stopping a run on banks by lending without limit, against good collateral, and at a penalty interest rate.[24] This process would allow the banks to cover withdrawals so that the run would stop. Once deposit insurance was added to the assurance of emergency lending, runs on demand deposits virtually stopped.[25]

However, as we have discussed, banks have increasingly financed their positions in assets by issuing a combination of uninsured deposits plus short-term nondeposit liabilities. Hence, the GFC actually began as a run on these nondeposit liabilities, which were largely held by other financial institutions. Suspicions about insolvency led to refusal to roll over short-term liabilities, which then forced institutions to sell assets. In truth, it was not simply a liquidity crisis but also a solvency crisis brought on by risky and in many cases fraudulent practices.[26]

Government response to a failing, insolvent bank is supposed to be much different than its response to a liquidity crisis: government is supposed to step in, seize the insolvent institution, replace the management, and begin a resolution. Indeed, in the case of the United States, there is a mandate to minimize costs to the Treasury (the FDIC maintains a fund to cover some of the losses so that insured depositors are paid dollar for dollar). Normally, stockholders lose, as do the uninsured creditors—which in the case of the GFC would have included other financial institutions.[27]

However, rather than resolving institutions that were probably insolvent, the Fed, working with the Treasury, tried to save them—purchasing troubled assets, recapitalizing them, and providing loans for long periods. Yet the crisis continued to escalate—with problems spilling over to insurers of securities, including the "monolines" (which specialized in providing private mortgage insurance), and then to AIG (which had provided "credit default swap" insurance), to all of the investment banks, and finally to the biggest commercial banks.[28]

With Congress reluctant to provide much funding,[29] the Fed and Treasury gradually worked out an alternative. The "bailout" can be characterized as "deal making through contracts" as the Treasury and Fed stretched the boundaries of law with behind-closed-doors, hard-headed negotiations. Where markets would shut down an insolvent financial institution, the government would instead find a way to keep it operating.[30]

The other unusual aspect of the approach taken this time was that assistance was provided through special facilities created by the Fed to provide loans as well as to purchase troubled assets (and to lend to institutions and even individuals that would purchase troubled assets). The Fed's actions went far beyond "normal" lender of last resort operations.

First, it is probable that the biggest recipients of funds were insolvent. Second, the Fed provided funding for financial institutions (and to financial markets in an attempt to support particular financial instruments) that were not the member banks that it is supposed to support. To do so, it had to make use of special sections of the Federal Reserve Act, some of which had not been used since the Great Depression.

The scale of this intervention was unprecedented, if we were to add up Fed lending through special facilities over time to obtain a cumulative measure of the Fed's response, counting every new loan originated over the course of the life of each special facility created to deal with the crisis. This scale indicates just how unprecedented the Fed's intervention was in terms of both volume and time—more than $29 trillion of loan originations through November 2011.[31] Borrowers were mainly the biggest financial institutions (including foreign banks), plus foreign central banks.

Most of these big banks borrowed over and over, for periods up to and exceeding two years. There are two reasons why these banks borrowed from the Fed day after day and year after year. First, they were having trouble borrowing in markets, which suspected that they were not healthy and therefore too risky. Second, the Fed was charging exceedingly low rates—well below market rates. The lending at heavily subsidized rates represents another kind of "bailout" for the biggest banks since they paid low rates on these loans relative to the interest they earned on their assets, generating profits and restoring health.

Finally, as it wound down the special facilities, the Fed undertook a new program—quantitative easing (QE). Through this program, the Fed embarked on a buying spree that saw its balance sheet grow from well under $1 trillion before the crisis to $4.5 trillion as the crisis dragged on; bank reserves increased by a similar amount as the Fed's balance sheet exploded. QE included asset purchases by the Fed that went well beyond treasuries—as the Fed bought troubled mortgage-backed securities. In the beginning of 2008, the Fed's balance sheet was $926 billion, of which 80 percent of its assets were U.S. Treasury bonds; in November 2010, its balance sheet had reached $2.3 trillion, of which almost half of its assets were MBSs.

What Would Minsky Think of the Response?

Surprisingly, though the Fed and Treasury intervened heavily to rescue troubled financial institutions, no significant financial reforms made it through Congress (we will not address in detail

Dodd–Frank legislation to "reform" banking, but its measures have been delayed, are too weak, and have already been weakened further on implementation).[32]

That situation was different from the experience in the 1930s, when the financial system was thoroughly revamped. What are banks to learn if they are rescued after engaging in exceedingly risky behavior that crashes the system? What they probably learned is that there are no consequences, and Congress will allow them to do it again. In short, the "bailout" promoted moral hazard.

What should have been done? If we had followed normal U.S. practice, we would have taken troubled banks into "resolution." The FDIC should have been called in (in the case of institutions with insured deposits), but in any case, the institutions should have been dissolved according to existing law—at least cost to Treasury and to avoid increasing concentration in the financial sector. Dodd–Frank does in some respects codify such a procedure (with "living wills," etc.), but it now appears unlikely that these measures will ever be implemented—and it is not clear that even if fully implemented they would be the best way to deal with a crisis.

It would be interesting to hear Minsky's views on the rescue of the system. There's little doubt that he would argue that the Big Government's deficit had played a tremendously important role in ensuring that the economy did not spiral downward into another Great Depression. He might argue that a more proactive fiscal policy would have limited the damage and might have even resulted in a smaller budget deficit.

Budget deficits can be generated in a "good" way or in a "bad" way. If government recognizes that the economy is slipping into a deep recession, it can use discretionary policy to ramp up spending and cut taxes. If the fiscal stimulus comes quick enough, it can prevent unemployment from rising so high that tax revenues plummet. In that case, only a small budget deficit might be sufficient to prop up profits, incomes, and employment—turning the economy around.

Alternatively, if the stimulus is too small or too late, the downturn will be more devastating—with unemployment rising toward double digits and profits collapsing. If pessimism sets in, private spending is curtailed and the budget deficit grows (tax revenues fall and social spending rises).

In the case of the response to the GFC, the deficit increased for both good and bad reasons. As discussed, Congress passed a fiscal stimulus of $800 billion spread over two years—that would lead to a "good" deficit. However, most of the increase of the deficit occurred the "bad" way—rising because spending increased for unemployment compensation and food stamps, even as tax revenue fell because of stubbornly high unemployment.

Turning to the "Big Bank," Minsky probably would give that mixed marks, too. He had long argued that in a crisis, the central bank needs to provide liquidity quickly and without limit. He also advocated extension of lender of last resort support to "nonbank banks"—what we call shadow banks. This is what the Fed did through its alphabet soup of special facilities. He would probably have supported the Fed's broad liquidity support.

Minsky would have criticized the Fed for taking too long to figure out how to provide the liquidity that markets needed. In most cases, the Fed made loans through the special facilities, auctioning predetermined amounts to bidders at interest rates that were supposed to mimic prices set in auctions. Effectively, this amounted to a quantity constraint, although the Fed would offer more funds in yet another auction.

Minsky might wonder why the Fed did not understand that it should offer an unlimited supply of funds at an announced "price" (interest rate)—rather than rationing the supply and taking bids on interest rates borrowers were willing to pay.

Furthermore, he would probably criticize the Fed for auctioning the funds rather than forcing borrowers to the discount window. As we'll see in the next chapter, Minsky advocated discount window lending over open market operations with reserves provided through Fed purchases of assets. This choice is because the Fed would get a chance to look at the "books" (assets and liabilities) of institutions borrowing at the discount window.

Apparently, the Fed developed the auctioning procedure because it feared that if financial institutions borrowed at the discount window, markets would take this as a signal that the borrowers were in trouble. That might hurt their stock prices and perhaps credit ratings—making it harder for them to raise funds in private markets. There is no doubt that this fear has some validity.

However, in a liquidity crisis, wide swaths of the financial system simultaneously face trouble. This was especially true given the degree of layering of the financial system by 2007. Since financial institutions owed each other, if one could not raise funds, it would not be able to make payments to another— which would then have knock-on, or secondary, effects as all financial institutions simultaneously faced trouble raising funds. This phenomenon is precisely why Minsky argued that lending would have to be available across the entire financial system. But rather than auctioning reserves, he would have opened the discount window widely, providing reserves without a quantity constraint but at a Fed-determined interest rate.

Minsky might object to the "bailout" because it looks like the Fed and Treasury were trying to save insolvent financial institutions. Back during the savings and loan crisis of the 1980s, Minsky had recalled the method used by President Roosevelt to resolve failing banks in the 1930s. First, Roosevelt imposed a "bank holiday" in which all banks were temporarily closed. He appointed Jesse Jones to oversee the process of reopening banks: healthy ones reopened quickly, and those deemed hopeless were permanently shut down.

Banks with some possibility of recovery were allowed to reopen but only after top management was replaced and after the government injected capital into them. This method effectively amounted to a "nationalization" of banks thought to be too unhealthy to make it on their own but possibly worthy of redemption. Surprisingly, this resolution worked extremely well—most of the nationalized banks recovered and paid back the equity funds provided by Uncle Sam with a profit!

Because Minsky died in 1996, we'll never know whether he would have recommended a similar procedure in dealing with troubled banks during the GFC, but it seems quite likely. One thing we can be sure of is that Minsky would not have advocated trying to "reboot" money manager capitalism by bailing out the biggest banks and the practices that had brought on the GFC.

Minsky always argued that one of the good things about great depressions accompanied by deep financial crises is that they "cleanse" the system of debt and risky practices. Highly indebted firms and financial institutions would fail, and the practices that brought them down would be avoided after recovery.

That does not mean that Minsky welcomed such crises because the economic costs are too great. In the era of the Big Bank and the Big Government, we had not had any great depressions—and Minsky thought that was a good thing. As emphasized above, Minsky would praise the Big Bank and Big Government for preventing another great depression this time.

However, he would worry that by rescuing those behemoths that had played the biggest role in bringing on the crisis, few lessons would have been learned. A half dozen years after the crisis began, those same institutions were engaging in many of the same dangerous practices. And money manager capitalism had essentially been restored—with little real reform.

In the next chapter, we look at Minsky's recommendations for reform of the financial sector. In the final chapter, we investigate his proposal to develop a better form of capitalism.

7

.

Minsky and Financial Reform

The only universal rule for Federal Reserve policy is that it cannot be dictated by any universal rule.
—*Minsky, 1977, p. 152*[1]

As the United States struggles with the problem of fixing the financial system policy, advocates of any particular proposal need to address three questions: 1. "What is it that is taken to be broke?" 2. "What theory about how our economy works underlies the proposal?" 3. What are the dire consequences of not fixing that which you assert is broke or alternatively how does the change you advocate make things better?
—*Minsky, 1992, p. 3*[2]

In this chapter, we examine Minsky's proposals for financial reform. First, we look at the prudent banker to examine good banking practices. We then turn to an examination of the financial services that are required for a well-functioning economy. We conclude with recommendations for reforms to reduce activities that promote financial fragility.

Good Banking: What Does a Prudent Banker Do?

In chapter 4, we examined Minsky's views on banking. As he put it, banks are in the business of accepting the IOUs of their borrowing customers and issuing their own IOUs to make payments for those customers. We call that first step "making a loan" and the second step "creating a deposit."

A good banker is a good underwriter—which means that the banker is good at assessing the creditworthiness of the borrower. The banker is successful only if the borrower can service the loan—paying interest and principal. Banks operate with high leverage (that is, with little of their "own money"), meaning that capital ratios are typically well below 10 percent. Since capital covers losses, that requires low loan default rates. Banking should not be like gambling because the bank needs to "win" around 98 percent of the time whereas a casino can be profitable if the house wins 52 percent of the bets.

Banks reduce their risks in several different ways. First, they develop expertise in underwriting. Second, they develop relationships with their borrowers that help them to decide when it makes sense to work with a debtor. Sometimes this might mean allowing late payments or debt restructuring (longer terms or lower rates). Third, they maintain loan loss reserves as well as capital to cushion losses so that they can avoid insolvency when some loans go bad.

Fourth, they hold a portion of their asset portfolio in safe, liquid assets that can be sold if they need to cover withdrawals from deposits or when they experience difficulty in rolling over other short-term liabilities. Fifth, they can turn to the central bank, which will act as lender of last resort when the bank's own liquidity cushion is insufficient. And sixth, government deposit insurance greatly reduces the incentive for depositors to cause a run on even a troubled bank. These three factors together help a bank to continue to finance its position in loans and other assets, even if their quality is suspect. That, in turn, ameliorates the need to sell troubled assets at falling prices—which would cause bank insolvency (as the value of assets falls below the bank's liabilities, wiping out capital).

That brings us to the relation between the bank and government regulators. The twin government backstops of deposit insurance and central bank lender of last resort facility means that an insolvent bank *could* continue to issue deposits and make loans. Market discipline, by itself, would not shut down an insolvent bank. This is quite different from the situation of a private firm operating without a government backstop—if it were insolvent, its stock price would fall and it would be attacked by creditors trying to recover at least part of what they were owed. The firm would be forced into bankruptcy court. Regulated banks are not really at the mercy of market discipline—they are at the mercy of the regulators.

Allowing an insolvent bank to continue to operate is called "forbearance" and is at the discretion of government regulators, who may simply do this implicitly by turning a blind eye to the bank's balance sheet. As we saw earlier, government can also choose to "nationalize" a bank by injecting capital (making it solvent). Or, government might "resolve" an insolvent bank while choosing how much pain to impose on the bank's creditors (other than insured depositors).

Regulators often seem to implicitly or even explicitly adopt a "too big to fail" doctrine, which is based on the belief that some banks are too important, too large, and possibly too connected to other financial institutions to be allowed to fail. This is the ultimate backstop! An institution that will not be allowed to fail has no need to worry about such things as underwriting, loan loss reserves, leverage ratios, or liquid assets. All that matters is currying favor with regulators.

It should go without saying that a too big to fail (TBTF) bank is not likely to be a well-run bank! It is a lot like a rich dad handing a sixteen-year-old the keys to a new Ferrari with an assurance that all damages, speeding tickets, and court summonses will be covered. You can safely assume that in the first case, the TBTF bank *will* need a bailout and in the second case, the kid *will* need the get-out-of-jail-free card. If you saw the film *The Wolf of Wall Street*, you will remember the scene in which the Leonardo DiCaprio character engages in some stupendously reckless, Quaalude-fueled driving. That's how the top management drove America's half dozen biggest TBTF financial institutions in the years leading up to the crisis. Hey, Uncle Sam, can you spare a $29 trillion loan?[3]

Setting to the side the TBTF banks, how would regulators evaluate the health of a bank? Minsky had worked since the late 1950s to improve bank evaluation. First, it is necessary to understand that banking is a profit-seeking business:

> A commercial bank is a business enterprise. The aim of its management is similar to the aim of the management of any other business: to maximize profits while paying due attention to the various constraints within which the firm operates. In banking the firm's business constraints deal with the maintenance of liquidity (the ability to pay debts when due) and solvency (the continual existence of a positive net worth). In addition to these constraints, a bank is subject to legal restrictions and controls. Hence, given the legal restrictions, a bank will maximize profits under liquidity and solvency constraints.[4]

Given liquidity and solvency constraints, how would a *prudent* banker behave? Minsky (1959) goes on: Such a banker

> uses an insurance principle to make allowances for such defaults and depreciations. That is each loan will carry some, albeit estimated, charge to compensate for possible losses due to default so that even if particular loans and investments do not turn out well, on the whole the loans and investments will be profitable. In addition to the risk

premium charged the issuer of the loans and securities the banker acquires, the prudent banker will insist that his loans and securities be properly secured so as to minimize the number and amount of default and depreciation losses. That is the assets that the banker acquires will be protected to serve extent [*sic*] against losses due to market prices.

The payments made by the borrower generate the cash flow received by the banker, out of which the banker, in turn, makes payments to its creditors to service its own debts (including deposits). The prudent banker wants the cash inflow to exceed the cash outflow by a margin sufficient to generate profits on bank equity but also to cover expected losses on bad loans.

Minsky stressed such "net cash flow analysis" over "net worth" analysis, which subtracts the bank's liabilities from the value of its assets. In his view, net worth analysis can be highly misleading. First, much of a bank's portfolio of assets is not liquid and hence cannot be sold to cover liabilities. This is because the bank has confidential information obtained in the underwriting process that led the bank to make the loan; revealing that information erodes trust:

> Such a violation of confidence could result in the loss of the customer as the customer could object to having his financial condition made public. In addition, the banker has exercised his own judgment as to the capabilities of the customer. Whoever is willing to acquire such a customer's loan from the banker would expect the banker to back up his judgment by endorsing the note and hence accepting a contingent liability. In times when a banker is sorely pressed for banker's cash, his endorsement may be relatively worthless. Hence a banker cannot depend upon the sale of

customers' loans to provide for the cash flows needed to off-set an unusually large clearing loss.

For this reason, banks like to hold some marketable assets:

> The desire for impersonal and hence marketable earning as-sets takes two directions; one is the purchase of securities, the other is the making of impersonal loans. As both secu-rities and impersonal loans make it possible for the prudent banker to have a smaller ratio of banker's[5] cash to deposits than if he had only customer's loans as his assets, he is will-ing to acquire such assets at a lower interest rate than he receives from his customers loans. The actual type of securi-ties and impersonal loans that bankers acquire at any time and place will depend upon the usages and institutions. However two assets which bankers have usually acquired are short dated government debt and if an appropriate mar-ket exists, call loans.

This is precisely the direction that banks have taken since the early 1980s as they began to securitize loans (especially mort-gages) to make them marketable.

Returning to our prudent banker's two main constraints, the bank faces much tighter liquidity and solvency constraints than a typical nonfinancial firm. The liquidity obligation is se-vere because it issues deposits, many of which are convertible on demand while its assets usually cannot be converted quickly without loss of value:

> Whereas an ordinary business has dated debts, debts which are not due until a specified date, the essential attribute of a bank is that its liabilities, aside from the owner's invest-ment, are demand liabilities. The initiative in making a

bank's liabilities current lies with the depositor, the owner of the bank's liabilities. As a result the banker must always keep sufficient banker's cash on hand to meet whatever clearing losses result from depositors' actions and in case of unexpectedly large clearing losses a banker must be able to replenish his stock of banker's cash.

The solvency constraint is severe because bank equity is low relative to assets, which "means that banks cannot survive as large a fall in the value of its assets as ordinary business firms can." Banks make loans against collateral or unsecured loans that "do not have specific assets as security, rather they are based upon the fact that the borrower's total assets are sufficiently in excess of his debts to protect the prudent banker." However, a prudent banker does not want to seize assets—seizure is costly and can be risky and time-consuming.

Normally, bank loans are made against the estimated income (cash inflow) of the borrower, although the borrower's portfolio of safe and liquid assets also plays a role. Again, cash flow analysis is the most important consideration in bank lending activity.

We will come back to Minsky's views on prudent banking when we examine his recommendations for reform.

What Should a Financial System Do?

Before we can reform the financial system, we need to understand what it *should* do. This section examines the later work of Hyman Minsky at the Levy Institute on his project titled "Reconstituting the United States' Financial Structure." This project led to a number of Levy working papers and also to a draft book manuscript by Minsky (which has since been edited and soon will be published).

Much of this work was devoted to his thoughts on the role that financial institutions should play in the economy. To put it as simply as possible, Minsky always insisted that the proper role of the financial system is to promote the "capital development" of the economy. By this, he did not simply mean that banks should finance investment in physical capital. Rather, he was concerned with creating a financial structure that would be conducive to economic development to improve living standards, broadly defined. We will return to other policies that would contribute to those goals in the final chapter.

Let us first enumerate the functions Minsky thought essential for the financial system to provide.

1. A safe and sound payments system;
2. Short-term loans to households and firms, and, possibly, to state and local government;
3. A safe and sound housing finance system;
4. A range of financial services, including insurance, brokerage, and retirement services; and
5. Long-term funding of purchases of expensive capital assets.

A Safe and Sound Payments System

In most wealthy nations, the payments system is largely run through the banking system that issues demand deposits and—increasingly—allows for electronic payments. Demand deposits exchange at par against one another and against currency, with government backstopping the banks. Par clearing was not always the case. In the nineteenth century, before deposit insurance and before the Fed was created, the liabilities of banks in the United States did not exchange at par. This situation was inefficient and unstable because a $5 note issued by one bank might be accepted at another for only $3.

The current system works well, although there are alternatives. One commonly used alternative is to have the government operate the payments system, often through postal savings banks. Households can pay bills through debits to their deposits at the public "bank" operated through the post office. Another possibility is to have special "narrow banks" that offer deposits and payments services but do not make loans. Instead, they hold only the safest assets—central bank reserves and cash or treasury bonds. The idea is that deposit insurance would no longer be needed to ensure that deposits maintain parity against currency—since the narrow banks do not take on risk.

Short-Term Loans

As discussed in chapter 4, commercial banks have traditionally made short-term loans to firms, although during the twentieth century they also moved into consumer loans. Another area is student loans, which are not exactly short term, but in the United States they came with government guarantees to make them safe for banks (but not necessarily for students who are now carrying an aggregate debt load of a trillion dollars!). Short-term loans have been ideally suited for commercial banks since their liabilities are short term. Furthermore, local branches know the local economic environment, which is important for assessing creditworthiness of small businesses. Also, there is little interest rate risk involved in making short-term loans.[6] Banks could also provide short-term loans to local government, although these can also obtain finance through bond issues (normally handled by investment banks).

There are alternatives to such loans. From the early 1970s, firms turned increasingly to the commercial paper market—skipping bank loans by selling their own short-term debt into financial markets. Creditworthiness was enhanced by getting a bank guarantee against the commercial paper (banks earned fees for this). Firms as well as consumers could also get vendor finance, in which the seller holds the debt of the buyer—again potentially bypassing banks (although, again, banks could get involved by guaranteeing debts or providing finance to the vendors). Credit cards play a similar role. Finally, government can provide loans to firms (e.g., Small Business Administration loans) and households (e.g., student loans).

Housing Finance

In the United States in the "old days," George Bailey thrifts made thirty-year fixed-rate mortgage loans; they held the mortgages to maturity and issued depositlike mutual shares to finance their positions in the mortgages. If you've seen the movie *It's a Wonderful Life*, you will remember that when a "run" against the thrift of George Bailey (played by Jimmy Stewart), the Bailey Building and Loan, began, he implored his customers to leave their deposits in the thrift because they were "invested" in the community's homes. He insisted that the deposits were all good because they were as good as the neighbors. In truth, George was right. Until the 1970s, U.S. homeowners virtually never defaulted on mortgages and the thrifts almost never failed. This is what a safe and sound home finance system looked like.

All of that changed after the early 1970s, as the thrifts were gradually "freed" to engage in riskier practices. Ownership rules were changed to allow those with little interest in the health of the community—or even in the thrift—to take over savings and loans. Believe it or not, even convicted criminals, drug runners, and gun smugglers moved in to cannibalize the thrifts and use them for their own nefarious purposes. By the early 1980s, thrifts were free to engage in virtually any kind of activity. Finally, they were driven into insolvency by Chairman Volcker's high interest rate policy. A severe financial crisis ensued (the worst postwar U.S. financial crisis until the GFC) that required an expensive bailout during the George H. W. Bush administration.

In the aftermath of that fiasco, banks and thrifts were wary of holding long-term fixed-rate mortgages, which fueled the model based on securitization—which as we've seen played a central role in creating the GFC. In truth, there is nothing necessarily wrong with securitization of mortgages—so long as it is done right. There needs to be good underwriting of the mortgages to ensure that home buyers are highly likely to make the payments; in addition, the securitization process itself needs to follow well-established procedures, including competent risk rating and documentation. Unfortunately, during the U.S. housing bubble, the underwriting was almost nonexistent, and proper procedures were not followed; documents were falsified or lost; and ratings agencies provided impossibly optimistic ratings.

In the United States, the federal government already provides guarantees for "conforming" loans—those that meet certain requirements. An alternative to bank finance would be for the government to make mortgage loans directly—since it already bears the risk. However, if banks and thrifts do better underwriting than government, then it makes sense for government to partner with them. The United States is unusual because most mortgages are fixed-rate, self-amortizing loans (payments are fixed throughout the term, with most of the interest paid off first). This type of mortgage reduces uncertainty for homeowners but, for technical reasons we will not get into, makes it very difficult to value the mortgages and the mortgage-backed securities (MBSs). Hence, another option is to move toward floating-rate mortgages, which reduces interest rate risks to financial institutions that hold them.

Range of Financial Services

Households need a range of financial services, from insurance to retirement savings. In the United States these were traditionally segmented across a spectrum of specialized financial institutions. Over time, the barriers were broken down so that a "big box" financial institution can offer the full range. The disadvantage of the multiservice bank is that customers might be duped through bait and switch tactics: the elderly grandmother thinks she's buying a government-insured certificate of deposit when the bank is actually selling her risky stocks.[7]

Some of these financial services are more risky than the traditional commercial banking business, which is why the New Deal reforms had purposely segmented the financial sector. In the next chapter, we look at an alternative proposal by Minsky— which would allow small, local banks to offer the full range of financial services but maintain segmentation for bigger national institutions.

To protect consumers from unsavory practices, the United States created the Consumer Financial Protection Bureau. It has promoted consumer education and promulgated new rules on financial practices. It is too early to determine how much power the bureau will have to reduce fraud.

In the aftermath of the GFC, virtually all of the largest global financial institutions have been fined for illegal practices, although no top managers have been prosecuted for crimes. These institutions have admitted to hundreds of thousands of criminal acts—from forging documents, to improper foreclosures against homeowners, to rigging markets, to assisting money laundering for drug lords and terrorists, to helping tax evaders, to helping firms evade international sanctions against pariah states.

Consolidation of financial services within a single institution makes it easier to defraud customers. For example, an institution might provide loans on unfavorable terms to a customer and put together another team that sells products that pay off if the customer defaults. That institution has an incentive to push the borrower into default. There are also potential problems of use of inside information across units within a big institution. Concentration within the financial services sector makes it increasingly likely that a big investment banker will represent both sides of a big merger or other big deal.

Investment Banking

Investment banks provide long-term finance to firms and state and local governments. As discussed in chapter 4, they either directly hold long-term debt or they place it into markets to be held in asset portfolios of households or managed money. Investment banks also float equity of firms as well as securitized loans, such as home mortgages, auto finance-related debt, student loans, and even housing rents. This is usually riskier than short-term debt because of uncertainty over distant horizons. There is both default risk (if the borrower's income in the future cannot service the debt) and interest rate risk (if interest rates rise, the value of long-term debt that pays a lower rate falls). New Deal reforms in the United States prohibited commercial banks from getting involved in such business; however, the restrictions were gradually relaxed and then eliminated in 1999.

There are four basic models: the stand-alone investment bank partnership; the stand-alone investment bank public corporation; the "big box" financial superstore that includes investment banking among its many services; and the bank holding company (BHC) model, in which the BHC includes an investment banking arm as a separate entity. In the United States after the New Deal reforms, the U.S. investment banks were partnerships, relatively small and conservative since the partners' money was at risk. By the late 1990s, the investment banks had gone public, issuing shares to take part in the stock market boom. Hired management was rewarded with stock options and so was incentivized to pump up share values. A similar phenomenon occurred in the 1920s, in which "pump and dump" schemes proliferated.[8] It was essentially "déjà vu" all over again in the 2000s. We take up some of these functions again in the concluding chapter when we address policies to promote the capital development of the economy.

According to Minsky, there is no reason why any single institution should provide all of these services, although as discussed above, the long-run trend has been to consolidate a wide range of services within the affiliates of a bank holding company.

The New Deal reforms had separated institutions by function (and state laws against bank branching provided geographic constraints). Minsky recognized that Glass–Steagall had already become anachronistic by the early 1990s. He insisted that any reforms must take account of the accelerated innovations in both financial intermediation and the payments mechanism. He believed that these changes are in large part market-driven and not solely caused by deregulation. The demise of commercial banking and the rise of shadow banking was mostly a consequence of the transition to money manager capitalism—and Minsky considered that to be more important than the demise of the Glass–Steagall separation by function.

How to Reform Banking

We conclude this chapter with an examination of Minsky's views on reforming banking. We begin with his thoughts on favoring smaller banks and returning to relationship banking.

TBTF Versus Relationship Banking

The "too big to fail" doctrine that dates back to the problems of Continental Illinois in 1984 gives an obvious advantage to the biggest banks. These are able to finance positions at the lowest cost because government stands behind them. The small local banks face higher costs as they try to attract local deposits by opening more offices than necessary and because it costs small banks more to attract "wholesale" brokered deposits in national markets. Even in the case of FDIC-insured deposits (which have no default risk), smaller banks pay more simply because of the market perception that they are riskier because the government does not fully backstop them.

Since the crisis, investment banks (like Goldman Sachs) are allowed to take the risks of a hedge fund but can obtain FDIC-insured deposits and can rely on Fed and Treasury protection should risky trades go bad. It is very hard for a small bank to compete with that.

How can the system be reformed to favor relationship banking that Minsky believed to be more conducive to promoting good practice and the public purpose?

Minsky argued that small to medium size banks are more profitable and relationship oriented, knowing their customers and therefore capable of doing better underwriting. In other words, there is no reason to allow, and even less reason to promote, the rise of hegemonic TBTF financial institutions with international markets and broad scope. As many others have long argued, the economies of scale associated with banking are achieved at the size of relatively small banks.

However, Minsky did recognize that banks would lose market share anyway because of competition from shadow banks. Hence the solution would not be found in promoting bigger, less profitable banks that are not interested in relationship-oriented banking. Rather, Minsky would allow greater scope to the activities of the small community banks. We might call this "intensifying" banking—allowing each small institution to provide a greater range of services—as opposed to promoting branching and concentration of power in the hands of a few large bank holding companies with a variety of subsidiaries.

In a prescient analysis of securitization of home mortgages, Minsky argued that

> Because of the way the mortgages were packaged it was possible to sell off a package of mortgages at a premium so that the originator and the investment banking firms walked away from the deal with a net income and no recourse from the holders. The instrument originators and the security underwriters did not hazard any of their wealth on the longer term viability of the underlying projects. Obviously in such packaged financing the selection and supervisory functions of lenders and underwriters are not as well done as they might be when the fortunes of the originators are at hazard over the longer term.[9]
>
> —*Minsky, 1992b, pp. 22–23*

The implication is rather obvious: good underwriting is promoted when the underwriter is exposed to the longer term risks. Securitization as practiced in the early 2000s essentially eliminated underwriting, which played a huge role in fueling the bubble that finally crashed.

This problem brings us to Minsky's skeptical banker:

> When we go to the theater we enter into a conspiracy with the players to suspend disbelief. The financial developments of the 1980s [and 1990s and 2000s!] can be viewed as theater: promoters and portfolio managers suspended

disbelief with respect to where the cash would come from that would [validate] the projects being financed. Bankers, the designated sceptic in the financial structure placed their critical faculties on hold. As a result the capital development was not done well. Decentralization of finance may well be the way to reintroduce the necessary scepticism.[10]
                                                              —*Minsky, 1992a, p. 37*

Decentralization and favoring smaller institutions, plus maintaining exposure to risk could reorient institutions back toward relationship banking. Unfortunately, most trends in recent years have favored concentration in the hands of the national (with global outreach) TBTF institutions. In the concluding chapter, we look at one of Minsky's specific proposals to support decentralization: creation of a system of community development banks.

Redirecting Government Protection against Bank Liquidity and Solvency Risks

As we have discussed, government provides a secure backstop for regulated banks and a looser safety net for the shadow banks. It would be useful to reduce government protection for less desirable banking activities. There are two important kinds of protection government currently provides to banks: liquidity and solvency.

Minsky adopted the view that "liquidity is not an innate attribute of an asset but rather that liquidity is a time-related characteristic of an ongoing, continuing economic institution"[11] (Minsky, 1967, p. 1). A liquid institution is able to "fulfill its payment commitments," which depends on "how its normal activities will generate both cash and payments, as well as the conditions under which its assets (including its ability to borrow as an 'honorary' asset) can be transformed into cash" (Minsky, 1967, p. 2). Finally, "[a]ny statement about the liquidity of an institution depends upon assumptions about the behavior of the economy and financial markets" (Minsky, 1967, p. 2).

A bank can face liquidity problems because of its own idiosyncratic problems or because of the behavior of the economy and financial markets. Furthermore, idiosyncratic problems can infect financial markets if the institution facing problems is sufficiently important and interconnected with other institutions. If problems are not widespread, liquidity can be supplied in overnight interbank lending markets (the fed funds market in the United States). Since modern central banks target overnight interest rates, however, any pressure on the overnight lending market rate generates an automatic central bank response.

When private markets cannot meet the demand for liquidity at the central bank's target, the central bank lends reserves at the discount window and buys assets (in the past, the Fed bought government debt, but in recent years it has bought private debt through quantitative easing) to keep the rate within target. In a crisis, it may need to lend on a huge scale not only to keep rates on target but also to stop runs.

Minsky always advocated extension of the discount window operations to include a wide range of financial institutions. If the Fed had lent reserves without limit to all financial institutions when the GFC first hit, it is probable that the liquidity crisis could have been resolved more quickly. Hence, this kind of government protection should not be restrained. In a run to liquidity, the government must lend without limit to stop the run.

The old idea that the central bank can exert control over banks by rationing reserves is wrong. In normal times, that would cause it to miss its target rate. In troubled times, it would worsen a crisis. The liability side of a bank balance sheet is the wrong side to try to exert control. If the central bank wants banks to lend less, it needs to discipline the asset side—that is, control the quantity or quality of loans directly (through credit controls, for example, that limit the growth rate of loans or set lower limits to down payments).

In summary, the central bank should, indeed must, accommodate the liquidity needs of banks. However, the central bank should supervise the balance sheet of banks, conduct cash flow analysis, and pursue policy that promotes macroeconomic and financial stability—as we discuss below.

It is the second kind of safety net, protection against default, that is more problematic. Deposit insurance guarantees that there is no default risk on certain classes of deposits—now up to $250,000 in the United States. This is essential for clearing at par and for maintaining a safe and secure payments system.

The question is about which types of institutions should be allowed to offer such deposits or which types of assets would be eligible for financing by issuing insured deposits. Some considerations would include riskiness of assets, maturity of assets, and whether purchase of the class of assets fulfills the public purpose—the capital development of the economy discussed in the next chapter.

Risky assets put the government insurer—the FDIC in the United States—on the hook since it must pay out dollar-for-dollar to protect insured deposits, but if it resolves a failing institution, it receives only cents on the dollar of assets. In his discussion of reforming the FDIC, Minsky made it clear that "cost to the Treasury" should not be a major concern. We can probably also conclude for the same reason that riskiness of assets financed through issuing insured deposits should not be the major concern.

Maturity of the assets is no longer a concern if the Fed stands ready to lend reserves as needed—a bank could always meet deposit withdrawals by borrowing reserves and so would not need to sell longer term assets.

Hence, the major argument for limiting financial institution ability to finance positions in assets by issuing insured deposits is that government has a legitimate interest in promoting the public purpose. Banks should be prevented from using financing obtained by issuing insured deposits in a manner that causes the public purpose to be "ill-done."

What about the other, uninsured, liabilities of financial institutions (both banks and shadow banks)? With TBTF institutions, the practice has been to effectively guarantee them, while allowing uninsured creditors of smaller institutions to lose in the case of institution insolvency. This is clearly unfairly biased to benefit big institutions, which are not necessarily more efficient than small ones. From a Minskian view, this is highly problematic and undesirable. Instead, troubled institutions should be resolved, and uninsured creditors plus owners should share the losses.

Four Reforms to Promote Prudent Banking

We described how the prudent banker behaves. It is clear that the real-world banker has moved far away from this ideal. How can we reform banking regulation and supervision to promote prudent banking? In this subsection, we look at four of Minsky's ideas: improving underwriting, raising capital requirements (a popular approach), enhancing bank evaluations through greater use of the discount window, and micro- and macroprudential regulation (another idea that has long had support).

IMPROVING UNDERWRITING

Banks that receive government protection in the form of liquidity and (partial) solvency guarantees are essentially public–private partnerships. They promote the public purpose by specializing in activities that they can perform more competently than government can do.

One of these activities is underwriting—assessing creditworthiness and building relations with borrowers that enhance borrower willingness to repay. Over the past decade, a belief that underwriting is unnecessary flowered and then exploded. In the aftermath of the crisis, financial institutions discovered that credit ratings, credit scores, and the credit default swap premium cannot substitute for underwriting—in part because those can be manipulated but also because elimination of relationship banking changes the behavior of borrowers and lenders. This situation means that past default rates become irrelevant (as credit raters discovered).

If banks are not doing good underwriting, it is difficult to see why government needs them as partners: it would be much simpler to have government directly finance activities it perceives to be in the public interest—home mortgages, student loans, state and local government infrastructure, and even small business activities (commercial real estate and working capital expenses). In other words, the government could just directly make the loans, rather than backstopping private banks that make them.

In the United States, the federal government has tended to favor guaranteeing private debt over directly making loans. There is a compelling argument for government reliance on guarantees over making loans directly if private financial institutions are better underwriters than government can be. However, if the private financial institutions are not doing good underwriting (as they did not do in the case of U.S. home mortgages), then bypassing guarantees in favor of direct lending makes sense. Indeed, there has been a movement in that direction, with government taking back control over student loans. When government guarantees both the deposits and the loans (for example, mortgages and student loans), it is difficult to see any role to be played by banks except underwriting—deciding who is sufficiently creditworthy to obtain a loan guaranteed by Uncle Sam.

The argument for direct lending is even stronger if there is a strong public purpose involved, where relatively high default rates are acceptable. For example, in the United States college students typically use student loans to pay for education. Unlike the case in most wealthy nations—where the national government provides almost free college education—the federal government of the United States spends relatively little (except for research grants). As a result, college is out of reach for many students, who must go into debt, with heavy reliance on federal government-guaranteed loans. If college education is highly valued, it might make sense to drop participation of private institutions because careful underwriting is less important. The net value to society as a whole could well be large enough to offset the losses caused by relatively high default rates. (Note that the federal government can avail itself of fairly robust debt collection services using the Internal Revenue Service to identify and tap future incomes of defaulters.)

INCREASING CAPITAL REQUIREMENTS

It has long been believed that capital requirements are a proper way to regulate bank lending: higher capital requirements not only make banks safer, but they also constrain bank lending unless the banks can raise capital. Unfortunately, according to Minsky neither claim is correct. Higher capital requirements were imposed in the aftermath of the savings and loan fiasco, and they were codified in the Basel agreements.[12] Rather than constraining bank purchases of assets, banks simply moved assets and liabilities off their balance sheets—putting them into special purpose vehicles, for example.

Basel also used risk-adjusted weightings for capital requirements to encourage banks to hold less risky assets for which they were rewarded with lower capital requirements. The idea is that the risk-weighted requirements would encourage banks to stay out of the riskiest activities, but even if they didn't, the higher capital ratio could absorb losses.

Unfortunately, banks gamed the system in two ways: since risk weightings were by class, banks would take the riskiest positions allowed in each class, and banks worked with credit ratings agencies to structure assets such as MBSs to achieve the risk weighting desired. For example, it was relatively easy to get triple-A rated tranches (as safe as sovereign government debt) out of packages of subprime and "liar loan" Alt-A mortgages—with 85–90 percent of the risky mortgages underlying investment-grade (supposedly very safe) tranches. But in reality, the credit raters were ignoring or at least downplaying risk.

Finally, Minsky (*Stabilizing*, 1986) argued that all else being equal, high capital ratios necessarily reduce return on equity (and, hence growth of net worth), so it is not necessarily true that higher capital ratios increase safety of banks because it means that they are less profitable.[13] Indeed, with higher capital ratios they need to choose a higher risk/return portfolio of assets to achieve a target return on equity. If regulators want to constrain the rate of growth of risky lending, it appears that direct credit controls are better. Regulators can either set maximum limits to the rate of growth of the volume of bank loans (or total assets) or discourage certain kinds of lending (for example, by requiring higher down payments or better collateral or higher loan-to-value ratios).

On the other hand, there is not much that can be done to encourage banks to lend when they do not want to. That is the old "you cannot push on a string" argument, and it describes the situation after the GFC quite well—when banks refused to lend no matter how much the government tried to induce them to make loans. Nor should government policy try to get banks to make loans they do not want to make! After all, if banks are our underwriters, and if their assessment is that there are no good loans to be made, then we should trust their judgment. In that case, lending is not the way to stimulate aggregate demand to get the economy to move toward fuller employment. Instead, fiscal policy is the way to do it.

EXAMINING BANKS AT THE DISCOUNT WINDOW

One of the reasons that Minsky wanted the Fed to lend reserves to all comers was because he wanted private institutions to be "in the bank"—that is, to be debtors to the Fed. As a creditor, the Fed would be able to ask the banker question: "How will you repay me?"—that is, what earning assets are you going to buy? As he put it,

> The Federal Reserve's powers to examine are inherent in its ability to lend to banks through the discount window . . . As a lender to banks, either as the normal provider of the reserve base to commercial banks (the normal operation prior to the great depression) or as the potential lender of last resort, central banks have a right to knowledge about the balance sheet, income and competence of their clients, banks and bank managements. This is no more than any bank believes it has the right to know about its clients.[14]
> —*Minsky, 1992c, p. 10*

The Fed would ask to see evidence for the cash flow that would generate the ability of the bank to service loans. It is common practice for a central bank to lend against collateral, using a "haircut" to favor certain kinds of assets (for example, a bank might be able to borrow one hundred cents on the dollar against government debt but only seventy-five cents against a dollar of mortgages—which incentivizes them to buy government debt that can be used as collateral). Collateral requirements and haircuts can be used to discipline banks—to influence the kinds of assets they purchase.

Examination of the bank's books also allows the central bank to look for risky practices and to keep abreast of developments. It is clear that the Fed was caught with its pants down, so to speak, by the crisis that began in 2007, in part because it mostly supplied reserves in open market operations rather than at the discount window. Forcing private banks "into the bank" (that is, forcing them to borrow directly from the Fed) gives the Fed more leverage over their activities. For this reason, Minsky opposed the Treasury's early 1990s proposal to strip the Fed of some of its responsibilities for regulation and oversight of institutions. If anything, Minsky would have increased the Fed's role and would use the discount window as an important tool for oversight.

Minsky rejected the old mainstream view that the central bank can constrain bank activity by rationing reserves. However, from the 1960s he argued against the monetarist view that reserves ought to be provided in open market operations (with the central bank creating reserves to buy assets—mostly treasury debt). Since that method simply puts reserves into the overnight market for reserves (the fed funds market in the United States), it provides little useful information on the health of the financial system. If instead, banks needing reserves would have to go individually to the central bank and submit assets as collateral, the central bank would know what they had as collateral. Minsky emphasized that the central bank can get more nosey because as a creditor it can ask the borrower to open the books. The idea here is not that the central bank would refuse to lend the reserves but that it would gain a window to financial practices.

MICROPRUDENTIAL AND
MACROPRUDENTIAL REGULATION

Minsky's views are relevant to recent discussions in the aftermath of the GFC about the creation of the "super" systemic regulator, and he probably would have sided with those who wanted to increase the Fed's power. Indeed, as has happened after almost every major financial crisis experienced in the United States, the Fed "failed upward"—after failing to prevent a crisis, its power was increased after the crisis. After both the Great Crash of 1929 and the Global Financial Crisis of 2007–2008, much more emphasis was placed on central bank control of the macroeconomic environment in which banks operate, rather than on microlevel bank supervision.

The traditional approach to regulating financial institutions is to protect the system from "[i]diosyncratic failures" that "can trigger an epidemic of bank failures, imparting an adverse 'depression-creating' shock to the economy" (p. 255).[15] The focus, then, is on preventing incompetent or fraudulent management at individual banks from causing a bank failure that then brings down other banks, either by sparking a run or by defaulting on its liabilities to them. However, Minsky stressed that though a "particular bank fails because of its own, idiosyncratic attributes," this failure is unlikely to create a serious financial crisis unless the system as a whole is fragile. Minsky criticized regulators and bank supervisors for failing to adopt a theory of financial instability and argued that simply examining individual bank behavior without attempting to contain the macro environment's evolution toward instability would fail to prevent major financial crises.

Minsky felt vindicated when the savings and loan crisis hit the U.S. economy in the early 1980s. To be sure, bank examination in that period was lax, and, as discussed earlier, the thrift sector had been freed of most regulation. Still, regulators had failed to recognize that a number of macro factors had put the financial system at risk: the high interest rate policy of Volcker, rapid growth of exposure of U.S. financial institutions to developing country debt, a U.S. commercial real estate bubble, and regional housing bubbles caused by an oil boom. As Kregel (2014) discusses, that crisis led to the development of a "risk-focused examination process" to identify individual bank risks and to assess what each bank had done to manage the risks. That approach was also adopted internationally in the Basel Accords.

According to Minsky, however, "In the position-making view, bank failures do not arise simply because of incompetence or corrupt management. They occur mainly because of the interdependence of payment commitments and position-making transactions across institutions and units" (Campbell and Minsky, 1987, p. 255). One unit's ability to make its payments on time depends on the ability of its creditors to make their payments; but these creditors also rely on the well-being of their own debtors.

By the 2000s, things were much more complicated, as it had become common to hedge risks with "insurance"—credit default swaps—which in turn depended on the financial situation of the seller of the insurance (counterparty risk), who generally had no loss reserve but instead had also hedged, buying the same kind of "insurance" (again, credit default swaps). When the crisis hit, it was discovered that a unit of AIG was responsible for much of the system's "insurance." AIG defaulted, and Uncle Sam was left to cover much of the loss.

For this reason, it is not sufficient to put in place effective bank examinations—microprudential regulation—but equally essential is macroprudential regulation of the system as a whole. After the GFC, this notion became almost a mantra in the regulatory community. However, as Kregel (2014) argues, even

macroprudential regulation is insufficient if it is not based on
a theory that recognizes the evolution of the financial system
toward instability.

What Minsky had developed from the early 1970s could
be called dynamic macroprudential regulation with the perspective of "a dynamic, evolving set of financial institutions
and relations."[16] Effective regulation must "be reassessed frequently and made consistent with evolving market and financial structures."[17]

> Over time the initially apt pattern of regulation and super-
> vision becomes increasingly inept: the inherited structure
> of regulation and the supervision first becomes not quite
> right and later becomes perverse. A cumulative effect of the
> institutional and usage changes that occur is that the in-
> stitutions which are supposed to contain the endogenous
> disequilibrating forces of our economy lose much of their
> power to do so.
>
> —*Minsky, 1994, p. 4*[18]

In other words, the regulators and supervisors need to have their
fingers on the pulse of the entire financial system—not just the
regulated banks but also the largely unregulated shadow banking system. And regulations must evolve, along with financial
practices.

But how could the central bank closely follow developments
in the shadow banking sector? After all, it almost completely
missed what was going wrong in the home mortgage securitization business through 2006.

Minsky believed that because "a central bank needs to have
business, supervisory and examination relations with banks
and markets if it is to be knowledgeable about what is happening" reducing its responsibility for examining and supervising

banks would inhibit its "ability to perform its monetary policy function. This is so because monetary policy operations are constrained by the Federal Reserve's views of the effect such operations would have upon bank activities and market stability" (Minsky, 1992a, p. 10). The Fed would be better informed to the extent that it supervised and examined banks. One way for the central bank to keep tabs would be for it to force banks to the discount window, as discussed. Opening the discount window to at least part of the shadow banking sector would also inform the Fed of activities outside banking.

In the next chapter, we conclude with Minsky's recommendations for general policy reform.

8

∎

Conclusion: Reforms to Promote Stability, Democracy, Security, and Equality

[A] fundamental flaw exists in an economy with capitalist financial institutions, for no matter how ingenious and perceptive Central Bankers may be, the speculative and innovative elements of capitalism will eventually lead to financial usages and relations that are conducive to instability.

—*Minsky, 1977* [1]

The problems we face now may well be the result of a misspecification by the theories that guided past policies of the processes that determine what happens in our type of economy.

—*Minsky, 1992, p. 21* [2]

When designing and advocating policies economists and practical men alike have to choose between the Smithian theory, that markets always lead to the promotion of the public welfare, and the Keynesian theory, that market processes may lead to the capital development of the economy being ill-done, i.e. to other than the promotion of the public welfare.

—*Minsky, 1992, p. 5*

In this final chapter, we examine Minsky's proposals for reform, focusing in particular on those reforms that would help to stabilize the economy while promoting democracy, security, and equality.

The Three Fundamental Faults of Capitalism

Keynes's *General Theory* (1936) identified two fundamental flaws of the capitalist system: chronic unemployment and excessive inequality. The two are linked: excessive inequality puts too much of the income into the hands of the rich, who prefer high rates of saving rather than spending. That depresses demand and keeps jobs scarce.[3]

Minsky added a third: instability is a normal feature of modern capitalism, which is a *financial* system. Furthermore, persistent stability cannot be achieved—even with apt policy—because it changes behavior in ways that make "it"—a depression and debt deflation—likely. As Minsky put it,

> One can read almost all of the textbooks, and most of the current journal literature without being made aware that the overriding issue in monetary economics is whether capitalism is flawed in that it is inherently subject to booms and busts. However this was clearly the concern of Keynes and the Chicago school of the 1930's.
> —*Minsky, 1972, p. 2*

Although it is true that other interpreters of Keynes emphasize that economies can experience downturns—even severe ones—almost all of them see these as deviations from equilibrium brought on by a wide variety of "shocks" to the system. Or, to put it another way, they presume that the capitalist system is naturally stable. When it moves away from equilibrium, government can use monetary and fiscal policy to push it back.

Minsky argued that the situation is precisely the reverse: the *system* is fundamentally unstable but instability can be *constrained* by apt use of fiscal and monetary policy. However, this is no simple matter. First there is uncertainty over the effectiveness of policy. More importantly, adopting a policy is likely to change behavior. And to the degree that policy actually constrains instability, it is *more* certain to induce behavior changes that will make the stabilizing policy less effective. Stability is destabilizing!

For this reason, Minsky rejected any notion of "fine-tuning"—even if policy did manage to achieve transitory stability, that would set off processes to reintroduce instability. Hence, "[t]he policy problem is to devise institutional structures and measures that attenuate the thrust to inflation, unemployment, and slower improvements in the standard of living without increasing the likelihood of a deep depression" (Minsky, 1986, p. 295). However, success could never be permanent; policy would have to continually adjust to adapt to changing circumstances. As Neil Young put it, *rust never sleeps*. Policy formation must be dynamic, always evolving to adapt to behavioral adaptations that the policy induces.

After his *Stabilizing* book was published in 1986, Minsky argued that the relative stability of the postwar period had led to development of money manager capitalism—a much more unstable version of the "57 Varieties of Capitalism." In a prescient piece written in 1987, Minsky had predicted the explosion of home mortgage securitization that eventually led to the financial meltdown in 2007.[4] Indeed, he was one of the few commentators who understood the true potential of securitization: in principle, all mortgages (as well as many other kinds of assets) could be packaged into a variety of risk classes, with differential pricing to cover risk; as he put it in that piece: "That which can be securitized, will be securitized."

Minsky argued that securitization reflects two developments. First, it is part and parcel of the globalization of finance because securitization creates financial paper that is freed from national boundaries. German investors with no direct access to America's homeowners could buy a slice of the action in booming U.S. real estate markets. As Minsky was fond of pointing out, the unparalleled post–World War II, depression-free expansion in the developed world (and even in much of the developing world) created a global glut of managed money seeking returns. Packaged securities with risk weightings assigned by respected rating agencies were appealing for global investors trying to achieve the desired proportion of dollar-denominated assets.

It would be no surprise to Minsky to find that the value of securitized American mortgages at the peak in 2007 exceeded the value of the market for federal government debt, nor that the U.S. mortgage problems quickly spread around the world after mid-2007—from a German bank (IKB) that required a bailout in July of that year, to problems in BNP Paribas (France's biggest bank), and to a run on Northern Rock in the United Kingdom.

The second development assessed by Minsky is the relative decline of the importance of banks (narrowly defined as financial institutions that accept deposits and make loans) in favor of "markets." (The bank share of all financial assets fell from around 50 percent in the 1950s to around 25 percent in the 1990s.) The global casino needed fuel, and it was the movement away from traditional banking to the "originate to distribute" model that opened the floodgates to risky mortgage products to serve as the basis for speculative bets.

The whole housing sector, which had been made very safe by the New Deal reforms, was transformed by shadow banking into a huge global casino—with bets on bets. High-risk mortgages were securitized to produce tranched, trashy mortgage-backed securities, the worst pieces of which were resecuritized as collateralized debt obligations (CDOs), which could be re-resecuritized for CDOs squared, and then even cubed! In this way, a single risky mortgage could underlay any number of bets—with gamblers choosing whether to bet on success or on failure. The structure of the U.S. real estate market resembled the story of Yertle the Turtle,[5] with poor little homeowner turtle Mack struggling to support a pile of turtles reaching to the sky. When Mack burped, missing a few of his mortgage payments, the whole pile came crashing down. And Mack lost his home.

In a much earlier paper, Minsky had worried that "[a]ll too often it seems as if the Federal Reserve authorities have been surprised by changes in financial practices"[6] (p. 150). Indeed, the Fed—as well as most mainstream economists—had missed the rise of the entire shadow banking system.[7] Through his links with real-world bankers, Minsky was well aware of the evolution of financial practices and of the financial system itself.

The declining role played by traditional banking was spurred by continual erosion of the portion of the financial sphere that had been allocated by rules, regulations, and tradition to banks. The growth of competition on both sides of banking business—checkable deposits at nonbank financial institutions, which could pay market interest rates, and the rise of the commercial paper market, which allowed firms to bypass commercial banks—squeezed the profitability of banking.

Minsky observed that banks appear to require a spread of about 450 basis points[8] between interest rates earned on assets less rates paid on liabilities. This spread covers the normal rate of return on bank capital, plus the required reserve "tax" imposed on banks,[9] and the costs of servicing customers (staffing the bank, for example). By contrast, "shadow banks" can operate with much lower spreads precisely because they are exempt from required reserve ratios, regulated capital requirements, and much of the costs of relationship banking. At the same time, the financial markets were freer from the New Deal regulations that had made banks safer.

Not only did this situation mean that a growing portion of the financial sector was free of most regulations but also that the competition forced policy makers to relax regulations on banks. By the time of the real estate boom that eventually led to the financial crisis, there was no longer any essential difference between a "commercial bank" and an "investment bank."

It is noteworthy that Minsky argued that the New Deal reforms related to home finance had been spurred by a common belief that short-term mortgages (typically with large balloon payments) had contributed to the Great Depression. Ironically, the "innovations" in home mortgage finance leading up to the speculative boom of the 2000s largely recreated those conditions—with new and risky types of mortgages displacing the old fixed-rate, self-amortizing, thirty-year mortgage that built America's robust housing market.[10]

The Greenspan "put" (a belief that the Fed would not allow bad things to happen, with evidence drawn from the arranged Long-Term Capital Management hedge fund rescue, as well as the quick reduction of interest rates in the aftermath of the dot-com bust), plus the new operating procedures adopted by the Fed (the new monetary consensus, which adopts gradualism, transparency, and expectations management—meaning, no surprises), tipped the balance of sentiments away from fear and toward greed.[11] The Clinton boom and the shallow George W. Bush recession led to a revised view of growth, according to which expansions could be more robust without inflation and recessions would be brief and relatively painless—Bernanke's "Great Moderation."

All of this moderation increased the appetite for risk, reduced risk premia, and encouraged ever more leverage. In addition, securitization, hedging, and various kinds of insurance (such as credit default swaps) appeared to move risk to those best able to bear it. If Minsky had been able to observe the decade after his death that preceded the Global Financial Crisis (GFC), he would have labeled it a period with *a radical suspension of disbelief*—a phrase he invoked to describe those who convinced themselves to "disbelieve" that something bad could happen.

All of these developments cast doubt on the direction that policy has taken over the past three decades. In the following sections, we examine the direction that policy might take if it were to follow Minsky's suggestions. These are designed to deal with all three of the fundamental faults of capitalism: unemployment, inequality, and instability.

Promoting the Capital Development of the Economy

In his proposal for development of the newly independent eastern European nations, Minsky argued that the critical problem is to "create a monetary and financial system which will facilitate economic development, the emergence of democracy and the integration with the capitalist world"[12] (p. 28). Except for the last goal, this statement applies equally well to promotion of the capital development of the Western nations.

Minsky used the term "capital development" in a very broad way to include public and private infrastructure investment, technological advance, and development of human capacities (through education, training, and improvements to health and welfare). Note that Minsky always included full employment, greater equality, and stability as goals of policy, so pursuing the capital development of the economy must take a path that ensures those goals are met, too.

Minsky argued that there are two main ways in which the capital development of the economy can be "ill done": the "Smithian" and the "Keynesian." The first refers to what might be called "misallocation": the wrong investments are financed. The second refers to an insufficiency of investment, which leads to a level of aggregate demand that is too low to promote high employment and with insufficient productive capacity to promote living standard improvements.

The 1980s suffered from both, but most importantly from inappropriate investment—especially in excessive commercial real estate investment. We could say that the 2000s again suffered from "Smithian" ill-done capital development because far too much finance flowed into the residential real estate sector. In both cases, Minsky would point his finger at securitization. In the 1980s, because the thrifts were not holding mortgages (they securitized them, instead), they had funding capacity that flowed into commercial real estate (in that case, REITs—real estate and investment trusts—were part of the problem); in the 2000s, the mania for risky (high return) asset-backed, securities-fueled subprime and Alt-A lending. At the same time, we faced unemployment that is chronically too high—even in the bubble-fueled booms. As a result, aggregate demand is chronically too low—only exacerbated by rising inequality that puts too much of the nation's income in the hands of the rich (who save rather than spending).

Hence, in designing reform, we face both the "Smithian" problem and the "Keynesian" problem. We first deal with the Keynesian problem that financial institutions might not provide the right amount of finance; then we turn to the Smithian problem of allocating the right amount of finance to the activities that actually promote capital development.

Opening the discount window to provide an elastic supply of reserves ensures that banks *can* finance positions in as many assets as they desire, borrowing at the central bank's target rate. This method does not ensure that we have solved the Keynesian problem because banks might finance too much or too little activity to achieve full employment while promoting the capital development of the economy.

It is somewhat easier to resolve the "too much" part of the Keynesian problem because the central bank or other responsible bank regulators can impose constraints on bank purchases of assets when it becomes apparent that they are financing too much activity. For example, in the past U.S. real estate boom, it was obvious (except, apparently to mainstream economists and many at the Fed) that lending should be curtailed. The Fed had the authority to do so but refused to intervene.

The problem is that the orthodox response to too much lending is to raise the Fed's target rate. And because borrowing is not very interest sensitive, especially in a euphoric boom, rates must rise sharply to have much effect. Furthermore, raising rates conflicts with the Fed's goal of maintaining financial stability because—as the Volcker experiment from 1979 showed—interest rate hikes that are sufficiently large to kill a boom also are large enough to cause severe financial disruption (approximately three-quarters of all thrifts were driven to insolvency). There is no real-world smooth relationship between higher rates and reduction of loan demand. When rates get sufficiently high to induce insolvency, defaults finally snowball through the economy, causing panic and collapse of spending.

Indeed, this recognition is part of the reason that the Greenspan/Bernanke Fed turned to "gradualism"—a series of very small rate hikes that are well telegraphed. Unfortunately, this method means that markets have plenty of time to prepare and to compensate for rate hikes, which means that the policy has less effect. For these reasons, rate hikes are not an appropriate means of controlling the quantity of bank lending. Instead, the controls used by government supervisors (the Fed, the FDIC, and the Office of the Comptroller of the Currency) ought to be direct: raising down payments and collateral requirements, and even issuing cease and desist orders to prevent further financing of some activities.

On the other hand, lowering rates does not necessarily encourage borrowing and spending—as we've seen in the aftermath of the GFC, with rates near zero and private spending remaining sluggish. It is difficult to get private institutions to lend when they cannot find good borrowers; and when pessimism reigns, the good borrowers do not want to borrow and spend. The saying goes "you cannot push on a string," meaning that low rates do not push up aggregate demand. In the slump, monetary policy is impotent, and government needs to turn to fiscal policy.

Many economists, both orthodox and heterodox, insist that the time to ramp up public infrastructure investment is in the slump. Private spending is depressed, labor and machines are idle (and so can be redirected to the public sphere), and interest rates are low (so that national, state, and local government bonds can be floated at low rates). The only thing holding back public spending is an irrational fear of national government budget deficits.

However, it should be said that Minsky put more emphasis on automatic stabilizers to ramp up government spending in a slump and to cool it down in a boom. This emphasis works because these stabilizers kick in automatically, without requiring elected representatives to go through a long and potentially acrimonious process of choosing programs and authorizing spending. The most important automatic stabilizer Minsky advocated was the job guarantee—what he called the employer of last resort program.

Solving the Smithian problem—getting banks to make loans that promote the capital development of the economy—requires direct oversight of bank activity on the asset side of their balance sheets. Financial activities that further the capital development of the economy need to be encouraged; those that cause it to be "ill done" need to be discouraged. Moreover, there is no reason to rely solely on banks and shadow banks to provide all the finance needed to support the capital development. There is also a role to be played by government provision of finance—something we discuss in more detail below.

Minsky's Agenda for Reform

In his 1986 book, *Stabilizing an Unstable Economy*, Minsky had offered an agenda for reform that focused on four main areas:

- Big Government (size, spending, taxing);
- Employment strategy (employer of last resort);
- Financial reform; and
- Market power.

This section summarizes his agenda, and in the following sections we bring this agenda up to date, drawing on his writings from the 1990s.

Minsky argued that all kinds of capitalism suffer from flaws (and any form of capitalism that relies on privately owned expensive capital assets exhibits the three fundamental flaws discussed at the beginning of this chapter: unemployment, inequality, and instability) but that we can develop one in which the flaws are less evident.

As discussed earlier in this book, Minsky favored a capitalism with lower investment and higher consumption, one that maintains full employment, and one that fosters smaller organizations. He wanted to shift the focus of policy away from transfers and toward employment. He was skeptical that anything close to full employment could be attained without direct job creation by government.

Thus, Minsky pointed to various New Deal employment programs, such as the Civilian Conservation Corps and the National Youth Administration, as examples to guide creation of a comprehensive employer of last resort program—arguing that only government can offer an infinitely elastic demand for labor, which is necessary for full employment.

Minsky estimated a comprehensive program's costs at about 1.25 percent of national output—which is in line with more recent estimates of others promoting such programs (Philip Harvey 1989, Wray 1998) and with the real-world experience in Argentina and India. In addition, Minsky would offer a universal child allowance,[13] also equal to about 1.25 percent of GDP. Together, these programs would replace most welfare and unemployment compensation spending, providing more opportunity and dignity for participants than current programs do.[14]

He argued that his programs would be less inflationary. Unlike welfare, which pays people not to work and thereby increases demand for output without increasing supply, a jobs program would be geared to produce useful output as well as to enhance productivity. This is because some of the jobs would be focused on promoting the capital development of the economy (discussed above—this development includes public infrastructure). Furthermore, keeping people employed and providing training on the job would improve human capacity.

Minsky also anticipated the objection that full employment must be inflationary by proposing a relatively fixed and uniform program wage that would actually help to stabilize wages by providing an anchor. All of these arguments have been taken up in recent years by advocates of employer of last resort policies.

Finally, he would reduce barriers to labor force participation by eliminating the payroll tax and by allowing retirees to work without losing Social Security benefits. He would have endorsed President Obama's "payroll tax holiday" that reduced taxes on all workers by two percentage points (unfortunately, the holiday ended with the compromises the president made with Republicans in the "fiscal cliff" negotiations of early 2013). Minsky would have gone further by eliminating the payroll tax on both workers and their employers. He could not see a public purpose in discouraging work, and especially by doing so with a regressive tax (the payroll tax is designed to hit low- and middle-income earners hardest because of the "cap"—wages above a certain level are not taxed, and nonwage income is not taxed at all). However, the other component of his proposal actually has been followed as Social Security recipients have been able to continue to work with more of their earnings exempt from taxes.

Because Minsky believed that bank size is related to the size of firms with which banks do business, he favored policy to support small-to-medium size banks. He would have loosened some of the New Deal constraints for these smaller banks so that they could provide a broader range of the services required by their smaller customers.

Instead, U.S. policy moved in the opposite direction, exempting the largest banks from Glass–Steagall regulations before finally gutting the New Deal reforms. Hence, banking became much more concentrated than it was when Minsky made these proposals—precisely the opposite of the direction he would have taken.

At the same time, as discussed above, policy and innovations have favored "markets" over "banks," which has also promoted even further consolidation. When the financial crisis hit in 2007, the Fed and the Treasury used bailout methods that actually increased concentration in the hands of the few remaining behemoth institutions. After the crisis, the biggest institutions were far bigger than they had been, and they had far less competition. Furthermore, markets had learned the lesson that government would backstop the "too big to fail" banks, which actually increases their competitive advantages, but would let smaller banks fail. So in all these ways, policy made things worse.

Minsky's "Big Government" would help stabilize the economy through countercyclical movement of its budget. As discussed already, Minsky rejected the mainstream Keynesian notion that a big government can fine-tune the economy through pump priming. Minsky advocated targeted spending (the job guarantee is an example; it creates jobs directly rather than by priming the pump and hoping that jobs are created). And he also argued that pump priming would be unsustainable—if it did achieve anything close to full employment, it would be inflationary and so would have to be stopped (the start–stop policy discussed earlier). Finally, he argued that traditional Keynesian policy would worsen inequality by favoring those sectors that are oligopolized and unionized and hence operate with administered prices that rise quickly when faced with high demand.

The government's budget should be "big"—as discussed earlier, the swings of its budget need to be large enough to offset swings of private investment, as well as the current account balance. This size allows the government's budget to contribute to stabilization of aggregate demand, income, consumption, and profits. We have discussed Godley's sectoral balance approach, so we understand that the budget deficit needs to be larger than the current account deficit to allow the domestic private sector to run a surplus; this approach contributes to financial stability.

Minsky wanted to shift the weight of government spending away from transfers and toward employment and investment-type spending. Again, this method is used to promote the capital development of the economy, which will help to reduce the inflation pressures of big government spending.

Minsky wanted to favor small firms over big corporations, but he advocated elimination of the corporate profits tax—which might seem to be inconsistent. However, he would have the tax authorities impute all profits to owners of corporations for the purpose of calculating personal income taxes. This accounting would reduce the incentive for corporations to retain earnings (allowing owners to avoid taxes), reduce the use of stock options for executive compensation (their taxes would be based on profits imputed to ownership), and also reduce the bias toward use of debt (currently corporations use debt finance instead of equity finance because they can write interest off taxes).

Reform of the Payments System

In the 1990s, Minsky focused much of his attention on "reconstituting finance"; we have already covered some of his proposals. After the savings and loan crisis (which was followed by problems in the big banks in the late 1980s and early 1990s), there was a lot of discussion in the United States about deposit insurance. The complaint was that with government insurance standing behind banks and thrifts, there is no reason for depositors to discipline the financial institutions—Uncle Sam will pay for their mistakes. This problem led to calls to either reform or even to eliminate deposit insurance. Minsky brought his own ideas to that debate.

According to Minsky, the problem banks have faced over the past three or four decades is the "cream skimming" of their business by shadow banks (or, as Minsky called it, managed money). Uninsured checkable deposits in managed funds (such as money market mutual funds) offer a higher earning but relatively convenient alternative to insured deposits, allowing much of the payments system to bypass banks.

As Minsky argued, credit cards have also diverted the payments system out of banking (although the larger banks capture a lot of the credit card business). At the same time, banks were squeezed on the other side of their balance sheets by the development of the commercial paper market, which allows firms to borrow short-term at interest rates below those on bank loans (sometimes, firms could even borrow more cheaply than banks could). Again, banks recaptured some of that business by earning fees for guaranteeing commercial paper. But these competitive pressures caused banks to jettison expensive underwriting and relationship banking, replaced by the "originate to distribute"[15] model.

There is no simple solution to these competitive pressures, although Minsky offered some ideas. In several publications, Minsky argued that policy should move to make the payments system a profit center for banks.

> One weakness of the banking system centers around the American scheme of paying for the payments system by the differential between the return on assets and the interest paid on deposits. In general the administration of the checking system costs some 3.5% of the amount of deposits subject to check. If the checking system were an independent profit center for banks then the banks would be in a better position to compete with the money funds.
> —*Minsky, 1992a, p. 36*

It may not be desirable to return to the early postwar period in which banks and thrifts monopolized the payment system. However, in the 1800s, the federal government eliminated private banknotes by placing a tax on them. In a similar manner, preferential treatment of payments made through banks could restore a competitive edge. Transactions taxes could be placed on payments made through managed funds—raising the payments system costs of shadow banks relative to those of traditional banks. In addition, banks could be offered lower, subsidized fees for use of the Fed's clearing system. Minsky also held out some hope that by substituting debit cards for checks, banks could substantially lower their costs of operating the payments system—something that does seem to be happening.[16]

Some called for a return to the 100 percent money proposal of Irving Fisher and Milton Friedman—often called the Chicago Plan. As a student at Chicago, Minsky had been exposed to these ideas and was favorably disposed (he wrote a supportive introduction to a book[17] promoting the idea). Briefly, the proposal by Levy scholar Ronnie Phillips would create a system of narrow banks that would offer deposits while holding only the safest assets (Treasury securities). Here the idea is that we can carve off a portion of the financial system and keep it perfectly safe. Anyone who wanted to avoid the "casino economy" could keep deposits in the safe narrow banks. This is a partial answer to critics who argue that it is "impossible" to regulate the modern financial sector because institutions innovate or move headquarters offshore to escape regulation. The narrow banking proposal segments the financial sector into a "safe" segment and a "risky" one.

However, Minsky argued that this method loses

sight of the main object: the capital development of the economy. The key role of banking is lending or, better, financing. The questions to be asked of any financial system are what do the assets of banks and other financial institutions represent, is the capital development of the economy

better served if the proximate financiers are decentralized local institutions, and should the stricture lean towards compartmentalized or broad jurisdiction institutions.
—*Minsky, 1992a, pp. 36–37*

In a sense, the Chicago Plan "fixes what is not broken." It is important to note that in the GFC, the runs were not on insured deposits—deposit insurance did precisely what it was supposed to do: stop runs. The real problems were in the uninsured "depositlike" money market mutual funds. The government had to extend its guarantee to them to stop the run. It seems that it would be better to prohibit those uninsured funds from pretending that their "deposits" are as safe as insured bank deposits and to make it clear that government will never again protect holders of those uninsured funds.

To be sure, Minsky did not categorically reject the narrow bank proposal—he simply believed that it addresses only a peripheral problem, safety and soundness of the payments and saving systems. It does not address promotion of the capital development of the economy. So, yes, he thought that we can have narrow banks, but we are still stuck with the bigger problem of what to do with the financial institutions that are not narrow.

Minsky also was not swayed by the argument that elimination of deposit insurance would cause depositors to discipline wayward banks. This is simply not possible. Not only do depositors lack the time and expertise to do so but they also have no access to detailed bank balance sheets. No bank can open its loan book to depositors (or anyone else, except government regulators) due to confidentiality requirements. It is thus literally impossible for a depositor to determine whether assets are good. While supporters of relying on market discipline claim that credit ratings agencies can provide the information needed, we now know that is ludicrous—they failed miserably to properly assess risks in the run-up to the GFC.

Institutional Design to Promote
Stability, Security, and Democracy

Later, while at the Levy Economics Institute, Minsky continued his policy work advocating designing institutions for modern capitalism. He argued that capitalism is dynamic and comes in many forms and that the 1930s reforms are no longer appropriate for the money manager form of capitalism.

It is not a coincidence that this stage of capitalism has seen the rise of neoconservative ideology (or what is called neoliberalism outside the United States) that wants to dismantle what is left of New Deal and "Keynesian-era" policies. Everything from financial institution regulation to public provision of retirement income has been under attack by privatizers. A Democratic president, Bill Clinton, even "ended welfare as we know it," substituting temporary assistance with lifetime limits. While Minsky was not a huge fan of welfare (for reasons already discussed), Clinton provided a stick but no carrot—he took away the "entitlement" but did not provide jobs, preferring to rely on free markets to provide them.

However, Minsky argued that free-market ideology is dangerous, particularly at this stage of capitalism. Ironically, the "invisible hand" could not do too much damage in the early postwar period, given the low level of private debt, with private portfolios full of government debt, and with memories of the Great Crash of 1929 generating conservative behavior. However, now, with private debt ratios much higher and after decades of leveraging in an environment that promoted greed over fear, the invisible hand promoted increasingly risky behavior.

Thus, Minsky's alternative policy proposals in the 1990s were designed to reduce insecurity, promote stability, and encourage democracy. He continued to support job creation, policy to promote greater equality of wages, and child allowances.

With other Levy scholars, he pushed President Clinton to adopt a program that would create a system of small community development banks. His proposal went much farther than the program that was actually adopted early in the Clinton administration (apparently influenced by Minsky's proposal)—to increase the range of financial services provided to underserved neighborhoods.

Minsky worried that the trend to megabanks "may well allow the weakest part of the system, the giant banks, to expand, not because they are efficient but because they can use the clout of their large asset base and cash flows to make life uncomfortable for local banks: predatory pricing and corners [of the market] cannot be ruled out in the American context" (Minsky, 1992a, p. 12). Furthermore, since the size of loans depends on capital base, big banks have a natural affinity for the "big deals," while small banks service smaller clients: "A 1 billion dollar[18] bank may well have 80 million dollars in capital. It therefor would have an 8 to 12 million dollar maximum line of credit . . . in the United States context this means the normal client for such banks is a community or smaller business: such banks are small business development corporations" (Minsky, 1992a, p. 12).

The Community Development Bank Proposal

For this reason, Minsky advocated a proactive government policy to create and support small community development banks (CDBs).[19] Briefly, the argument advanced was that the capital development of the nation and of communities in a nation is fostered via the provision of a broad range of financial services. Unfortunately, many communities, lower income consumers, and smaller and start-up firms are inadequately provisioned with these services.[20]

For example, in many communities there are far more check cashing outlets and pawnshops than bank offices. Many households do not even have checking accounts. Small businesses often finance activities using credit card debt. These are all expensive alternatives.

Hence, Minsky's proposal would have created a network of small community development banks to provide a full range of services (a sort of universal bank[21] for underserved communities):

1. a payment system for check cashing and clearing, and credit and debit cards;
2. secure depositories for savings and transaction balances;
3. household financing for housing, consumer debts, and student loans;
4. commercial banking services for loans, payroll services, and advice;
5. investment banking services for determining the appropriate liability structure for the assets of a firm and for placing these liabilities; and
6. asset management and advice for households.

—Minsky et al., 1993, pp. 10–11

This list of services to be performed by CDBs is similar to the list of the essential functions to be performed by the financial system, as discussed in the previous chapter. For that reason, the CDB proposal really provides an overview for fundamental reformation of the financial system.

The institutions would be kept small, local, and profitable. They would be public–private partnerships, with a new Federal

Bank for Community Development Banks created to provide equity and to charter and supervise the CDBs. Each CDB would be organized as a bank holding company; one example of its composition would be

a. a narrow bank to provide payments services;
b. a commercial bank to provide loans to firms and mortgages to households;
c. an investment bank to help place equity issues and long-term debt of firms; and
d. a trust bank to act as a trustee and to provide financial advice.

As mentioned earlier, President Clinton did help to pass and sign an act creating community banks, but the scale and scope of the system actually created fell far short of what Minsky had advocated.

Reform of Shadow Banking

Reform of the financial system needs to address the "shadow banks" of money manager capitalism. Minsky focused especially on pension funds because he believed that they were largely responsible for the leveraged buyout (LBO)[22] boom (and bust) of the 1980s; similarly, there is strong evidence that pension funds drove the commodities boom and bust of the mid-2000s. To be sure, this is just a part of managed money, but it is a government-protected and -supported portion—both because it gets favorable tax treatment and because it has quasigovernmental backing through the Pension Benefit Guaranty Corporation.[23]

Hence, it is yet another public–private partnership that ought to serve the public purpose. Minsky wondered, "Should the power of pension funds be attenuated by having open ended IRA's? (No limit to contributions, withdrawals without penalty but all withdrawals taxed, interest and dividend accruals not taxed except as they are spent)" (Minsky, 1992a, p. 35). He favored policy to promote IRAs that would compete with pension fund managers, reducing their influence.

He also advocated regulation by function rather than by institution type. In other words, if a shadow bank offers a financial product that is subject to regulation when offered by a bank, the shadow bank should also be regulated. For example, any type of financial institution that originates mortgages ought to be regulated in the same manner as a bank or thrift that originates mortgages. That approach would impose similar costs and reduce the "race to the bottom" incentives.

Downsizing Finance to Address Unemployment, Inequality, and Insecurity

Finally, returning to Minsky's views on unemployment, poverty, inequality, and insecurity, he certainly would be appalled at recent financial sector trends.

First, there has been an important shift away from the wage share and toward gross capital income (that is, the profit share). Many have argued that stagnant wages played a role in promoting growth of household indebtedness over the past three decades, with rapid acceleration since the mid-1990s.

As many at the Levy Institute have been arguing since Minsky's death in 1996, the shift to a private sector deficit that was unprecedentedly large and persistent would prove to be unsustainable. The mountains of debt still crushing households is in part caused by the shift of national income away from wages as households tried to maintain living standards. That shift largely benefited Wall Street's "1 percent."

According to a study by Pavlina Tcherneva, 95 percent of the benefits of the recovery from the GFC have gone to the top 1 percent of the income distribution.[24] Another study finds that the top one-thousandth (top 0.1 percent) of the U.S. population now owns a fifth of all wealth.[25]

Equally problematic is the allocation of profits toward the financial sector—just before the crisis, the finance, insurance, and real estate, or FIRE[26] sector got 40 percent of all corporate profits, and its share has returned to that level. This level contrasts with a 10 to 15 percent share until the 1970s, and a 20 percent share until the 1990s. Whereas value added by the FIRE sector also grew, from about 12 percent in the early postwar period to almost 20 percent today, its share of profits was twice as high as its share of value added by the time of the bubble in the 2000s.

Hence, three interrelated problems hinder the capital development of the economy: the profit share is too high and the wage share is too low—this depresses demand, causing unemployment; the share of GDP coming from the financial sector is too large, at 20 percent of value added—increasing instability; and the share of corporate profits allocated by the financial sector to itself is far too large.

Downsizing finance is necessary to ensure that the capital development of the economy can be well done. With 40 percent of corporate profits going to finance, not only does this leave too little to other sectors but it also encourages entrepreneurial effort and innovations to be directed to the financial sector rather than to the real economy. Much of this excess financialization is concentrated in the hands of TBTF institutions. They need to be taken into conservatorship and split up; alternatively, they should be asked to choose between losing their banking charter or downsizing.

Policy to Promote a Successful Twenty-First Century Capitalism

As Minsky put it in one of his last papers, "Our current difficulties make it necessary to consider not only how we measure the success of an economy but also the institutional prerequisites for a successful 21st-Century capitalism."[27] He went on to quickly recap his stages approach, describing the characteristics of postwar "paternalistic" capitalism as including

> countercyclical fiscal policy, which sustained profits when the economy faltered: low interest rates and interventions by the Federal Reserve unconstrained by gold-standard considerations; deposit insurance for banks and thrifts; establishment of a temporary, national investment bank (the Reconstruction Finance Corporation) to infuse government equity into transportation, industry and finance; and interventions by specialized organizations created to address sectoral concerns (such as those in housing and agriculture).
> —*Minsky and Whalen, 1996, p. 3*

In the early postwar period, memories of the Great Depression ensured

> cautious use of debt. But as the period over which the economy did well began to lengthen, margins of safety in indebtedness decreased and the system evolved toward a greater reliance on debt relative to internal finance, as well as toward the use of debt to acquire existing assets. As a result, the once robust financial system became increasingly fragile.
> —*Minsky and Whalen, 1996, p. 4*

Money manager capitalism gradually replaced the paternalistic stage, eroding these institutions that had offered security.

> When one considers the pressures due to both the rapidly evolving financial system and the economy's other structural changes, it is no surprise that economic insecurity is widespread. With the passing of the paternalistic financial structure, corporate paternalism has also faded. Workers at nearly all levels are insecure, as entire divisions are bought and sold and as corporate boards exhibit a chronic need to downsize overhead and to seek out the least expensive set of variable inputs.
> —*Minsky and Whalen, 1996, pp. 5–6*

> Many families cannot distinguish recession from recovery. Despite strong profits and recent productivity gains, chief economist Stephen Roach of Morgan Stanley summarizes the view of most Americans when he writes, "Recovery or not, the 1990s are still all about downsizing, longer workdays, white-collar shock and relatively limited opportunities for new employment."
> —*Minsky and Whalen, 1996, p. 8*

> The task before today's economists and policymakers is to meet the challenges of the coming millennium without forgetting the valuable lessons of the past, lessons that include: 1) capitalism comes in many varieties; 2) the institutions established through public policy play a vital role in determining what form capitalism takes; and 3) laissez-faire is a prescription for economic disaster.
> —*Minsky and Whalen, 1996, p. 8*

Minsky goes on to argue that there are two alternative futures: a hostile and uncivilized "fortress" capitalism or an optimistic and humane "shared-prosperity" capitalism. It is clear that since his death, we have pursued the first. That is a path to disaster because, as Minsky argues, "[c]apitalism can be successful only if economists and policymakers recognize that people have a limited tolerance for uncertainty and insecurity" (Minsky and Whalen, 1996, p. 9). The task ahead is to reduce insecurity while ensuring "the civilized standards of an open and democratic society" (Minsky and Whalen, 1996, p. 10). These are complementary goals.

In the short run, societies can choose to compete pursuing a "high-performance" path or a "low-wage" path. Post-unification Germany is an example of the first, although it is far from perfect (it has held its own wages constant while those of its European Monetary Union member neighbors have risen, making Germany the low-cost producer; in many respects, so is China, although it too is imperfect because it began from a position as a very low wage competitor—and China's growth has boosted inequality between urban and rural living standards). The low-wage path has been taken in much of the developing world and also in the United States.

This path is not sustainable for any large country that desires to support its population. The United States is rapidly falling behind the world's leaders by many measures. Its public infrastructure is by no means up to developed country standards. It stands almost alone in its refusal to supply cheap and universal health care and education through college (which is now a bare minimum level of schooling for advanced nations). Its retirement security system is not up to the tasks of caring for an aging society in which most workers have no significant personal financial savings—and with its Social Security program under continual attack by would-be privatizers who want to turn it over to Wall Street's management.

Minsky also continually bemoaned the state of "public consumption" in the United States. As a part-time resident of Bergamo, Italy, Minsky loved to take his evening *passeggiata* (strolling the cobbled streets and piazzas) while remarking how impoverished Americans only had their sterile shopping malls (many of which are now bankrupted and closed). That might have been a bit of a Pollyanna-ish view of Italy, and while living standards there have declined since the Euro crisis began, anyone who has traveled to Europe (or even the UK!) understands what Minsky meant.[28]

Conclusion

Over the past decades, the belief that "markets work to promote the public interest" gained in popularity. Minsky questioned: but what if they don't? Then a system of constraints and interventions can work better. He wanted to develop institutional "ceilings and floors" to help constrain the natural, inherent instability of the modern economy.

He also believed that we need to make "industry" dominate over "speculation" (recalling Keynes's famous dichotomy), and not vice versa, or the capital development of the economy will be ill-done in two ways: the Smithian/neoclassical way or the Keynes/ aggregate demand way. If investment is misdirected (the Smithian problem), we not only waste resources, but we also get boom and bust. If investment is too low (the Keynesian conundrum), we not only suffer from unemployment, but also profits are too low to support payment commitments—leading to default.

Furthermore, when profits are low in "industry," then problems arise in the financial sector because commitments of that sector cannot be met either. In that case, individual profit-seeking behavior leads to incoherent results as financial markets, labor markets, and goods markets all react in a manner that causes wages and prices to fall, generating debt deflation.

The Smithian ideal is that debt deflations are not endogenous, rather they must result from exogenous factors, including "black swans with fat tails," but also because of too much government regulation and intervention. So the solution is said to be deregulation, downsizing government, tax cuts, and making markets more flexible so that they can respond quickly to "shocks" like unexpected black swan events.

The Minskian view is that the financial structure is transformed over a run of good times from a robust to a fragile state as a result of the natural reaction of agents to the successful operation of the economy. If policy makers understood this, they could formulate policy to attenuate the transformation and then to deal with a crisis when it occurs. Relying on the Smithian ideal is, for Minsky, nothing more than believing in "invisible hand-waves."

Minsky acknowledged that pessimism permeates his approach: stability is destabilizing. There is no final solution to the problem of instability. However, Minsky was fundamentally optimistic in his outlook: we can do better than we have done so far.

NOTES

Preface

1. http://www.bard.edu/library/archive/minsky/.

Introduction

1. Hyman P. Minsky, *John Maynard Keynes* (New York: Columbia University Press, 1975).
2. Minsky, *John Maynard Keynes.*
3. The title of his 1982 book was *Can "It" Happen Again?*—a question that he answered with a conditional "no"—however, he later worried that the transformation of the financial system after 1980 made it increasingly possible that the conditional answer might be "yes."
4. *The Financial Crisis Inquiry Report: Final Report of the National Commission on the Causes of the Financial and Economic Crisis in the United States*, http://www.gpo.gov/fdsys/pkg/GPO-FCIC /content-detail.html.
5. William K. Black, *The Best Way to Rob a Bank is to Own One: How Corporate Executives and Politicians Looted the S&L Industry* (Austin, TX: University of Texas Press, 2005).
6. See Joe Nocera, "Inquiry Is Missing Bottom Line," Talking Business, *New York Times*, January 28, 2011, www.nytimes. com/2011/01/29/business/29nocera.html; Gretchen Morgenson, "A Bank Crisis Whodunit, with Laughs and Tears," Fair Game, *New York Times*, January 29, 2011, www.nytimes.com/2011/01/30 /business/30gret.html.
7. See James A. Felkerson, "$29,000,000,000,000: A Detailed Look at the Fed's Bailout by Funding Facility and Recipient,"

Annandale-on-Hudson, NY: Levy Economics Institute, Working Paper No. 698, December 2011, http://www.levyinstitute.org/pubs/wp_698.pdf, and L. Randall Wray, "The Lender of Last Resort: A Critical Analysis of the Federal Reserve's Unprecedented Intervention after 2007," Annandale-on-Hudson, NY: Levy Economics Institute, Research Project Reports, April 2013, http://www.levyinstitute.org/publications/the-lender-of-last-resort-a-critical-analysis-of-the-federal-reserves-unprecedented-intervention-after-2007.

8. By selling everything, prices collapsed in what Irving Fisher described as a "debt deflation" that would bankrupt everyone— making the depression much worse.

9. http://en.wikipedia.org/wiki/Andrew_W._Mellon#Great_Depression.

10. He is referring to *Stabilizing an Unstable Economy,* 1986.

11. Paul Krugman, "Actually Existing Minsky," The Conscience of a Liberal, *New York Times*, May 19, 2009, http://krugman.blogs.nytimes.com/2009/05/19/actually-existing-minsky/?_php=true&_type=blogs&_r=0.

12. This is a conference on "reconstituting the financial system" that Minsky began at the Levy Economics Institute in the early 1990s; it has been held annually in his memory ever since.

13. Janet Yellen, 2009, http://www.frbsf.org/our-district/press/presidents-speeches/yellen-speeches/2009/april/yellen-minsky-meltdown-central-bankers/.

14. Paul Krugman, "Frustrations of the Heterodox," The Conscience of a Liberal, *New York Times*, April 25, 2014, http://krugman.blogs.nytimes.com/2014/04/25/frustrations-of-the-heterodox/?_php=true&_type=blogs&_r=0.

15. Hyman P. Minsky, "Securitization," 1987, published as Levy Policy Note 2008/2, June 2008, http://www.levyinstitute.org/publications/securitization.

16. In truth, policy makers were not as blind as orthodoxy now claims. At Federal Open Market Committee policy meetings, there was discussion of asset price bubbles as early as 1994; some members

warned of a housing bubble and of widespread fraud in the mortgage market in the early 2000s. The Fed had actually started raising interest rates in 2004, and by July 2006 its fed funds target was 5.25 percent. Whereas it seems to be true that the Fed was caught off guard by the extremely high leverage and interconnectedness of shadow banking balance sheets, anyone who was carefully watching the financial sector should have been aware that the regulated commercial banks were losing market share to the rapidly growing "nonbank banks," as they were called before McCulley renamed them shadow banks (http://media.pimco.com/Documents/GCB%20Focus%20May%2009.pdf).

17. Adam Smith, *An Inquiry into the Nature and Causes of the Wealth of Nations*, 5th ed., Edwin Cannan, ed. (London: Methuen and Co., Ltd., 1904).

18. Hyman P. Minsky, *John Maynard Keynes* (New York: Columbia University Press, 1975; New York: McGraw-Hill, 2008).

Chapter 1

1. Hyman P. Minsky, "Beginnings," in *Recollections of Eminent Economists, Volume 1,* Jan A. Kregel, ed. (New York: Macmillan Press, 1988): 169–79, originally published in *Banca Nazionale del Lavoro*, No. 154, September 1985, 172.

2. Minsky, 1992a, "Reconstituting."

3. Two good—albeit brief—references are Minsky, "Beginnings," in Kregel, 1988, and Dimitri B. Papadimitriou, "Minsky on Himself," in *Financial Conditions and Macroeconomic Performance: Essays in Honor of Hyman P. Minsky*, Steven Fazzari and Dimitri B. Papadimitriou, eds. (Armonk, NY: M. E. Sharpe, 1992). The discussion in this section draws on those references, plus my own memories.

4. Minsky, "Beginnings," in Kregel, 1988, 178.

5. Minsky, "Beginnings," in Kregel, 1988, 172.

6. Minsky knew many of the postwar greats who won the Nobel Prize for economics, including Samuelson, Franco Modigliani,

Tobin, Robert Solow, and Kenneth Arrow. Sadly, he was not seriously considered for the prize, largely because he was too far outside the mainstream, and perhaps because he stopped writing the types of articles favored by the most prestigious academic journals. Whereas he had published in many of the top journals in his early years in academia, he soon became dissatisfied with the simplistic math models those journals demanded. He found that he could explain much more complicated ideas using English rather than math. That might be why Krugman complained about the "long slog through turgid writing" as he read Minsky's 1986 book. Most economic theories are rather simple, which makes it easier to put them into math; to an important degree, the limits of math constrain the theory. Like Keynes, Minsky gave up the math (both took college degrees in math) so that he would be free to explore more complicated ideas. Unfortunately, economists today are unaccustomed to "turgid writing"—and Krugman candidly admitted that "it took me several decades before I learned to appreciate Keynes in the original."

7. See John G. Gurley and Edward S. Shaw, *Money in a Theory of Finance* (Washington, DC: Brookings Institution, 1960). Minsky credited Gurley and Shaw for recognizing that we should not make a sharp distinction between commercial banks and what Minsky called "nonbank banks" (later called shadow banks by Paul McCulley). Minsky's views were influenced by Gurley and Shaw's insistence that the liabilities issued by nonbank banks compete with bank deposits. As Minsky would later say, anyone can create money.

8. Last year's version was held at the National Press Club in Washington, DC, on April 11 and 12, 2014.

9. Much of his work in that area was published in a book after his death, Minsky, *Ending Poverty: Jobs, Not Welfare*, (Annandale-on-Hudson, NY: Levy Economics Institute, 2013). http://www.amazon.com/Ending-Poverty-Jobs-Not-Welfare/dp/1936192314/ref=sr_1_1?ie=UTF8&qid=1366125357&sr=8-1&keywords=ending+poverty+jobs+not+welfare.

10. Hyman P. Minsky, *Stabilizing an Unstable Economy* (New York: McGraw-Hill, 2008): 255. Originally published in 1986 by Yale University Press, New Haven, CT.

11. Minsky, *Stabilizing an Unstable Economy*, 255.

12. Minsky, "Central Banking and Money Market Changes," *Quarterly Journal of Economics* 71, no. 2 (May 1957): 171–87.

13. Stephanie Bell and Wray updated Minsky's work, showing the importance of full-time work for poverty reduction (discussed in chapter 5): Stephanie Bell and L. Randall Wray, "The War on Poverty after 40 Years: A Minskyan Assessment," Public Policy Brief No. 78, June 2004, http://www.levyinstitute.org/publications /the-war-on-poverty-after-40-years.

14. In Europe, this stage of capitalism is often called social democracy; while the New Deal was American, most of the developed Western nations adopted policies regulating financial institutions that were similar to those of the United States.

15. L. Randall Wray, "Ford–Levy Institute Projects: A Research and Policy Dialogue Project on Improving Governance of the Government Safety Net in Financial Crisis," *Levy Economics Institute Research Project Report*, Annandale-on-Hudson, NY: Levy Economics Institute, April 2012. http://www.levyinstitute.org /ford-levy/governance/.

16. Hyman P. Minsky, *Stabilizing an Unstable Economy* (New Haven, CT: Yale University Press, 1986; New York: McGraw-Hill, 2008), 297.

17. A full explanation of this phenomenon gets complicated. The trade balance is the main portion of the current account balance. For reasons we will not go into now, when a nation runs a current account deficit together with a balanced government budget, this means by identity that its domestic private sector is running a deficit (spending more than its income). Private sector deficits tend to be destabilizing because they require the private sector to go ever-further into debt. This is precisely what happened in the United States from the late 1990s until the GFC. To avoid a private sector deficit while running a current account deficit requires that the

government's budget run a deficit at least as large as the current account deficit. This requirement is why it makes sense to consider the trade balance when thinking about the proper size of the "Big Government"—its deficit needs to offset fluctuations of investment but also to offset the current account deficit. Once we take these factors into account, we conclude that in the United States, federal government spending ought to be closer to 25 percent of GDP, while taxes should average about 20 percent—which means that a budget deficit would be the normal expectation.

18. Note that here Minsky was referring to the Glass–Steagall Act, which separated investment banking from commercial banking. In fact, that "segmentation" was ended in 1999. However, it mainly benefited the biggest banks—those that were largely responsible for the GFC only a few years later.

Chapter 2

1. Hyman P. Minsky, *Stabilizing an Unstable Economy* (New Haven, CT: Yale University Press, 1986).
2. We will put quotation marks around "Keynesian" when we are referring to mainstream Keynesians—what Joan Robinson called "Bastard Keynesians."
3. In 1937, John Hicks had created the ISLM model to present Keynes's theory in a simple framework that could be used to compare "Keynesian" and "classical" results.
4. John Maynard Keynes, *General Theory of Employment, Interest, and Money* (New York and London: Harcourt Brace Jovanovich, 1964); new edition has Krugman's introduction (London: Macmillan, 1936, reprinted 2007).
5. Throughout this section, I provide only a brief overview of the main tenets of orthodox approaches and spare the reader detailed citations. Thorough summaries as well as references are provided in many commonly used macroeconomics textbooks. The Samuelson (1973) text is useful for the "Keynesian" neoclassical synthesis; for the post-1970s developments, the text by Gregory Mankiw,

Macroeconomics, 8th ed., (New York: Worth Publishers, 2012), is good for undergraduates, and Brian Snowdon and Howard R. Vane, *Modern Macroeconomics: Its Origins, Development and Current State* (Cheltenham, UK: Edward Elgar Publishing, 2005), provides a more advanced examination.

6. Paul A. Samuelson, *Economics*, 9th ed. (New York: McGraw-Hill, 1973).

7. See Don Patinkin, *Money, Interest, and Prices: An Integration of Monetary and Value Theory,* 2nd ed. (New York: Harper & Row, 1965), and Minsky, *Stabilizing an Unstable Economy*, 1986.

8. Karl Brunner, "The Role of Money and Monetary Policy," *Federal Reserve Bank of St. Louis Review*, 1968; Milton Friedman, *The Optimal Quantity of Money and Other Essays* (Aldine: Chicago, 1969).

9. Robert Skidelsky, *Keynes: Return of the Master* (New York: Public Affairs, 2009): xiv.

10. Eugene Fama, "Efficient Capital Markets: A Review of Theory and Empirical Work," *Journal of Finance*, 25, no. 2 (1970).

11. Robert Skidelsky, *Keynes: Return of the Master* (New York: Public Affairs, 2009): xviii.

12. Stock and Watson concluded that most of the stability of the Great Moderation was attributable to unexplained factors instead of improvements in the structure of the economy or in monetary policy; luck was the main cause of the Great Moderation. (J. H. Stock and M. W. Watson, "Has the Business Cycle Changed and Why?" *NBER Macroeconomics*, 17 (2002): 159–218. J. H. Stock and M. W. Watson, "Understanding Changes in International Business Cycle Dynamics," *Journal of the European Economic Association*, 3, no. 5 (2005): 968–1006.)

13. This is not to say that orthodoxy has completely ignored money. Indeed, as discussed above, all but the real business cycle approach tried to find a way to make money matter—that is, to make it "non-neutral." However, money was never introduced in a convincing manner—as Hahn's lament (cited below) makes clear. None of the orthodox approaches makes money the *object* of production. In

Keynes's terminology, the subject of orthodox economics is not an entrepreneurial economy, so although money might be used, it is not essential.

14. See Frank H. Hahn, "The Foundations of Monetary Theory," (1987): 172–94 in L. Randall Wray, ed., *Theories of Money and Banking, Volume II: Alternative Approaches to Money, Financial Institutions and Policy* (Cheltenham, UK: Edward Elgar Publishing, 2012).

15. Charles A. E. Goodhart, "Money and Default," in Mathew Forstater and L. Randall Wray, eds., *Keynes for the Twenty-First Century: The Continuing Relevance of the General Theory* (New York: Palgrave Macmillan, 2008): 213–23.

16. "The End of Laissez-Faire," in John M. Keynes, *The Collected Writings of John Maynard Keynes: Essays in Persuasion*, vol. IX (London and Basingstoke: Royal Economic Society, 1978): 272–94.

17. It is often claimed that "Keynesian" policy of the 1960s led to the stagflation of the 1970s.

18. The idea, presented in all the textbooks of economic principles, is that if investment goes up by 100, aggregate income will go up by a multiple—say, four times as much. The reason is that as investment raises income and employment, those workers will consume most of their income, generating more sales and thus more employment and income. The "induced" consumption from the additional hiring is the "multiplier" effect of investment. (Government spending is said by Keynesians to have a similar effect.)

19. The stagnation thesis was recently endorsed by mainstream Keynesians, such as Larry Summers ("U.S. Economic Prospects: Secular Stagnation, Hysteresis, and the Zero Lower Bound," in *Business Economics* 49 (2014): 65–73) and Paul Krugman ("Three Charts on Secular Stagnation," The Conscience of a Liberal, *New York Times*, May 7, 2014, http://krugman.blogs.nytimes.com/2014/05/07/three-charts-on-secular-stagnation/?_r=0) To simplify, the problem is that although $100 of investment might raise demand through the spending multiplier by $400, the extra capacity resulting from that investment could be greater—say $600. This means that there is excess capacity, which then reduces the incentive to

invest more in the future. That depresses demand further—growth falters, and we get stagnation. Vatter and Walker (*The Rise of Big Government in the United States* (Armonk, NY: M. E. Sharpe, 1997)) argued, following Keynes, that one solution is to promote more government spending to provide the demand needed.

20. See Hyman P. Minsky, "Discussion," *American Economic Review*, 53, no. 2 (1963): 401–12, and Wynne Godley and L. Randall Wray, "Can Goldilocks Survive?" *Policy Notes* (1999) 1999/4, Annandale-on-Hudson, NY: Levy Economics Institute.

21. John M. Keynes, "How to Avoid the Slump," *The Times*, January 12–14, 1937. Reprinted in D. E. Moggridge, ed., *The Collected Writings of John Maynard Keynes*, vol. 21, (London: Macmillan, 1973): 384–95.

22. Minsky, *Ending Poverty: Jobs, Not Welfare* (Annandale-on-Hudson, NY: Levy Economics Institute, 2013).

23. Stephanie Bell, "Do Taxes and Bonds Finance Government Spending?" *Journal of Economic Issues*, 34, no. 3 (2000): 603–20; L. R. Wray, *Understanding Modern Money: The Key to Full Employment and Price Stability* (Northampton, MA: Edward Elgar, 1998).

24. Minsky, "The Reconsideration of Keynesian Economics," Working Paper, Washington University at St. Louis, April 7, 1970, in Hyman P. Minsky Archive, Paper 475, http://digitalcommons .bard.edu/hm_archive/475.

25. Abba Lerner, "Functional Finance and the Federal Debt," *Social Research: An International Quarterly* 10, no. 1 (Spring 1943): 38–51, and "Money as a Creature of the State," *The American Economic Review*, 37, no. 2 (May 1947), Papers and proceedings of the fifty-ninth annual meeting of the American Economic Association, 312–17.

Chapter 3

1. Hyman P. Minsky, *Stabilizing an Unstable Economy* (New Haven, CT: Yale University Press, 1986).

2. C. Campbell and Hyman P. Minsky, "How to Get Off the Back of a Tiger or, Do Initial Conditions Constrain Deposit Insurance Reform?" in Federal Reserve Bank of Chicago, ed., *Proceedings of*

a Conference on Bank Structure and Competition (Chicago: Federal Reserve Bank of Chicago, 1987): 252–66.

3. This is the Hicks–Hansen model discussed earlier that formalized Paul Samuelson's "neoclassical synthesis" version of Keynesian theory. The ISLM model is based on equilibrium in two "markets," the IS market (where equilibrium occurs when investment equals saving) and the LM market (where money demand equals money supply). There is a third market in the background, the bond market—which is supposed to represent financial assets more generally. Equilibrium there occurs where the demand for bonds equals the supply of bonds. It can be shown (by Walras's law) that if there are only three markets (investment and saving, money, and bonds) then if two are in equilibrium (IS and LM), the third must also be in equilibrium. There are many problems with this model, which was developed by Sir John Hicks in 1937 (J. R. Hicks, "Mr. Keynes and the "Classics": A Suggested Interpretation," *Econometrica*, 5, no. 2 (April 1937): 147–59). Late in his life he recanted (John Hicks, "IS-LM: An Explanation," *Journal of Post Keynesian Economics*, 3, no. 2 (Winter 1980–1981): 139–54), arguing that the model is incoherent. However, it is still taught in economics courses and has long been behind much real-world policy making. The modern version is the new monetary consensus, which replaced the LM curve with an interest-rate setting monetary policy curve (often following a Taylor rule). We won't go into the distinction because it remains institutionally truncated. And do not worry—the reader does not need to be familiar with these models to follow the discussion in this book!

4. Friedman argued that the central bank can, and should, fix the rate of growth of the money supply at a constant rate—say, 4 percent per year. This proposal was based on his revision of the quantity theory of money, which begins from the equation of exchange: $MV = PQ$. Here M is money supply, V is velocity of money, P is the overall price level, and Q is real output. Friedman supposed that V is fairly stable and that Q grows at a fairly constant rate determined by real capacity of the economy. In that case, the rate of growth of

the money supply determines the growth of *P*, which is inflation. Hence, by controlling money growth, the central bank controls inflation.

5. Hyman P. Minsky, "A Theory of Systemic Fragility," in E. I. Altman and A. W. Sametz, eds., *Financial Crises* (New York: Wiley, 1977): 138–52.

6. Hyman P. Minsky, "Central Banking and Money Market Changes," *Quarterly Journal of Economics*, 71, no, 2 (May 1957): 171.

7. Hyman P. Minsky, *John Maynard Keynes* (New York: Columbia University Press, 1975).

8. For example, assume that it costs $100 to produce a widget-making machine. The producer adds $50 as a markup to cover his or her own interest costs, overhead, and profits. A firm with sufficient internal funds can buy the machine for $150. However, if external funds are required, the supply price is higher—say $175—to cover interest and fees paid to the lender. Thus, one must pay $175 to obtain the externally financed capital asset, with the supply price covering production costs, including profits to the producer, and finance costs to cover lender's risk.

9. Alternatively, if asset prices rise sufficiently, a Ponzi unit might be able to sell assets to pay off the debt. In the hot real estate markets in the United States before 2006, many homeowners had Ponzi positions—their income was not sufficient to make mortgage payments. However, in some cases, the house price rose so quickly that they could sell out and repay the mortgage debt, or refinance on more favorable terms.

10. The Kalecki relation is named after Michał Kalecki, a Polish economist who worked with Keynes at Cambridge University. He showed that if we start from the GDP equals national income identity, we can show that at the aggregate level, profits equal investment plus the government's deficit plus net exports plus consumption out of profits, minus saving out of wages. He then proceeded to make this identity a causal relation by noting that profits are not under the control of businesses and other variables result from choices. The simplified, "classical" version assumes that the

last two terms are zero (workers do not save, and capitalists do not consume) so that profits equal and are determined by investment plus the budget deficit plus net exports. All else being equal, rising investment increases profits by the same amount at the aggregate level. See M. Kalecki, *Collected Essays on the Dynamics of the Capitalist Economy 1933–1970* (Cambridge, UK: Cambridge University Press, 1971).

11. Minsky, *Stabilizing an Unstable Economy* (New Haven, CT: Yale University Press, 1986).

12. See Hyman P. Minsky and Charles J. Whalen, "Economic Insecurity and the Institutional Prerequisites for Successful Capitalism," Levy Working Paper No. 165, May 1996.

13. See John Cassidy, "The Minsky Moment," *The New Yorker*, February 4, 2008. http://www.newyorker.com/magazine/2008/02/04/the-minsky-moment, and Edward Chancellor, "Ponzi Nation," *Institutional Investor*, February 7, 2007. http://www.institutionalinvestor.com/article.aspx?articleID=1234217#.VN-5cC7py1Q.

14. To be clear, in the more orthodox versions of Keynes (both the neoclassical synthesis as well as the new Keynesian economics), unemployment is caused by sticky wages (and prices). It is argued that if wages were perfectly flexible, markets would eliminate unemployment by lowering the real wage. Hence, in these versions of Keynes, the choice is either to make wages more flexible or to use policy to ameliorate the suffering caused by unemployment. By contrast, in Keynes's theory, greater flexibility of wages would likely cause unemployment to rise! For Keynes, relative stability of wages actually improves stability of markets.

15. See Piero Ferri and Hyman P. Minsky, "Market Processes and Thwarting Systems," Annandale-on-Hudson, NY: Levy Economics Institute, Working Paper No. 64, November 1, 1991, and Minsky, 1986.

Chapter 4

1. Hyman P. Minsky, "Suggestions for a Cash Flow-Oriented Bank Examination," in Federal Reserve Bank of Chicago, ed., *Proceedings*

of a Conference on Bank Structure and Competition (Chicago: Federal Reserve Bank of Chicago, 1975): 150–84.

2. Hyman P. Minsky, "Money, Other Financial Variables, and Aggregate Demand in the Short Run," in G. Horwich, ed., *Monetary Process and Policy* (Homewood, IL: Richard D. Irwin, 1967): 265–94.

3. Hyman P. Minsky, "Private Sector Asset Management and the Effectiveness of Monetary Policy: Theory and Practice," *Journal of Finance*, 24, no.2 (1969): 223–38. Published by John Wiley and Sons. © American Finance Association.

4. Paul Krugman, "Banking Mysticism, Continued," The Conscience of a Liberal, *New York Times*, March 30, 2012, http://krugman.blogs.nytimes.com/2012/03/30/banking-mysticism-continued/.

5. He used to go on to joke that a Chicago money lender breaks your leg for late payment. A money lender is a true intermediary, one who must obtain cash before lending it. Banks do not operate that way—they lend their own IOUs.

6. To be sure, retailers do deposit cash at the end of the day, but with so much of the cash circulating outside the United States and with a large portion of the domestic holdings circulating in illegal activities, the amount received and deposited by retailers is a tiny fraction of the total loans created on an average day by banks.

7. Today the entries are made through computer keystrokes. Before computers, they were written in pen and ink. In any event, it is not at all misleading to say that these entries are "created out of thin air," even if ink is used. The amount of real resources used up is insignificant—even in the case of paper notes.

8. Pizza Hut creates liabilities "out of thin air" all the time—coupons promising a free pizza. It does not have to make pizza before issuing the pizza coupons; it can create coupons out of thin air in an unlimited quantity (not that this would be a smart business decision).

9. See Paul McCulley, "The Shadow Banking System and Hyman Minsky's Economic Journey," Global Central Bank Focus, May 2009, http://www.pimco.com/EN/Insights/Pages/Global%20Central%20Bank%20Focus%20May%202009%20Shadow%20Banking%20and%20Minsky%20McCulley.aspx.

10. Negotiable Orders of Withdrawals and Money Market Mutual Funds, respectively.

11. "Break the buck" means that the value of a one-dollar deposit falls below a dollar. This cannot happen in the case of FDIC-insured deposits in banks because government guarantees parity with currency. However, MMMFs and other types of liabilities issued by shadow banks do not have government guarantees standing behind them.

12. We could call this an "advance" to avoid confusing the bank with a Chicago money lender. The bank lends its own IOU—it is not lending cash.

13. In today's environment of quantitative easing, the Fed is keeping massive quantities of excess reserves in the banking system. However, the Fed has moved to a policy of paying interest on excessive reserves, so the fed funds rate is pushed down to that rate but not below. The reason is that no bank would lend reserves in the fed funds market to earn a rate below what the Fed pays on excess reserves. So they just hold excess reserves and receive the interest that the Fed pays on them.

14. Basil Moore, *Horizontalists and Verticalists: The Macroeconomics of Credit Money* (Cambridge, UK: Cambridge University Press, 1988).

15. Hyman P. Minsky, "Reconstituting the United States' Financial Structure: Some Fundamental Issues," Working Paper No. 69. Annandale-on-Hudson, NY: Levy Economics Institute, January 1992a, p. 12.

16. Savings deposits are short-term time deposits. Banks can invoke thirty days' notice for withdrawal, unlike the case for demand deposits. Certificates of deposit (CDs) are longer term time deposits, for example, ninety-day CDs—which have penalties for early withdrawal.

17. Hyman P. Minsky, "Financial Crises: Systemic or Idiosyncratic," Annandale-on-Hudson, NY: Levy Economics Institute, Working Paper, No. 51, April 1991, p. 13, http://digitalcommons.bard.edu /cgi/viewcontent.cgi?article=1243&context=hm_archive.

18. For every creditor, there is a debtor; for every lender, there is a borrower.

19. Traditionally, savings and loans institutions in the United States issued mutual share deposits that in practice functioned like savings deposits of banks, although legally they were not.

20. For example, when the GFC hit, investment banks got stuck with mortgage-backed securities (MBSs) that they had planned to sell to investors.

21. If the firm fails to make payments on the loans, the bank could seize and sell the goods to reduce losses. However, that is a last resort; banks generally do not want to seize collateral, especially nonfinancial assets that can be hard to sell.

22. See Martin Mayer, "The Spectre of Banking," One-Pager No. 3, Annandale-on-Hudson, NY: Levy Economics Institute, May 2010.

23. An "ephor" is one who oversees.

24. J. Schumpeter, *The Theory of Economic Development* (New Brunswick, NJ: Transaction Publishers, 1997 [1934]).

25. In this case, the commercial bank provides short-term finance during the production phase of the capital (e.g., machines, buildings); the investment bank then provides long-term finance to enable the purchasers to buy the capital goods that they will use.

26. Rudolf Hilferding, *Finance Capital: A Study in the Latest Phase of Capitalist Development* (London: Routledge, 2006 [1910]).

27. The best and most entertaining account of the shenanigans of investment banks like Goldman Sachs in the run-up to the Great Depression is John Kenneth Galbraith's *The Great Crash 1929* (New York: Houghton Mifflin Harcourt, 2009 [1954]).

28. For those interested in Minsky's views on all of this, see this paper at the Levy Institute: L. Randall Wray, *What Should Banks Do? A Minskyan Analysis*, Public Policy Brief No. 115, September 2010, http://www.levyinstitute.org/publications/?docid=1301. Galbraith devoted an entire chapter to Goldman Sachs, and his description of that bank's activities reads like an account of its activities leading up to the GFC in 2007.

Chapter 5

1. Hyman P. Minsky, "Where Did the American Economy—and Economists—Go Wrong?" Unpublished manuscript, 1971. This is in the archives as "Further Rewrite" version of paper 428.

2. Hyman P. Minsky, "The Poverty of Economic Policy," Presented at the Graduate Institute of Cooperative Leadership, New York, July 14, 1975.

3. Hyman P. Minsky, "Institutional Roots of American Inflation," in N. Schmukler and E. Marcus, eds., *Inflation through the Ages: Economic, Social, Psychological and Historical Aspects* (New York: Brooklyn College Press, 1983): 265–77.

4. His papers are in his archive at the Levy Economics Institute of Bard College: http://www.bard.edu/library/archive/minsky/. Some of his work on poverty and employment was published after his death in Hyman P. Minsky, *Ending Poverty: Jobs, Not Welfare,* published by the Levy Economics Institute, Annandale-on-Hudson, NY, 2013.

5. Michael Harrington, *The Other America*, (New York: Macmillan,1962); reprint edition, paperback: (New York: Scribner, 1997).

6. This chapter draws on *The War on Poverty after 40 Years* by Stephanie Bell and L. Randall Wray, June 2004, Levy Institute Public Policy Brief No. 78, http://www.levyinstitute.org/publications /the-war-on-poverty-after-40-years.

7. Hyman P. Minsky, "The Role of Employment Policy," In *Poverty in America*, Margaret S. Gordon, ed. (San Francisco: Chandler Publishing Company, 1965), p. 175.

8. According to Josh Levin, who tried to track down the source of President Reagan's story used frequently in his campaign speeches in 1976, "Many accounts report that Reagan coined the term 'welfare queen,' and that this woman in Chicago was a fictional character." It turns out that there really was a Chicago woman— Linda Taylor—on whom the anecdote might have been based, but the true story is much more complicated than Reagan had implied. See http://www.slate.com/articles/news_and_politics

/history/2013/12/linda_taylor_welfare_queen_ronald_reagan
_made_her_a_notorious_american_villain.html. Twenty years
later, in 1996, President Clinton said, "Today, we are ending welfare as we know it," as he signed a bill ending the federal guarantee
of cash assistance to the poor and turning welfare programs over to
the states. See Barbara Vobejda, "Clinton Signs Welfare Bill amid
Division," *Washington Post*, August 23, 1996, p. A1, http://www
.washingtonpost.com/wp-srv/politics/special/welfare/stories
/wf082396.htm.

9. Recall the earlier discussion of orthodox Keynesians who adopted
   some of Keynes's ideas but "synthesized" them with neoclassical
   economics.

10. The metaphor commonly used is that "a rising tide of growth lifts all
    boats." For a critique, see Marc-Andre Pigeon and L. Randall Wray,
    "Can a Rising Tide Raise All Boats? Evidence from the Clinton-Era
    Expansion," *Journal of Economic Issues*, 34, no. 4 (2000): 811–45.

11. Pavlina Tcherneva has shown that the benefits of economic recov-
    ery (the rising tide) have always disproportionately benefited those
    at the top of the income distribution over the entire postwar pe-
    riod. And that bias has increased over each subsequent recovery; in
    the most recent recovery, more than all the benefits (116 percent)
    went to the top 10 percent. See Pavlina R. Tcherneva, "Growth for
    Whom?" One-Pager, No. 47, Annandale-on-Hudson, NY: Levy
    Economics Institute, October 6, 2014, http://www.levyinstitute
    .org/pubs/op_47.pdf.

12. Poverty rates for black Americans *did* fall, but they had been fall-
    ing even before the War on Poverty. However, this is largely due
    to migration out of the Southern United States to better jobs
    in the north, and then to Civil Rights legislation that reduced
    discrimination.

13. *Papers of U.S. Presidents*, Lyndon B. Johnson, 1963–1964.(Wash-
    ington, DC: U.S. Printing Office, 1965) 1: 375–80.

14. Judith Russell, *Economics, Bureaucracy, and Race: How Keynes-
    ians Misguided the WOP* (New York: Columbia University Press,
    2004).

15. Hyman P. Minsky, "The Role of Employment Policy," in *Poverty in America*, Margaret S. Gordon, ed. (San Francisco: Chandler Publishing Company, 1965).

16. Hyman P. Minsky, "The Poverty of Economic Policy," Presented at the Graduate Institute of Cooperative Leadership, New York, July 14, 1975.

17. Minsky used "Okun's law" to make this calculation, according to which each one percentage point reduction of unemployment raises GNP by 3 percent.

18. See L. Randall Wray and Stephanie Bell, "The War on Poverty after 40 Years: A Minskyan Assessment", Public Policy Brief, Annandale-on-Hudson, NY: Levy Economics Institute, No. 78, 2004; and "The War on Poverty Forty Years On," in *Challenge*, 47, no. 5 (September–October 2004): 6–29.

19. Hyman P. Minsky, "The Strategy of Economic Policy and Income Distribution," *Annals of the American Academy of Political and Social Science*, 409 (September 1973): 92–101.

20. What Minsky means is that consumption should be a higher share of GDP, while investment should be a lower share. In his view, high investment is associated with greater instability. Note also that he was not arguing for wasteful and environmentally destructive consumption.

21. Hyman P. Minsky, "Effects of Shifts of Aggregate Demand upon Income Distribution," *American Journal of Agricultural Economics*, 50, no. 2 (1968): 328–39.

22. For more on the ELR proposal, see Mathew Forstater, "Public Employment and Economic Flexibility," Public Policy Brief No. 50, Annandale-on-Hudson, NY: Levy Economics Institute; Phillip Harvey, *Securing the Right to Employment* (Princeton, NJ: Princeton University Press, 1989); Jan Kregel, "Currency Stabilization through Full Employment: Can EMU Combine Price Stability with Employment and Income Growth?" *Eastern Economic Journal*, 25, no. 1 (1999): 35–48; and L. Randall Wray, *Understanding Modern Money: The Key to Full Employment and Price Stability* (Northampton, MA: Edward Elgar, 1998).

23. See Nick Taylor, *American-Made: The Enduring Legacy of the WPA: When FDR Put the Nation to Work* (New York: Bantam, 2009).

24. Marc-Andre Pigeon and L. R. Wray, "Can a Rising Tide Raise All Boats? Evidence from the Clinton-Era Expansion," *Journal of Economic Issues*, 34, no. 4, December 2000.

25. See Marc-Andre Pigeon and L. R. Wray, "Demand Constraint and the New Economy," in *A Post Keynesian Perspective on Twenty-First Century Economic Problems*, Paul Davidson, ed. (Aldershot, UK: Edward Elgar, 2002), pp. 158–94.

26. We begin with the program wage set at the minimum wage because that is least disruptive. However, following Minsky, we would want to increase this wage over time to close the inequality gap—so it should rise faster than the general rate of wage increases as well as the rate of growth of labor productivity. That would tilt the distribution of income toward the bottom.

27. This helps to minimize corruption—since program employers would not have access to the wages paid.

28. This element would defray nonwage costs but would not be so high that projects would be created for the main purpose of obtaining federal funding of administrative and materials costs.

Chapter 6

1. Hyman P. Minsky, "Securitization," 1987, republished as Policy Note 2008/2, June 2008.

2. Hyman P. Minsky, "Securitization," 1987.

3. Hyman P. Minsky, "Securitization," 1987.

4. Hyman P. Minsky, "Reconstituting the United States' Financial Structure: Some Fundamental Issues," 1992, Annandale-on-Hudson, NY: Levy Economics Institute, Working Paper No. 69.

5. What Minsky means by this is that apparent stability encourages more risk-taking by investors, financial institutions, and entrepreneurs. They tend to borrow more relative to expected earnings, and innovate with riskier financial instruments. In addition, regulators might relax rules on the belief that downside risks have been

reduced. All of this increases financial fragility and hence enhances instability.

6. See L. Randall Wray, "The Rise and Fall of Money Manager Capitalism: A Minskian Approach," *Cambridge Journal of Economics*, 33, no. 4 (2009): 807–28, and Hyman P. Minsky, "The Transition to a Market Economy," Working Paper no. 66, 1991, Annandale-on-Hudson, NY: Levy Economics Institute.

7. Ben S. Bernanke, "The Great Moderation," Speech given at the meetings of the Eastern Economics Association, Washington, DC, February 20, 2004, www.federalreserve.gov/Boarddocs/Speeches /2004/20040220/default.htm.

8. Minsky sometimes called this the "industrial capitalism" stage. See Hyman P. Minsky and Charles J. Whalen, "Economic Insecurity and the Institutional Prerequisites for Successful Capitalism," Levy Working Paper No. 165, May 1996. The important point was that industry needed external finance for its expensive and long-lived capital assets—so they turned to investment banks.

9. See John Kenneth Galbraith, *The Great Crash 1929* (New York: Houghton Mifflin Harcourt, 2009 [1954]).

10. Minsky also called this the "paternalistic capitalism" stage—with both big government and big corporations taking care of workers and families. (Hyman P. Minsky and Charles J. Whalen, "Economic Insecurity and the Institutional Prerequisites for Successful Capitalism," Levy Working Paper no. 165, May 1996).

11. Susan Strange, *Casino Capitalism* (Manchester, UK: Manchester University Press, 1997), Jane D'Arista, *The Role of the International Monetary System in Financialization* (Amherst, MA: Financial Markets Center, 2001), http://www.peri.umass.edu/fileadmin/pdf /financial/fin_darista.pdf.

12. As Minsky put it, the financial structure "has evolved into its present stage of 'money-manager' capitalism, where financial markets and arrangements are dominated by managers of funds . . ." These managers work in "institutions that manage large portfolios of financial instruments" (Minsky and Whalen, 1996, pp. 3–4).

13. Gresham's law is usually applied to coins: "Bad money drives out good money," referring to the days in which precious metal such as

gold was coined. One would prefer to spend the low-weight coins (gold coins could be clipped or rubbed to collect precious metal) and hold the high-weight coins. Here we use the term to refer to competitive pressures that favor "bad practices" to "drive out the good practices."

14. The capital ratio is net worth divided by assets; the higher that ratio, the more losses the bank can suffer before it becomes insolvent. Banks also keep loan loss reserves to cover the first losses; once depleted, losses come out of net worth. Reducing either the capital ratio or the loan loss reserve increases bank profitability but also increases risk of insolvency.

15. See Wray, 2009.

16. See Minsky and Whalen, 1996.

17. Thus, the War on Poverty was consistent with the "culture of poverty" thesis of Daniel Patrick Moynihan ("The Negro Family: The Case for National Action." Office of Policy Planning and Research, U.S. Department of Labor, March 1965, http://www.dol.gov/dol/aboutdol/history/webid-meynihan.htm).

18. An NPR report, "Stopping the 'Brain Drain' of the U.S. Economy," is here: http://www.scpr.org/news/2012/02/06/31135/stopping-the-brain-drain-of-the-us-economy/.

19. See L. Randall Wray, "Surplus Mania: A Reality Check," Policy Notes, 1999/3, Annandale-on-Hudson, NY: Levy Economics Institute; Wynne Godley and L. Randall Wray, "Can Goldilocks Survive?" Policy Notes, 1999/4, Annandale-on-Hudson, NY: Levy Economics Institute; and Wynne Godley and L. Randall Wray, "Is Goldilocks Doomed?" *Journal of Economic Issues*, 34, no. 1 (March 2000): 201–206.

20. However, the U.S. federal government had gone into surplus at the end of the 1920s, and American households had discovered that they could use credit to finance consumption purchases (for electric appliances—the technological innovation of the time). The economy quickly went into a tailspin in 1930, the government's budget turned back toward deficit, and households stopped borrowing. The Great Depression was off and running. It is interesting that the late 1920s was the last time the federal government ran a

sustained budget surplus—until the Clinton years. It was déjà vu all over again!

21. This debt figure includes all debt—government, households, and private financial and nonfinancial institutions. By contrast, the comparable figure had only reached 300 percent before the "Great Crash" that led to the Great Depression. So the debt ratio was much higher this time.

22. See Yeva Nersisyan and L. R. Wray for a critique of empirical work that purported to show that government debt ratios beyond a certain threshold slow growth ("Does Excessive Sovereign Debt Really Hurt Growth? A Critique of 'This Time Is Different,' by Reinhart and Rogoff," Annandale-on-Hudson, NY: Levy Economics Institute, Working Paper No. 603, June 2010, http://www.levyinstitute.org/pubs/wp_603.pdf). The research was based on flawed theory and errors in the empirical analysis: "This Time is Different: Eight Centuries of Financial Folly," *Challenge*, 54, no. 1 (January–February 2011): 113–20.

23. Walter Bagehot, *Lombard Street: A Description of the Money Market* (London: CreateSpace Independent Publishing Platform, 2012 [1873]).

24. The recommendation to lend at a penalty rate and only against good collateral was to ensure that the lending was to solvent banks with good assets—and not to insolvent banks with no good assets to pledge. A healthy bank would have good, earning assets and would be able to afford to pay a penalty rate; it needed to borrow only because it was facing a run on liquidity.

25. A much more detailed critical analysis of the response to the crisis is provided in Eric Tymoigne and L. Randall Wray, *The Rise and Fall of Money Manager Capitalism: Minsky's Half Century from WWII to the Great Recession* (New York: Routledge, 2013).

26. See Tymoigne and Wray, 2013.

27. The Treasury (through the FDIC) is responsible for resolution. There are alternative ways to resolve insolvent banks, ranging from shutting them and selling assets to try to cover liabilities, to subsidizing a merger with a healthy institution.

28. All of this process can get quite technical and complicated. See Tymoigne and Wray, 2013, for details.

29. Treasury Secretary Hank Paulson had managed to obtain more than $700 billion from Congress to rescue financial institutions early in the crisis, but that was not nearly enough.

30. See L. Randall Wray, "The Lender of Last Resort: A Critical Analysis of the Federal Reserve's Unprecedented Intervention after 2007," Annandale-on-Hudson, NY: Levy Economics Institute, Research Project Reports, April 2013, http://www.levyinstitute .org/publications/the-lender-of-last-resort-a-critical-analysis-of -the-federal-reserves-unprecedented-intervention-after-2007.

31. See James Felkerson, "$29,000,000,000,000: A Detailed Look at the Fed's Bailout by Funding Facility and Recipient," Annandale-on-Hudson, NY: Levy Economics Institute, Working Paper No. 698, December 2011, http://www.levyinstitute.org/pubs /wp_698.pdf.

32. See the Ford–Levy Institute Project on "Financial Instability and the Reregulation of Financial Institutions and Markets," http:// www.levyinstitute.org/ford-levy/.

Chapter 7

1. Hyman P. Minsky, "A Theory of Systemic Fragility," in E. I. Altman and A. W. Sametz, eds., *Financial Crises* (New York: Wiley, 1977): 138–52. © John Wiley and Sons.

2. Hyman P. Minsky, "Reconstituting the United States' Financial Structure: Some Fundamental Issues," Annandale-on-Hudson, NY: Levy Economics Institute, Working Paper No. 69, January 1992a.

3. Some people call them "too big to jail," rather than TBTF because none of the top executives of the biggest financial institutions has been prosecuted for fraud, even though their banks have all admitted to multiple frauds and paid tens of billions of dollars in fines each.

4. Hyman P. Minsky. "Bank Portfolio Determination," from Hyman P. Minsky Archive, Annandale-on-Hudson, NY: Levy

Economics Institute, January 1, 1959. All the quotes in this section come from this early paper.

5. By "banker's cash," Minsky means reserves at the central bank, which are used to cover clearing against other banks and also cash withdrawals by depositors. Here he's arguing that a bank will accept a lower interest rate on marketable assets than on loans, in part because they save the cost of borrowing reserves as needed to cover losses through withdrawal (and clearing) since the bank can just sell the securities to obtain reserves.

6. Interest rate risk generally increases with time to maturity. If a bank makes a loan today at, say, 4 percent and is paying near zero on deposits, that loan can be profitable. But if interest rates generally rise so that banks are forced to pay 2 percent on deposits, a 4 percent loan no longer looks good. The best example of the damage that can be done is the savings and loan crisis in America in the early 1980s. Banks and thrifts typically made thirty-year fixed-rate mortgage loans at 6 or 7 percent, which was fine when it cost banks 2 or 3 percent to issue deposit liabilities. When Fed Chairman Volcker pushed short-term rates above 20 percent to fight inflation, banks had to pay much more to issue short-term liabilities, but they were still stuck with the low-earning mortgages—accumulating huge losses on every mortgage they had made. This is one of the reasons the "originate-to-distribute" model was created—to shift that kind of interest rate risk to the holder of the securitized mortgages.

7. Lincoln Savings & Loan actually did this, under the stewardship of one of the most notorious crooks of the thrift crisis, Charles Keating—who also curried favor with five U.S. senators, known as the Keating Five; among the five was John McCain, a perennial presidential candidate.

8. See Galbraith's *The Great Crash 1929*, 1954. "Pump and dump" refers to management pursuing strategies to push stock prices up temporarily so that they can sell their shares before markets realize that the price rise was unwarranted.

9. Hyman P. Minsky, "The Capital Development of the Economy and the Structure of Financial Institutions," Annandale-on-Hudson,

NY: Levy Economics Institute, Working Paper No. 72, January 1992b.

10. Hyman P. Minsky, "Reconstituting the United States' Financial Structure: Some Fundamental Issues," Annandale-on-Hudson, NY: Levy Economics Institute, Working Paper No. 69, January 1992a.

11. Hyman P. Minsky, "Suggestions for a Cash Flow Oriented Bank Examination," Paper No. 175, Hyman P. Minsky Archive, Annandale-on-Hudson, NY: Levy Economics Institute, 1967.

12. The Basel Accords are formulated by the Basel Committee on Banking Supervision and are used as the basis for aligning international banking and supervision. While these are only recommendations, the nations of the G-20 generally follow these guidelines as they regulate and supervise banks operating in their countries. The focus has tended to be on use of capital ratios as well as external risk ratings (from ratings agencies) to keep banks safe.

13. The more capital a bank holds against assets, the lower the return on equity—all else being equal—because the profit rate is determined by the flow of income on assets divided by net worth.

14. Hyman P. Minsky, "Reconstituting the Financial Structure: The United States," Paper No. 18, Hyman P. Minsky Archive, Annandale-on-Hudson, NY: Levy Economics Institute, 1992c, http://digitalcommons.bard.edu/hm_archive/18.

15. C. Campbell and Hyman P. Minsky, "How to Get Off the Back of a Tiger, or, Do Initial Conditions Constrain Deposit Insurance Reform?" in Federal Reserve Bank of Chicago, ed., *Proceedings of a Conference on Bank Structure and Competition* (Chicago: Federal Reserve Bank of Chicago, 1987): 252–66. For a detailed discussion of Minsky's views, see Jan A. Kregel, "Minsky and Dynamic Macroprudential Regulation," Annandale-on-Hudson, NY: Levy Economics Institute, Public Policy Brief No. 131, 2014.

16. Hyman P. Minsky, "Regulation and Supervision," Paper No. 443, Hyman P. Minsky Archive, Annandale-on-Hudson, NY: Levy Economics Institute, 1994, p. 6.

17. C. Campbell and Hyman P. Minsky, "Getting Off the Back of the Tiger: The Deposit Insurance Crisis in the United States,"

Working Paper No. 121, Department of Economics, Washington University, February 1988, p. 6.

18. Again, see Kregel, 2014, for a detailed discussion of this approach.

Chapter 8

1. Hyman P. Minsky, "Banking and a Fragile Financial Environment," *Journal of Portfolio Management*, 3, no. 4 (Summer 1977): 22.

2. Hyman P. Minsky, "Reconstituting the United States' Financial Structure: Some Fundamental Issues," Working Paper No. 69. Annandale-on-Hudson, NY: Levy Economics Institute, January 1992a, p. 21.

3. It is a bit more complicated than this because if the rich saved in the form of productive capital (machines and factories), that would create jobs. The problem is that they prefer to save in liquid—money, broadly defined—form, which does not create jobs. As Keynes put it, unemployment results because "men want the moon," i.e., money.

4. Hyman P. Minsky "Securitization," Annandale-on-Hudson, NY: Levy Economics Institute, Policy Note 2008/2, (1987) June 2008, http://www.levyinstitute.org/pubs/pn_08_2.pdf.

5. A character in a Doctor Seuss book: Dr. Seuss [Theodor Seuss Geisel], *Yertle the Turtle and Other Stories* (New York: Random House, April 12, 1958).

6. Hyman P. Minsky, "Suggestions for a Cash Flow-Oriented Bank Examination," in Federal Reserve Bank of Chicago, ed., *Proceedings of a Conference on Bank Structure and Competition* (Chicago: Federal Reserve Bank of Chicago, 1975): 150–84.

7. Recall the Krugman quote from the introduction, which admitted that conventional economists failed "to notice the rising importance of shadow banking. Economists looked at conventional banks, saw that they were protected by deposit insurance, and failed to realize that more than half the de facto banking system didn't look like that anymore." http://krugman.blogs.nytimes.com/2014/04/25/frustrations-of-the-heterodox/?_php=true&_type=blogs&_r=0.

8. Hyman P. Minsky, "Securitization," Annandale-on-Hudson, NY: Levy Economics Institute, Policy Note No. 2, May 12, 1987 (2008c). One percentage point equals 100 basis points. Hence, the difference between earning 6.5 percent interest on assets and paying 2 percent on deposits equals 450 basis points.

9. At that time, reserves were nonearning assets that must be held against deposits; today, reserves earn a very low but positive rate, slightly reducing the cost of issuing deposits.

10. A large portion of the "subprime" and "Alt-A" risky loans were adjustable-rate mortgages—if rates went up, borrowers could be in trouble. Furthermore, many of them had "teaser" rates—exceptionally low rates for the first two to three years—that would then "blow up" to very high rates. They were called "neutron bomb" mortgages in the industry that would "kill" the borrower but leave the home standing (to be foreclosed and resold). The only hope for the borrower was that home prices would rise, market rates would not rise, and that the borrower would qualify for a better loan before the rates blew up. Unfortunately for those who bought homes after 2004, that was a pipe dream. When rates rose, they could not refinance, and they lost their homes.

11. *Gradualism* means that when the Fed decides to change interest rates, it does so in a long series of small steps—typically 25 to 50 basis points spread over a period of up to a year. *Transparency* means that the Fed communicates with markets about its intentions. It does so to manage expectations—so that it will not surprise markets by a rate change. There is also a strong presumption that monetary policy affects the economy mostly by changing expectations. The belief is that if the Fed can get markets to *expect* low inflation and robust growth, the economy will *experience* low inflation and robust growth. As markets bought into this trust in a Wizard of Oz–like Federal Reserve chairman (first, Maestro Greenspan and then, Uncle Ben Bernanke), all caution was thrown out the window.

12. Hyman P. Minsky, "The Economic Problem at the End of the Second Millennium: Creating Capitalism, Reforming Capitalism and

Making Capitalism Work," prospective chapter, May 13, 1992d. Hyman P. Minsky Archive.

13. Almost all developed nations offer a child allowance.

14. Social spending to deal with poverty and unemployment, and social problems closely related to them already account for 10 percent of GDP, without eliminating poverty and unemployment!

15. Banks and mortgage lenders originate mortgage loans with no intention of holding them. Rather, they quickly sell them to investment banks that package and securitize them for sale to investors. Neither the originator nor the securitizer has an interest in assessing creditworthiness of the borrower.

16. Hyman P. Minsky, "Reconstituting the United States' Financial Structure: Some Fundamental Issues," Working Paper No. 69. Annandale-on-Hudson, NY: Levy Economics Institute, January 1992a, p. 12.

17. Ronnie Phillips, *The Chicago Plan and New Deal Banking Reform* (New York: M. E. Sharpe, 1995).

18. A billion dollars of assets might sound like a lot, but that is a small bank by today's standards. Remember that the United States has banks with over $2 trillion in assets.

19. Hyman P. Minsky, Dimitri B. Papadimitriou, Ronnie J. Phillips, and L. Randall Wray, "Community Development Banking: A Proposal to Establish a Nationwide System of Community Development Banks," Public Policy Brief No. 3, Annandale-on-Hudson, NY: Levy Economics Institute, 1993.

20. As reported in the *New York Times*, "many low-income people are 'unbanked' (not served by a financial institution), and thus nearly eaten alive by exorbitant fees. As the *St. Louis Federal Reserve* pointed out in 2010, 'Unbanked consumers spend approximately 2.5 to 3 percent of a government benefits check and between 4 percent and 5 percent of payroll check just to cash them. Additional dollars are spent to purchase money orders to pay routine monthly expenses. When you consider the cost for cashing a bi-weekly payroll check and buying about six money orders each month, a household with a net income of $20,000 may pay as much as $1,200

annually for alternative service fees—substantially more than the expense of a monthly checking account.'" Charles M. Blow, "How Expensive It Is to Be Poor," *New York Times*, January 18, 2015, http://www.nytimes.com/2015/01/19/opinion/charles-blow -how-expensive-it-is-to-be-poor.html?hp&action=click&pgtype =Homepage&module=c-column-top-span-region&region=c -column-top-span-region&WT.nav=c-column-top-span-region.

21. A universal bank model is generally one with a handful of huge banks, each of which provides the full range of services; at the time that Minsky was writing, the German banking system was closer to the universal bank model, and the United States still had some segmentation. However, what he was proposing was that *only* the small CDBs would be allowed to be universal banks; the big financial institutions would still be subject to some segmentation by function. After Minsky's death, however, the United States went in the opposite direction—eliminating the Glass–Steagall Act, which required segmentation.

22. Leveraged buyouts are often hostile takeovers undertaken by financiers like Michael Milken, who target corporations with little debt. The takeover is financed by risky debt that leaves the takeover target saddled with heavy debt and high interest payments. The financiers walk away with fee income. Though Milken served jail time for fraud, LBOs remain with us. Indeed, the LBO boom of the 2000s dwarfed that of the 1980s.

23. Yeva Nersisyan and L. Randall Wray, "The Trouble with Pensions," Levy Public Policy Brief, No. 109, March 2010. See also Y. Nersisyan and L. R. Wray, "Transformation of the Financial System: Financialization, Concentration, and the Shift to Shadow Banking," in *Minsky, Crisis and Development*, D. Tavasci and J. Toporowski, eds. (Basingstoke, UK: Palgrave Macmillan, 2010): 32–49, for a general discussion of the long-term transformation to money manager capitalism.

24. See Pavlina Tcherneva, "Growth for Whom?" One-Pager No. 47, October 2014, http://www.levyinstitute.org/publications/growth -for-whom.

25. Scott Bixby, "This Terrifying Chart Shows the Unstoppable Rise of the 0.1%", News.Mic, January 3, 2015, http://mic.com/articles /107622/this-terrifying-chart-shows-the-unstoppable-rise-of-the -point-one-percent.

26. In today's economy, these lines of business are closely interrelated lines that we can label the "financial sector." After Obamacare, we could almost include the health-care sector because it has become thoroughly "financialized," too.

27. Hyman P. Minsky and Charles J. Whalen, "Economic Insecurity and the Institutional Prerequisites for Successful Capitalism," Levy Working Paper No. 165, May 1996.

28. For an amusing, yet telling, account of American myopia, see "Is This Country Crazy? Inquiring Minds Elsewhere Want to Know," by Ann Jones, TomDispatch, January 11, 2015, http://www.tom dispatch.com/blog/175941/tomgram%3A_ann_jones%2C _answering_for_america/. Only about a tenth of Americans own passports, which probably explains why they have no idea how far behind the rich nations their country has fallen.

FURTHER READING

References cited in the text as well as other relevant readings are cited here. An extended list of Minsky's collected writings follows this chapter.

Financial Instability and Money Manager Capitalism

Cassidy, J. 2008. "The Minsky Moment," *The New Yorker*, February 4, http://www.newyorker.com/magazine/2008/02/04/the-minsky -moment.

Chancellor, E. 2007. "Ponzi Nation," *Institutional Investor*, February 7.

Galbraith, John Kenneth. *The Great Crash 1929*, New York: Houghton Mifflin Harcourt, 2009 [1954].

McCulley, P. 2007. "The Plankton Theory Meets Minsky," Global Central Bank Focus, March. PIMCO Bonds, Newport Beach, CA: http://media.pimco.com/Documents/GCB%20Focus%20MAR%2007%20WEB.pdf.

Minsky, Hyman P. and Charles J. Whalen. "Economic Insecurity and the Institutional Prerequisites for Successful Capitalism," Levy Working Paper No. 165, May 1996.

Papadimitriou, D. B., and Wray, L. R. 1998. "The Economic Contributions of Hyman Minsky: Varieties of Capitalism and Institutional Reform," *Review of Political Economy*, 10, no. 2, pp. 199–225.

Whalen, C. 2007. "The U.S. Credit Crunch of 2007: A Minsky Moment," Levy Economics Institute, Public Policy Brief, No. 92, http://www.levyinstitute.org/publications/the-us-credit-crunch-of-2007.

Wray, L. Randall. "Financial Markets Meltdown: What Can We Learn from Minsky?" Levy Public Policy Brief No. 94, April 2008a.

Wray, L. Randall. "The Commodities Market Bubble: Money Manager Capitalism and the Financialization of Commodities," Levy Public Policy Brief No. 96, October 2008b.

Wray, L. Randall 2009. "The Rise and Fall of Money Manager Capitalism: A Minskian Approach," *Cambridge Journal of Economics*, 33, no. 4, pp. 807–28.

Poverty, Unemployment, and Employer of Last Resort

Anderson, W. H. Locke. 1964. "Trickling Down: The Relationship between Economic Growth and the Extent of Poverty among American Families," *Quarterly Journal of Economics*, 78, no. 4, 511–24.

Brady, David. 2003. "The Poverty of Liberal Economics." *Socio-Economic Review*, 1, no. 3, 369–409.

Council of Economic Advisers. 1965. "Economic Report of the President," Washington, DC: U.S. Government Printing Office.

Forstater, Mathew. 1999. "Public Employment and Economic Flexibility." Public Policy Brief No. 50, Annandale-on-Hudson, NY: Levy Economics Institute.

Harvey, Phillip. 1989. *Securing the Right to Employment*, Princeton, NJ: Princeton University Press.

Keynes, J. M. [1936] 1973. *The General Theory of Employment, Interest and Money*, New York: Harcourt Brace Jovanovich.

Kregel, Jan. 1999. "Currency Stabilization through Full Employment: Can EMU Combine Price Stability with Employment and Income Growth?" *Eastern Economic Journal*, 25, no. 1, 35–48.

Pigeon, Marc-Andre and L. R. Wray. 2000. "Can a Rising Tide Raise All Boats? Evidence from the Clinton-Era Expansion," *Journal of Economic Issues*, 34, no. 4.

Wray, L. Randall. 1998. *Understanding Modern Money: The Key to Full Employment and Price Stability*, Northampton, MA: Edward Elgar.

Wray, L. Randall. 2003. "Can a Rising Tide Raise All Boats? Evidence from the Kennedy–Johnson and Clinton-era expansions," in *New Thinking in Macroeconomics: Social, Institutional and Environmental Perspectives*, Jonathan M. Harris and Neva R. Goodwin, eds., Northampton, MA: Edward Elgar, pp. 150–81.

Hyman P. Minsky, Selected Works
at Levy Economics Institute

Levy Working Papers

"Reconstituting the United States' Financial Structure: Some Fundamental Issues," Working Paper No. 69, January 1992a.

"The Capital Development of the Economy and the Structure of Financial Institutions," Working Paper No. 72, January 1992b.

"Regulation and Supervision," Paper No. 443, Levy Economics Institute, 1994.

"Uncertainty and the Institutional Structure of Capitalist Economies," Working Paper No. 155, April 1996.

Minsky, Hyman P., Dimitri B. Papadimitriou, Ronnie J. Phillips, and L. Randall Wray, "Community Development Banking: A Proposal to Establish a Nationwide System of Community Development Banks," Public Policy Brief No. 3, Levy Economics Institute, 1993.

Manuscripts in Minsky Archives at Levy Institute
(http://digitalcommons.bard.edu/hm_archive/)

"The Essential Characteristics of Post-Keynesian Economics", April 13, 1993.

"Financial Structure and the Financing of the Capital Development of the Economy", The Jerome Levy Institute Presents Proposals for Reform of the Financial System, Corpus Christie, TX, April 23, 1993.

"The Economic Problem at the End of the Second Millennium: Creating Capitalism, Reforming Capitalism and Making Capitalism Work," prospective chapter, May 13, 1992.

"Reconstituting the Financial Structure: The United States," prospective chapter, four parts, May 13, 1992.

"Where Did the American Economy—and Economists—Go Wrong?" unpublished manuscript, May 20, 1971, further rewrite of Paper No. 428.

"Economic Issues in 1972: A Perspective," October 6, 1972, Paper No. 427.

Other Published Works by Minsky

1963. "Discussion." *American Economic Review*, 53, no. 2, 401–12.
1965. "The Role of Employment Policy," in *Poverty in America*, Margaret S. Gordon, ed., San Francisco: Chandler Publishing Company.
1968. "Effects of Shifts of Aggregate Demand upon Income Distribution," *American Journal of Agricultural Economics*, 50, no. 2, 328–39.
1973. "The Strategy of Economic Policy and Income Distribution." *The Annals of the American Academy of Political and Social Science*, 409 (September), 92–101.
1975. "The Poverty of Economic Policy." An unpublished paper, presented at the Graduate Institute of Cooperative Leadership, July 14.
1986. *Stabilizing an Unstable Economy*, New Haven, CT: Yale University Press.
1987. (with Claudia Campbell) "How to Get Off the Back of a Tiger or, Do Initial Conditions Constrain Deposit Insurance Reform?" in *Merging Commercial and Investment Banking* (Proceedings of a Conference on Bank Structure and Competition), Chicago: Federal Reserve Bank of Chicago, 252–66.
1996. "Uncertainty and the Institutionalist Structure of Capitalist Economies: Remarks upon Receiving the Veblen–Commons Award," *Journal of Economic Issues*, XXX, no. 2, June 1996, 357–68.
2013. *Ending Poverty: Jobs, Not Welfare*, Annandale-on-Hudson, NY: Levy Economics Institute.

THE COLLECTED WRITINGS
OF HYMAN P. MINSKY

This list contains most of Minsky's published articles, books, and working papers; however, the reader should also consult the Minsky Archive at the Levy Economics Institute for a large number of unpublished manuscripts—especially from Minsky's later years.

Books

Minsky, Hyman P. *John Maynard Keynes* (New York: Columbia University Press, 1975; New York: McGraw-Hill, 2008).

———. *Can "It" Happen Again?* (Armonk, NY: M. E. Sharpe, 1982).

———. *Stabilizing an Unstable Economy* (New Haven, CT: Yale University Press, 1986; New York: McGraw-Hill, 2008).

———. *Ending Poverty: Jobs, Not Welfare* (Annandale-on-Hudson, NY: Levy Economics Institute, 2013).

Articles

Minsky, Hyman P. 1957. "Central Banking and Money Market Changes," *Quarterly Journal of Economics*, 71 (2), May: 171–87.

———. 1957. "Monetary Systems and Accelerator Models," *American Economic Review*, 47 (6), December: 859–83.

———. 1959. "A Linear Model of Cyclical Growth," *Review of Economics and Statistics*, 41 (2), Part 1, May: 133–45.

———. 1961. "Employment, Growth and Price Levels: A Review Article," *Review of Economics and Statistics*, 43 (1), February: 1–12.

———. 1962. "Financial Constraints upon Decisions, an Aggregate View," *Proceedings of the Business and Economic Statistics Section*, Washington, DC: American Statistical Association, 256–67.

———. 1963. "Can 'It' Happen Again?" in *Banking and Monetary Studies*, Dean Carson, ed. (Homewood, IL: Richard D. Irwin). Reprinted in *Can "It" Happen Again?* Hyman P. Minsky, ed., 1982: 3–13.

———. 1964. "Financial Crisis, Financial System and the Performance of the Economy," in *Private Capital Markets*, Commission on Money and Credit, ed., Englewood Cliffs, NJ: Prentice-Hall, 173–380.

———. 1964. "Long Waves in Financial Relations: Financial Factors in the More Severe Depression," *American Economic Review*, 54 (3), May, 324–35.

———. 1965. "The Role of Employment Policy," in *Poverty in America*, Margaret S. Gordon, ed., San Francisco: Chandler Publishing Company.

———. 1965. "The Integration of Simple Growth and Cycle Models," in *Patterns of Market Behavior, Essays in Honor of Philip Taft*, Michael J. Brennan, ed., Lebanon, NH: University Press of New England. Reprinted in *Can "It" Happen Again?* Hyman P. Minsky, ed., 1982: 258–77.

———. 1966. "Tight Full Employment: Let's Heat Up the Economy," in *Poverty: American Style*, Herman P. Miller, ed., Belmont, CA: Wadsworth Publishing Company, 294–300.

———. 1967. "Financial Intermediation in the Money and Capital Markets," in *Issues in Banking and Monetary Analysis*, Giulio Pontecorvo, Robert P. Shay, and Albert G. Hart, eds., New York: Holt, Rinehart and Winston, Inc.

———. 1967. "Money, Other Financial Variables, and Aggregate Demand in the Short Run," in *Monetary Process and Policy*, George Horwich, ed., Homewood, IL: Richard D. Irwin, 265–93.

———. 1968. "Aggregate Demand Shifts, Labor Transfers, and Income Distribution," *American Journal of Agricultural Economics*, 50 (2), May: 328–39.

———. 1969. "Private Sector Asset Management and the Effectiveness of Monetary Policy: Theory and Practice," *Journal of Finance*, 24 (2), May: 223–38.

———. 1969. "The New Uses of Monetary Power," *Nebraska Journal of Economics and Business*, 8 (2), Spring. Reprinted in *Can "It" Happen Again?* Hyman P. Minsky, ed., 1982: 179–91.

———. 1972. "Financial Instability Revisited: The Economics of Disaster," in *Reappraisal of the Federal Reserve Discount Mechanism*, Board of Governors, ed., Washington, DC, 95–136. Partly reprinted in *Can "It" Happen Again?* Hyman P. Minsky, ed., 1982.

———. 1972. "An Evaluation of Recent Monetary Policy," *Nebraska Journal of Economics and Business*, 11 (4), Autumn: 37–56.

———. 1972. "An Exposition of a Keynesian Theory of Investment," in *Mathematical Methods in Investment and Finance*, Giorgio Szegö and Karl Shell, eds., Amsterdam, New York, London: North-Holland. Reprinted in *Can "It" Happen Again?* Hyman P. Minsky, ed., 1982: 203–30.

———. 1973. "The Strategy of Economic Policy and Income Distribution," *The Annals* (of the American Academy of Political and Social Science), 409, September, 92–101.

———. 1973. "Devaluation, Inflation and Impoverishment: An Interpretation of the Current Position of the American Economy," *One Economist's View*, 1 (1): 1–7. St. Louis: Mark Twain Economic and Financial Advisory Service.

———. 1974. "The Modeling of Financial Instability: An Introduction," *Modeling and Simulation*, 5, Part 1 (Proceedings of the Fifth Annual Pittsburgh Conference), 267–72. Reprinted in *Compendium of Major Issues in Bank Regulation*, Washington, DC: U.S. Government Printing Office, 1975, 354–64.

———. 1975. "Financial Resources in a Fragile Financial Environment," *Challenge*, July–August: 6–13.

———. 1975. "Financial Instability, the Current Dilemma, and the Structure of Banking and Finance," in *Compendium of Major Issues in Bank Regulation* (Washington, DC: U.S. Government Printing Office), 310–53.

———. 1975. "Suggestion for a Cash Flow-Oriented Bank Examination," *Proceedings of a Conference on Bank Structure and Competition*, Chicago: Federal Reserve Bank of Chicago, 1975, 150–84.

———. 1977. "A Theory of Systemic Fragility," in *Financial Crises*, Edward I. Altman and Arnold W. Sametz, eds., New York: Wiley, 138–52.

———. 1977. "An 'Economics of Keynes' Perspective on Money," in *Modern Economic Thought*, Sidney Weintraub, ed., Philadelphia: University of Pennsylvania Press, 295–307.

———. 1977. "The Financial Instability: An Interpretation of Keynes and an Alternative to 'Standard' Theory," *Nebraska Journal of Economics and Business*, 16 (1), Winter: 5–16. Reprinted in *Challenge*, March–April: 20–27, and in *Can "It" Happen Again?* Hyman P. Minsky, ed., 1982.

———. 1977. "How 'Standard' Is Standard Economics?" *Society*, March–April: 24–29.

———. 1977. "Banking and a Fragile Financial Environment," *Journal of Portfolio Management*, Summer: 16–22.

———. 1978. "The Financial Instability Hypothesis: A Restatement," *Thames Papers in Political Economy*, Autumn. Reprinted in *Post Keynesian Economic Theory*, Philip Arestis and Thanos Skouras, eds., New York: M. E. Sharpe, 1985, 24–55.

———. 1979. "Financial Interrelation and the Balance of Payments, and the Dollar Crisis," in *Debt and the Less Developed Countries*, Jonathan David Aronson, ed., Boulder, CO: Westview Press, 103–22.

———. 1980. "The Federal Reserve: Between a Rock and a Hard Place," *Challenge*, May–June: 30–36.

———. 1980. "Capitalist Financial Processes and the Instability of Capitalism," *Journal of Economic Issues*, 14 (2), June: 505–23.

———. 1980. "Finance and Profit: The Changing Nature of American Business Cycles," in *The Business Cycle and Public Policy, 1929–1980*, Joint Economic Committee, ed., Washington, DC: U.S. Government Printing Office. Reprinted in *Can "It" Happen Again?* Hyman P. Minsky, ed., 1982: 14–59.

———. 1980. "Money, Financial Markets, and the Coherence of a Market Economy," *Journal of Post Keynesian Economics*, 3 (1), Fall: 21–31.

———. 1980. "La Coerenza dell'Economia Capitalistica: I Fondamenti Marshalliani della Critica Keynesiana della Teoria Neo-Classica," *Giornale degli Economisti e Annali di Economia*, 34, March–April: 3–181.

———. 1981. "Financial Markets and Economic Instability, 1965–1980," *Nebraska Journal of Economics and Business*, 20 (4), Autumn: 5–17.

———. 1981. "The Breakdown of the 1960s Policy Synthesis," *Telos*, (50): 49–58.

———. 1982. "Can 'It' Happen Again? A Reprise," *Challenge*, July–August: 5–13.

———. 1982. "The Financial-Instability Hypothesis: Capitalist Process and the Behavior of the Economy," in *Financial Crises*, Charles P. Kindlerberger and Jean-Pierre Lafargue, eds., New York: Cambridge University Press, 13–39.

———. 1982. "Debt Deflation Processes in Today's Institutional Environment," *Banca Nazionale del Lavoro Quarterly Review*, (143), December: 375–93.

———. 1983. "Institutional Roots of American Inflation," in *Inflation through the Ages: Economic, Social, Psychological and Historical Aspects*, Nathan Schmukler and Edward Marcus, eds., New York: Brooklyn College Press, 266–77.

———. 1983. "Pitfalls Due to Financial Fragility," in *Reaganomics in the Stagflation Economy*, Philadelphia: University of Pennsylvania Press, 104–19.

———. 1983. "The Legacy of Keynes," *Metroeconomica*, 35, February–June: 87–103. Reprinted in *Journal of Economic Education*, 16 (1), Winter 1985: 5–15.

———. 1984. "Banking and Industry between the Two Wars: The United States," *Journal of European Economic History*, 13 (Special Issue): 235–72.

———. 1984. (with Steve Fazzari). "Domestic Monetary Policy: If Not Monetarism, What?" *Journal of Economic Issues*, 18 (1), March: 101–16.

———. 1984. (with Piero Ferri). "Prices, Employment, and Profits," *Journal of Post Keynesian Economics*, 6 (4), Summer: 480–99.

———. 1984. "Financial Innovations and Financial Instability: Observations and Theory," *Financial Innovations*, Federal Reserve Bank of St. Louis, ed., Boston: Kluwer-Nijhoff, 21–45.

———. 1985. "Money and the Lender of Last Resort," *Challenge*, March–April: 12–18.

———. 1985. "Beginnings," *Banca Nazionale del Lavoro Quarterly Review*, (154), September: 211–21.

———. 1986. "An Introduction to Post-Keynesian Economics," *Economic Forum*, 15, Winter: 1–13.

———. 1986. "The Crises of 1983 and the Prospects for Advanced Capitalist Economies," in *Marx, Schumpeter, Keynes*, Suzanne W. Helburn and David F. Bramhall, eds., New York: M. E. Sharpe, 284–96.

———. 1986. "The Evolution of the Financial Institutions and the Performance of the Economy," *Journal of Economic Issues*, 20 (2), June: 345–53.

———. 1986. "Global Consequences of Financial Deregulation," in *The Marcus Wallenberg Papers on International Finance*, Washington, DC: International Law Institute and School of Foreign Service, Georgetown University, 2 (1): 1–19.

———. 1986. "Money and Crisis in Schumpeter and Keynes," in *The Economic Law of Motion of Modern Society*, Cambridge, UK: Cambridge University Press, 112–22.

———. 1986. "Stabilizing an Unstable Economy: The Lessons for Industry, Finance and Government," in *Weltwirtschaft and Unterrelmerische Strategien*, Karl Aiginger, ed. (Vienna, Austria: Österreichisches Institut für Wirtschaftsforschung), 31–44.

———. 1986. "Conflict and Interdependence in A Multipolar World," *Studies in Banking and Finance*, 4: 3–22.

———. 1987. (with Claudia Campbell) "How to Get Off the Back of a Tiger or, Do Initial Conditions Constrain Deposit Insurance Reform?" in *Merging Commercial and Investment Banking* (Proceedings of a Conference on Bank Structure and Competition), Chicago: Federal Reserve Bank of Chicago, 252–66.

———. 1989. "Financial Structures: Indebtedness and Credit," in *Money Credit and Prices in a Keynesian Perspective*, Alain Barrère, ed., New York: St. Martin's Press, 49–70.

———. 1989. (with Piero Ferri). "The Breakdown of the IS-LM Synthesis: Implication for Post-Keynesian Economic Theory," *Review of Political Economy*, 1 (2), July: 123–43.

———. 1989. "The Macroeconomic Safety Net: Does It Need to Be Improved?" in *Research in International Business and Finance*, Vol. 7, H. Peter Gray, ed., Greenwich, CT: JAI Press, 17–27.

———. 1989. "Financial Crises and the Evolution of Capitalism: The Crash of '87—What Does It Mean?" in *Capitalist Development and Crisis Theory: Accumulation, Regulation and Spatial Restructuring*, Market Gottdiener and Nicos Komninos, eds., New York: St. Martin's Press, 391–403.

———. 1990. "Schumpeter: Finance and Evolution," in *Evolving Technology and Market Structure*, Arnold Heertje and Mark Perlman, eds., Ann Arbor, MI: University of Michigan Press, 51–74.

———. 1990. "Sraffa and Keynes: Effective Demand in the Long Run," in *Essays in Piero Sraffa*, Krishna Bharadwaj and Bertram Schefold, eds., London: Unwin Hyman, 362–71.

———. 1990. "Money Manager Capitalism, Fiscal Independence and International Monetary Reconstruction," in *The Future of the Global Economic and Monetary System*, M. Szabó-Pelsőczi, ed., Budapest, Hungary: Institute for World Economics of the Hungarian Academy of Sciences.

———. 1990. "Debt and Business Cycles," *Business Economics*, 25 (3), July: 23–28.

———. 1991. "The Instability Hypothesis: A Clarification," in *The Risk of Economic Crisis*, Martin Feldstein, ed., Chicago: University of Chicago Press, 158–66.

———. 1991. "The Endogeneity of Money," in *Nicholas Kaldor and Mainstream Economics*, Edward J. Nell and Willi Semmler, eds., New York: St. Martin's Press, 207–20.

———. 1992. (with Piero Ferri). "Market Processes and Thwarting Systems," *Structural Change and Economic Dynamics*, 3 (1): 79–91.

———. 1992. (with Piero Ferri). "The Transition to a Market Economy: Financial Options," in *The Future of the Global Economic and Monetary Systems with Particular Emphasis on Eastern European Developments*, M. Szabó-Pelsőczi, ed., Budapest, Hungary: International Szirak Foundation, 107–22.

———. 1992. "Profits, Deficits and Instability: A Policy Discussion," in *Profits, Deficits, and Instability*, Dimitri B. Papadimitriou, ed., New York: St. Martin's Press, 11–22.

———. 1993. "Schumpeter and Finance," in *Market and Institutions in Economic Development*, Salvatore Biasco, Alessandro Roncaglia, and Michele Salvati, eds., New York: St. Martin's Press, 103–15.

———. 1993. "On the Non-Neutrality of Money," *Federal Reserve Bank of New York Quarterly Review*, 18 (1), Spring: 77–82.

———. 1993. "Community Development Banks: An Idea in Search of Substance," *Challenge*, March–April: 33–41.

———. 1994. "The Financial Instability Hypothesis," in *The Elgar Companion to Radical Political Economy*, Philip Arestis and Malcom Sawyer, eds., Aldershot, UK: Edward Elgar.

———. 1994. "Full Employment and Economic Growth as an Objective of Economic Policy: Some Thoughts on the Limits of Capitalism," *Employment, Growth and Finance*, Paul Davidson and Jan A. Kregel, eds., Aldershot, UK: Edward Elgar.

———. 1994. "Integração Financeira e Política Monetária," *Economia e Sociedade*, No. 3.

———. 1994. "Financial Instability and the Decline (?) of Banking Public Policy Implications," in *Proceedings of a Conference on Bank Structure and Competition*, Chicago: Federal Reserve Bank of Chicago, 55–64.

———. 1995. "Longer Waves in Financial Relations: Financial Factors in the More Severe Depression II," *Journal of Economic Issues*, 29 (1), March: 83–96.

———. 1995. "The Creation of a Capitalist Financial System," in *The Global Monetary System after the Fall of the Soviet Empire*, M. Szabó-Pelsőczi, ed., Aldershot, UK: Avebury, 153–70.

———. 1995. "Financial Factors in the Economics of Capitalism," *Journal of Financial Services Research*, 9, 197–208. Reprinted in *Coping with Financial Fragility and Systemic Risk*, Harald A. Benink, ed., Boston: Ernst and Young, 1995, 3–14.

———. 1996. "The Essential Characteristics of Post-Keynesian Economics," in *Money in Motion*, Edward J. Nell and Ghislain Deleplace, eds., New York: St. Martin's Press, 70–88.

———. 1996. "Uncertainty and the Institutional Structure of Capitalist Economies," *Journal of Economic Issues*, 30 (2), June: 357–68.

———. 1996. (with Dimitri B. Papadimitriou, Ronnie J. Phillips, and L. Randall Wray). "Community Development Banks," in *Stability in the Financial System*, Dimitri B. Papadimitriou, ed., New York: St. Martin's Press, 385–99.

———. 1996. (with Domenico D. Gatti and Mauro Gallegati). "Financial Institutions, Economic Policy, and the Dynamic Behavior of the Economy," in *Behavioral Norms, Technological Progress, and*

Economic Dynamics: Studies in Schumpeterian Economics, Ernst Helmstädter and Mark Perlman, eds., Ann Arbor, MI: University of Michigan Press, 393–412.

———. 1997. (with Charles J. Whalen). "Economic Insecurity and the Institutional Prerequisites for Successful Capitalism," *Journal of Post Keynesian Economics*, 19 (2), Winter: 155–70.

Interviews, Replies, Comments, Discussions, Forewords

Minsky, Hyman P. 1958. Reply to Colin D. Campbell, *Quarterly Journal of Economics*, 72 (2), May: 297–300.

———. 1963. Comments on Friedman and Schwartz's *Money and the Business Cycle*, *Review of Economics and Statistics*, 45 (1), Part 2, Supplement, February: 64–72.

———. 1963. Financial Institutions and Monetary Policy—Discussion, *American Economic Review*, 53 (2), May: 401–12.

———. 1969. Financial Model Building and Federal Reserve Policy—Discussion, *Journal of Finance*, 24 (2), May: 291–97.

———. 1971. The Allocation of Social Risk—Discussion, *American Economic Review*, 61 (2), May: 388–91.

———. 1979. The Carter Economics: A Symposium, *Journal of Post Keynesian Economics*, 1 (1): 42–45.

———. 1980. Discussion of the Taylor Paper, *Federal Reserve Bank of St. Louis Review*, April: 113–26.

———. 1988. Interview: "Back from the Brink," *Challenge*, January–February, 22–28.

———. 1989. Comments on Benjamin M. Friedman and David I. Laibson's "Economic Implications of Extraordinary Movements in Stock Prices; Comments and Discussion," Brookings Papers on Economic Activity, 2: 173–89.

———. 1989. Foreword in *Financial Dynamics and Business Cycles*, Willi Semmler, ed., New York: M. E. Sharpe, vii–x.

———. 1995. Foreword in *The Chicago Plan & New Deal Banking Reform*, Ronnie J. Phillips, ed., New York: M. E. Sharpe.

———. 1999. A Letter to the Conference in *Economic Theory and Social Justice*, Giancarlo Gandolfo and Ferruccio Marzano, eds., New York: St. Martin's Press, 253–54.

Book Reviews

Minsky, Hyman P. 1952. *Cyclical Movements in the Balance of Payments* in *Journal of Political Economy*, 60 (2), April: 164–65.

———. 1959. *Business Cycle and Economic Growth* in *American Economic Review*, 49 (1), March: 161–62.

———. 1961. *Money in a Theory of Finance* in *Journal of Finance*, 16 (1), March: 138–40.

———. 1961. *Collected Economic Papers, Vol. I* in *Journal of Political Economy*, 69 (5), October: 497–98.

———. 1972. *The Demand for Money: Theories and Evidence* in *Econometrica*, 40 (4), July: 778–79.

———. 1972. *Money and Banking* in *Journal of Finance*, 27 (5), December: 1184–86.

———. 1973. *American Monetary Policy, 1928–1941* in *Journal of Economic Literature*, 11 (2), June: 543–44.

———. 1974. *Money and the Real World* in *Quarterly Review of Economics and Business*, 14, Summer, 7–17.

———. 1974. *Issues in Monetary Economics* in *Economic Journal*, 84 (336), December: 996–97.

———. 1976. *Did Monetary Forces Cause the Great Depression?* in *Challenge*, September–October: 44–46.

———. 1977. *Stagflation and the Bastard Keynesians* in *Journal of Economic Literature*, 15 (3), September, 955–56.

———. 1981. *Essays on Economic Stability and Growth* in *Journal of Economic Literature*, 19 (4), December: 1574–77.

———. 1981. "James Tobin's *Asset Accumulation and Economic Activity*: A Review Article," *Eastern Economic Journal*, 7 (3–4), July–October: 199–209.

———. 1983. *Our Overloaded Economy* in *Journal of Economic Issues*, 17 (1), March: 228–32.

———. 1984. "Frank Hahn's *Money and Inflation*: A Review Article," *Journal of Post Keynesian Economics*, 6 (3): 449–57.

———. 1985. *The Second Industrial Divide* in *Challenge*, July–August: 60–64.

———. 1985. *The Great Depression, 1929–1938: Lessons for the 1980s* in *Journal of Economic Literature*, 23 (3), September: 1226–27.

———. 1986. *The Zero-Sum Solution: Building a World-Class American Economy* in *Challenge*, July–August: 60–64.

———. 1987. *Financial Crises and the World Banking System* in *Journal of Economic Literature*, 25 (3), September: 1341–42.

———. 1987. *Casino Capitalism* in *Journal of Economic Literature*, 25 (4), December: 1883–85.

———. 1988. *Secret of the Temple: How the Federal Reserve Runs the Country* in *Challenge*, May–June: 58–62.

———. 1990. *The Debt and the Deficit: False Alarms/Real Possibilities* in *Journal of Economic Literature*, 28 (3), September: 1221–22.

Working Papers and Memos

Minsky, Hyman P. 1965. "Poverty: The 'Aggregate Demand' Solution and Other Non-Welfare Approaches," Institute of Government and Public Affairs, University of California, MR-41.

———. 1969. "The Macroeconomics of a Negative Income Tax."

———. 1971. *Notes on User Cost.*

———. 1982. "On the Control of the American Economy."

———. 1984. "Conflict and Interdependence in a Multipolar World," Washington University, WP No. 74, December.

———. 1986. "Global Consequences of Financial Deregulation," Washington University, WP No. 96, December.

———. 1991. "Financial Crises: Systemic or Idiosyncratic," Levy Economics Institute, WP No. 51, April.

———. 1991. "Market Processes and Thwarting Systems," Levy Economics Institute, WP No. 64, November.

———. 1991. "The Transition to a Market Economy: Financial Options," Levy Economics Institute, WP No. 66, November.

———. 1992. "Reconstituting the United States' Financial Structure: Some Fundamental Issues," Levy Economics Institute, WP No. 69, January.

———. 1992. "The Capital Development of the Economy and the Structure of Financial Institutions," Levy Economics Institute, WP No. 72, January.

———. 1992. "The Financial Instability Hypothesis," Levy Economics Institute, WP No. 74, May.

———. 1992. (with Dimitri B. Papadimitriou, Ronnie J. Phillips, and L. Randall Wray). "Community Development Banks," Levy Economics Institute, WP No. 83, May.

———. 1993. "Finance and Stability: The Limits of Capitalism," Levy Economics Institute, WP No. 93, May.

———. 1993. (with Dimitri B. Papadimitriou, Ronnie J. Phillips, and L. Randall Wray). "Community Development Banking: A Proposal to Establish a Nationwide System of Community Development Banks," Levy Economics Institute, Public Policy Brief No. 3.

———. 1994. "The Essential Characteristics of Post-Keynesian Economics," Milken Institute for Job and Capital Formation, WP No. 94-2, February.

———. 1994. (with Domenico Delli Gatti and Mauro Gallegati). "Financial Institutions, Economic Policy, and the Dynamic Behavior of the Economy," Levy Economics Institute, WP No. 126, October.

———. 1994. "Financial Instability and the Decline (?) of Banking Public Policy Implications," Levy Economics Institute, WP No. 127, October.

———. 1996. "Uncertainty and the Institutional Structure of Capitalist Economies," Levy Economics Institute, WP No. 155, April.

———. 1996. (with Charles J. Whalen). "Economic Insecurity and the Institutional Prerequisites for Successful Capitalism," Levy Economics Institute, WP No. 165, May.

INDEX

Topics

Names